Building an RPG with Unreal 4.x

Get to grips with building the foundations of an RPG using Unreal Engine 4.x

Steve Santello

Alan R. Stagner

BIRMINGHAM - MUMBAI

Building an RPG with Unreal 4.x

First published: January 2016

Production reference: 2100816

Published by Packt Publishing Ltd.
Livery Place
35 Livery Street
Birmingham B3 2PB, UK.

ISBN 978-1-78217-563-6

www.packtpub.com

Credits

Authors
Steve Santello
Alan R. Stagner

Reviewers
Patrick Dinklage
Scott Hafner
Marcin Kamiński
Alankar Pradhan

Commissioning Editor
Edward Bowkett

Acquisition Editor
Tushar Gupta

Content Development Editor
Divij Kotian

Technical Editor
Taabish Khan

Copy Editors
Trishya Hajare
Rashmi Sawant

Project Coordinator
Neha Bhatnagar

Proofreader
Safis Editing

Indexer
Hemangini Bari

Production Coordinator
Shantanu N. Zagade

Cover Work
Shantanu N. Zagade

About the Authors

Steve Santello is a well-seasoned educator and veteran of the game industry from Chicago, Illinois, USA. His cross-disciplinary study in art, design, programming, and project management has allowed him to explore every facet of game development. As an educator, he has used his passion to teach others about game development, and has populated the game industry with many talented developers over the years. He has worked on over 10 different titles as a 2D and 3D artist for the Chicago game developer Babaroga. With Babaroga, he worked as one of the four artists on many mobile titles published by EA such as *Spore Origins*, *The Godfather Game*, and *Pictionary: The Game of Quick Draw*. He also worked on many mobile titles published by Disney Interactive, such as *Hannah Montana In Action* and *Meet the Robinsons*. He and his development team also developed a number of original IPs such as *Babaroga Eats Children* and *BEES!*.

Since 2006, Steve has also been a university professor. He helped pioneer the *Digital Entertainment and Game Design* program at ITT Technical Institute in St. Rose, LA, and also the *Game and Simulation Programming* program at DeVry University in Addison, IL. He has also served as an adjunct professor at the Illinois Institute of Art, Chicago, where he taught game prototyping as a team manager and acting producer. On the side, he developed game and simulation prototypes and plans to release his first two independent games, which were developed with Unreal Engine 4 sometime in 2015. He has writing contributions in *Game Development Essentials: Game Interface Design 2nd Edition, Kevin Saunders and Jeannie Novak, Delmar Cengage Learning*. In that book, he wrote about the past, present, and future of the user interface in games, which included breaking down the HUD in games such as *Deadspace*, and talked about how he and his team designed the user interface in *Spore Origins*.

Steve is currently working towards tenure as a CIS gaming instructor at the College of DuPage in Glen Ellyn, Illinois, USA. Although he is very proud of his success, he knows that all his combined experiences have played a major role in where he resides today.

Alan R. Stagner is an independent developer. He was introduced to programming by his father; he sought out different ways to create games in a variety of languages. Most recently, he found the Unity game engine and was instantly hooked, and discovered his love of multiplayer game development. He has also dabbled in database and server programming from time to time, mostly involving PHP and MySQL, with recent forays into ASP.NET.

About the Reviewers

Patrick Dinklage was born in 1987 in Datteln and now lives in Dortmund, Germany. He is a professional software developer, music producer, and music label owner who has also gathered experience in game development through modding, university, and projects in his free time.

Patrick started working with games by modifying them, starting with the Nintendo 64 using a gameshark for RAM hacking. He went on to found a successful modular C++ modding system for *Command & Conquer: Red Alert 2 – Yuri's Revenge*. The system is still being developed to date under the name *Ares* by a new team.

In the mid 2000s, he started work on several *Unreal Tournament 2004* mods, including *VCTF4*—a version of capture the flag with vehicles and four teams. The more outstanding *TitanRPG* is a standalone role-playing game system tailored for the packed online action of *UT2004*, with features such as leveling to power up abilities, item inventory, healing, creature summoning, construction, and so on. This way, he could gather a deep knowledge of the Unreal Engine concepts.

Besides modding, he developed a Java binding to the C++ multimedia library SFML that can be used as a core to build games.

Professionally, he worked as a Java developer for seven years in an established service enterprise that develops phone, computer network, and system management solutions. Currently, he is studying IT at the technical university in Dortmund, Germany, with the goal of obtaining a master's degree and then a dissertation. Here, he has worked on several experimental game projects using the Unity 3D engine, and is currently helping to develop a virtual reality biking game with the aim of motivating cardiac patients to do their daily training.

Finally, he is a keen gamer (explorer type—in love with huge and deep worlds); furthermore, he produces music under the name Veasna and runs a small music label called Goa Trance Music in the relatively niche genre of Goa trance.

Scott Hafner is a professional game designer with over 10 years of experience in the video game industry. Over the course of his career, he has worked as a producer, game designer, and level designer on a range of platforms and genres including MMOs, third-person shooters, and RPGs.

I would like to thank my fiancée for her continued encouragement and support in all that I do!

Marcin Kamiński works for Nordic Games as a programming consultant and has his own company, Digital Hussars. Previously, he worked for Artifex Mundi, CI Games, CTAdventure, and Vivid Games. His main fields of expertise are artificial intelligence and network programming. For 14 years, he has helped develop great games for PC, consoles, and mobiles.

Marcin was also the reviewer of the book *Blueprints Visual Scripting for Unreal Engine*, *Brenden Sewell*; *Unity iOS Essentials*, *Robert Wiebe*; and *Unity 2D Game Development Cookbook*, *Claudio Scolastici*; all published by Packt Publishing.

Alankar Pradhan is from Mumbai, Maharashtra, and he did his schooling at I.E.S.'s CPV High School. He is an ambitious person who loves interacting with new people, dancing, kickboxing, traveling, spending leisure time with friends, or playing games on a PC and mobile. Games have been always a passion in his life. More than just playing the game, how things work was his main curiosity. Hence, he decided to pursue his career in game development. He graduated with a BSc (Hons) in software development from Sheffield Hallam University, UK. He received his master's in video game programming and management (videogame director) (BAC+5 equivalent) from DSK Supinfogame where he undertook industry-oriented projects to increase his skill sets and gave his best to do so. He worked as a game programming intern at The Walt Disney India Pvt Ltd. During his internship, he worked on a live project called *Hitout Heroes*. His name was added to the credits due to the notable work he accomplished. He also interned as a game programmer with DSK Green Ice Games and then continued working as a video game programmer on a game targeted for PC and consoles. The game *Death God University (D.G.U.)* was released on 1st July 2015. Another project he is working on is *The Forsaken Mountains*.

Alankar has worked on many small projects in a team and also individually so as to sharpen his own skills in various languages such as C#, C++, Java, Unreal Script, Python, Lua, Groovy/Grails, HTML5/CSS, and so on. He is familiar with engines such as Unity 3D, Unreal Development Kit, Visual Studio, and also SDKs such as NetBeans, Eclipse, and Wintermute. In 2013, his dissertation on *Comparison between Python and Lua in Gaming Industry* was published as a book. He has even worked as a technical reviewer on the books *Creating E-Learning Games with Unity, David Horachek*, and *Learning Unreal Engine iOS Game Development, Muhammad A. Moniem.*

Alankar likes to read, listen to music, and write poems and short stories at times. He has his own website (`http://alan.poetrycraze.com`) where he posts his poems and has also published a book called *The Art Of Lost Words*, which is available through Amazon. He can be reached at `alankar.pradhan@gmail.com`. His portfolio site is `alankarpradhan.wix.com/my-portfolio`. He is available on Facebook at `www.facebook.com/alankar.pradhan`.

We are so often caught up in our aim that we forget to appreciate the journey, especially the people we meet on the way. Appreciation is a wonderful feeling, it's way better if we don't overlook it. I hereby take this opportunity to acknowledge the people who directed me and inspired me in this initiative.

I would like to express my sincere thanks to my parents who always instilled and believed in me. I am also thankful to my loving other half, Supriya, for her constant support and encouraging words that helped me to reach this level.

Last but not the least, I would like to thank all the people who are directly or indirectly involved with this book and who helped me in some way.

www.PacktPub.com

Support files, eBooks, discount offers, and more

For support files and downloads related to your book, please visit www.PacktPub.com.

Did you know that Packt offers eBook versions of every book published, with PDF and ePub files available? You can upgrade to the eBook version at www.PacktPub.com and as a print book customer, you are entitled to a discount on the eBook copy. Get in touch with us at service@packtpub.com for more details.

At www.PacktPub.com, you can also read a collection of free technical articles, sign up for a range of free newsletters and receive exclusive discounts and offers on Packt books and eBooks.

https://www2.packtpub.com/books/subscription/packtlib

Do you need instant solutions to your IT questions? PacktLib is Packt's online digital book library. Here, you can search, access, and read Packt's entire library of books.

Why subscribe?

- Fully searchable across every book published by Packt
- Copy and paste, print, and bookmark content
- On demand and accessible via a web browser

Free access for Packt account holders

If you have an account with Packt at www.PacktPub.com, you can use this to access PacktLib today and view 9 entirely free books. Simply use your login credentials for immediate access.

Table of Contents

Preface

Now that Unreal Engine 4 has become one of the most cutting-edge game engines in the world, developers both AAA and Indie alike are looking for the best ways of creating games of any genre using the engine. Upon Unreal's first release, it was known as a great first-person shooter game engine, but with the success of games such as WB's *Mortal Kombat*, Chair Entertainment's *Shadow Complex*, and Epic Games' *Gears of War*, along with highly anticipated upcoming games such as Capcom's *Street Fighter 5*, Comcept's *Mighty No. 9*, and Square Enix's *Final Fantasy VII Remake*, Unreal has proven itself to be one of the greatest engines to use when creating virtually any genre of game. This book will lay the foundations of creating a turn-based RPG in Unreal Engine 4.

What this book covers

Chapter 1, *Getting Started with RPG Design in Unreal*, alerts the reader to the various preparation steps required to make an RPG before jumping into Unreal. In order to avoid potential obstacles to progress, the example content is provided and briefly introduced.

Chapter 2, *Scripting and Data in Unreal*, walks the reader through using C++ to program gameplay elements in Unreal, creating Blueprint graphs, and working with custom game data in Unreal.

Chapter 3, *Exploration and Combat*, walks the reader through creating a character that runs around the game world, defining character data and party members, defining enemy encounters, and creating a basic combat engine.

Chapter 4, *Pause Menu Framework*, covers how to create a pause menu with inventory and equipment submenus.

Chapter 5, *Bridging Character Statistics*, covers how to keep track of the player's stats within the menu system.

Chapter 6, NPCs and Dialog, covers adding interactive NPCs and dialogue to the game world. The reader will learn how to use Blueprints to define what happens when an object or NPC is interacted with, including using a set of custom Blueprint nodes to create dialogue trees.

Chapter 7, Gold, Items, and a Shop, covers adding interactive NPCs and objects to the game world. The reader will learn how to use Blueprint to define what happens when an object or NPC is interacted with, including using a set of custom Blueprint nodes to create dialogue trees. The user will also be creating items that can be bought in a shop using the gold dropped by enemies.

Chapter 8, Inventory Population and Item Use, covers populating an inventory screen with items and using the items when not in combat.

Chapter 9, Equipment, covers the creation of equipment and equipping weapons and armor from an equipment screen.

Chapter 10, Leveling, Abilities, and Saving Progress, covers adding abilities to the game, keeping track of experience for each party member, awarding experience to party members after combat, defining leveling and stat updates for a character class, and saving and loading player progress.

What you need for this book

The required software: all chapters require Unreal Engine 4 version 4.12 or above along with either Visual Studio 2015 Enterprise/Community or above or XCode 7.0 or above.

The required OS: Windows 7 64-bit or above, or Mac OS X 10.9.2.

The required hardware: Quad-core 2.5 GHz or faster, 8 GB of RAM, and NVidia GeForce 470 GTX or AMD Radeon 6870 HD or above.

Who this book is for

If you are new to Unreal Engine and always wanted to script an RPG, you are this book's target reader. The lessons assume that you understand the conventions of RPG games and have some awareness of the basics of using the Unreal editor to build levels. By the end of this book, you will be able to build upon core RPG framework elements to create your own game experience.

Conventions

In this book, you will find a number of text styles that distinguish between different kinds of information. Here are some examples of these styles and an explanation of their meaning.

Code words in text, database table names, folder names, filenames, file extensions, pathnames, dummy URLs, user input, and Twitter handles are shown as follows: "We can include other contexts through the use of the `include` directive."

A block of code is set as follows:

```
if( DataTable != NULL )
{
  FTestCustomData* row = DataTable->FindRow<FTestCustomData>(
    TEXT( "2" ), TEXT(" LookupTestCustomData"  ) );
  FString someString = row->SomeString;
  UE_LOG( LogTemp, Warning, TEXT( "%s" ), *someString );
}
```

Any command-line input or output is written as follows:

```
LogTemp: Combat started
```

New terms and **important words** are shown in bold. Words that you see on the screen, for example, in menus or dialog boxes, appear in the text like this: "Compile and save the Blueprint and then press **Play**."

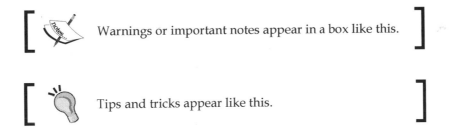

Warnings or important notes appear in a box like this.

Tips and tricks appear like this.

Reader feedback

Feedback from our readers is always welcome. Let us know what you think about this book—what you liked or disliked. Reader feedback is important for us as it helps us develop titles that you will really get the most out of.

To send us general feedback, simply e-mail feedback@packtpub.com, and mention the book's title in the subject of your message.

If there is a topic that you have expertise in and you are interested in either writing or contributing to a book, see our author guide at www.packtpub.com/authors.

Customer support

Now that you are the proud owner of a Packt book, we have a number of things to help you to get the most from your purchase.

Downloading the example code

You can download the example code files from your account at http://www.packtpub.com for all the Packt Publishing books you have purchased. If you purchased this book elsewhere, you can visit http://www.packtpub.com/support and register to have the files e-mailed directly to you.

Downloading the color images of this book

We also provide you with a PDF file that has color images of the screenshots/ diagrams used in this book. The color images will help you better understand the changes in the output. You can download this file from http://www.packtpub.com/sites/default/files/downloads/BuildingAnRPGWithUnreal_ColorImages.pdf.

Errata

Although we have taken every care to ensure the accuracy of our content, mistakes do happen. If you find a mistake in one of our books—maybe a mistake in the text or the code—we would be grateful if you could report this to us. By doing so, you can save other readers from frustration and help us improve subsequent versions of this book. If you find any errata, please report them by visiting http://www.packtpub.com/submit-errata, selecting your book, clicking on the **Errata Submission Form** link, and entering the details of your errata. Once your errata are verified, your submission will be accepted and the errata will be uploaded to our website or added to any list of existing errata under the Errata section of that title.

To view the previously submitted errata, go to https://www.packtpub.com/books/content/support and enter the name of the book in the search field. The required information will appear under the **Errata** section.

Piracy

Piracy of copyrighted material on the Internet is an ongoing problem across all media. At Packt, we take the protection of our copyright and licenses very seriously. If you come across any illegal copies of our works in any form on the Internet, please provide us with the location address or website name immediately so that we can pursue a remedy.

Please contact us at copyright@packtpub.com with a link to the suspected pirated material.

We appreciate your help in protecting our authors and our ability to bring you valuable content.

Questions

If you have a problem with any aspect of this book, you can contact us at questions@packtpub.com, and we will do our best to address the problem.

1
Getting Started with RPG Design in Unreal

Role-playing games are highly complex things. Even within the RPG genre, there is a diverse range of games with wildly different mechanics and controls.

Before even a single line of code is written, it's important to figure out what kind of RPG you want to make, how the game is played, whether the game should be turn-based or real-time, and what stats the player will have to concern themselves with.

In this chapter, we will cover the following topics which show how to design an RPG before you begin making it:

- Tools for game design
- The design and concept phase
- Describing the game's features and mechanics
- Tropes in existing RPGs
- RPG design overview

Tools for game design

While you can always type everything in Notepad and keep track of design decisions that way, there are a variety of tools available that can help when working on the design document.

Of particular note is the Google suite of tools. These tools come free with a Google account and have many applications, but in this case, we'll take a look at applying them to game design.

Google Drive

Google Drive is a cloud-based file storage system like Dropbox. It comes free with a Google account and has up to 15 GB of space. Google Drive makes sharing files with others very easy, as long as they also have a Google account. You can also set up permissions, such as who is allowed to modify data (maybe you only want someone to read but not change your design document).

Google Docs

Integrated with Google Drive is Google Docs, which is a fully featured online word processing application. It includes many features such as live collaborative editing, comments, and a built-in chat sidebar.

The bulk of your design document can be written in Google Docs and shared with any potential collaborators easily.

Google Spreadsheets

Just as with Google Docs, Google Spreadsheets is also directly integrated with Google Drive. Google Spreadsheets provides an Excel-style interface that can be used to keep track of data in a handy row/column format. You can also enter equations and formulas into cells and calculate their values.

Spreadsheets might be used, for example, to keep track of a game's combat formulas and test them with a range of input values.

Additionally, you can use spreadsheets to keep track of lists of things. For example, you may have a spreadsheet for weapons in your game, including columns for name, type, damage, element, and so on.

Pencil and paper

Sometimes, nothing beats the trusty method of actually writing things down. If you have a quick idea popped up in your head, it's probably worth quickly jotting it down. Otherwise, you'll most likely forget what the idea was later (even if you think you won't—trust me, you probably will). It doesn't really matter whether you think the idea is worth writing down or not—you can always give it more thought later.

The design and concept phase

Just as how a writer works from an outline or mind map, or an artist works from a rough sketch, nearly all games start from some sort of a rough concept or design document.

A design document's purpose is to describe nearly everything about a game. In the case of an RPG, it would describe how the player moves around the game world, how the player interacts with enemies and NPCs, how combat works, and more. The design document becomes the basis upon which all the game code is built.

Concept

Usually, a game starts with a very rough concept.

For example, let's consider the RPG we'll be making in this book. I might have the idea that this game would be a linear turn-based RPG adventure. It's a very rough concept, but that's OK—while it may not be a terribly original concept, it's enough to begin fleshing out and creating a design document from.

Design

The design document for the game is based on the previous rough concept. Its purpose is to elaborate on the rough concept and describe how it works. For example, while the rough concept was *linear turn-based RPG adventure*, the design document's job is to take that further and describe how the player moves around the world, how the turn-based combat works, combat stats, game over conditions, how the player advances the plot, and a lot more.

You should be able to give your design document to any person and the document should give them a good idea of what your game will be like and how it works. This, in fact, is one of the big strengths of a design document—it's incredibly useful, for example, as a way of ensuring that everyone on a team is on the same page so to speak.

Describing the game's features and mechanics

So, assuming you have a very rough concept for the game and are now at the design phase, how do you actually describe how the game works?

There are really no rules for how to do this, but you can divide your theoretical game into the important core bits and think about how each one will work, what the rules are, and so on. The more information and the more specific, the better it is. If something is vague, you'll want to expand on it.

For instance, let's take *combat* in our hypothetical turn-based RPG.

Combatants take turns selecting actions until one team of combatants is dead.

What order do combatants fight in? How many teams are there?

Combatants are divided into two teams: the player team and the enemy team. Combatants are ordered by all players and followed by all enemies. They take turns in order to select actions until one team of combatants is dead (either the enemy team or the player team).

What sort of actions can combatants select?

Combatants are divided into two teams: the player team and the enemy team. Combatants are ordered by all players and followed by all enemies. Combatants take turns in order to select actions (either attacking a target, casting an ability, or consuming an item) until one team of combatants is dead (either the enemy team or the player team).

And so on.

Tropes in existing role-playing games

Even though RPGs can vary wildly, there are still plenty of common themes they frequently share—features that a player expects out of your game.

Stats and progression

This one goes without saying. Every RPG—and I do mean *every* RPG—has these basic concepts.

Statistics, or *stats*, are the numbers that govern all combat in the game. While the actual stats can vary, it's common to have stats such as max health, max MP, strength, defense, and more.

As players progress through the game, these stats also improve. Their character becomes better in a variety of ways, reaching maximum potential at (or near) the end of the game. The exact way in which this is handled can vary, but most games implement experience points or XP that are earned in combat; when enough XP has been gained, a character's *level* increases, and with it, their stats increase as well.

Classes

It's common to have *classes* in an RPG. A class can mean a lot, but generally it governs what a character's capabilities are and how that character will progress.

For instance, a *Soldier* class might define that, as an example, a character is able to wield swords, and mainly focuses on increased attack power and defense power as they level up.

Special abilities

Very few role-playing games can get away with not having magic spells or special abilities of some sort.

Generally, characters will have some kind of *magic* meter that is consumed every time they use one of their special abilities. Additionally, these abilities cannot be cast if the character does not have enough magic (the term for this varies—it might also be called *mana*, *stamina*, or *power*—really, anything to fit the game scenario).

RPG design overview

With all that aside, we're going to take a look at the design for the RPG we will be developing over the course of this book, which we'll call *Unreal RPG*.

Setting

The game is set in an open field. Players will encounter enemies who will drop loot experience, which will increase the player's stats.

Exploration

While not in combat, players explore the world in an isometric view, similar to games such as Diablo. In this view, players can interact with NPCs and props in the world, and also pause the game to manage their party members, inventory, and equipment.

Dialogue

When interacting with NPCs and props, dialogue may be triggered. Dialogue in the game is primarily text-based. Dialogue boxes may be either linear, the player simply presses a button to advance to the next dialogue page, or multiple-choice. In the case of multiple-choice, the player is presented with a list of options. Each option will then proceed to a different page of dialogue. For instance, an NPC might ask the player a question and allow the player to respond "Yes" or "No", with different responses to each.

Shopping

A shop UI can also be triggered from a dialogue. For example, a shopkeeper might ask the player whether they want to buy items. If the player chooses "Yes", a shop UI is displayed.

While in a shop, players can buy items from the NPC.

Gold

Gold can be attained by defeating monsters in battle. This gold is known as a type of enemy drop.

The pause screen

While the game is paused, players can do the following:

- View a list of party members and their statuses (health, magic, level, effects, and so on)
- View abilities that each party member has learned
- View the amount of gold currently carried
- Browse an inventory and use items (such as potions, ethers, and so on) on their party members
- Manage items equipped to each party member (such as weapons, armor, and so on)

Party members

The player has a list of *party members*. These are all the characters currently on the player's team. For instance, the player may meet a character in a tower who joins their party to aid in combat. Note that in this book, we will only be creating a single party member, but this will lay the foundations of creating additional party members in your future developments.

Equipment

Each character in the player's party has the following equipment slots:

- **Armor**: A character's armor generally increases defense
- **Weapon**: A character's weapon generally provides a boost to their attack power (as given in the attack formula in the *Combat* section of this chapter)

Classes

Player characters have different classes. A character's class defines the following elements:

- The experience curve for leveling up
- How their stats increase as they level up
- Which abilities they learn as they level up

The game will feature one player character and class. However, based on this player character, we can easily implement more characters and classes, such as a healer or black mage, into the game.

Soldier

The Soldier class focuses on increasing attack, max HP, and luck. Additionally, special abilities revolve around dealing with lots of damage to enemies.

Therefore, as the Soldier class levels up, they deal more damage to enemies, withstand more hits, and also deliver more critical blows.

Combat

While exploring the game world, random encounters may be triggered. Additionally, combat encounters can also be triggered from cut scenes and story events.

When an encounter is triggered, the view transitions away from the game world (the field) to an area specifically for combat (the battle area), an arena of sorts.

Combatants are divided into two teams: the enemy team and the player team (consisting of the player's party members).

Each team is lined up, facing each other from the opposite ends of the battle area.

Combatants take turns, with the player team going first, followed by the enemy team. A single round of combat is divided into two phases: decision and action.

Firstly, all combatants choose their action. They can either attack an enemy target or cast an ability.

After all combatants have decided, each combatant executes their action in turn. Most actions have a specific target. If, by the time the combatant executes their action, this target is not available, the combatant will pick the next available target if possible, or else the action will simply fail and the combatant will do nothing.

This cycle continues until either all enemies or players are dead. If all enemies are dead, the player's party members are awarded with XP, and loot may also be gained from the defeated enemies (usually, a random amount of gold).

However, if all players have died, then it is game over.

Combat stats

Every combatant has the following stats:

- **Health points**: A character's **health points (HP)** represents how much damage the character can take. When HP reaches zero, the character dies.

  HP can be replenished via items or spells, as long as the character is still alive. However, once a character is dead, HP cannot be replenished — the character must first be revived via a special item or spell.

- **Max health**: This is the maximum amount of HP a character can have at any given time. Healing items and spells only work up to this limit, never beyond. Max health may increase as the character levels up, and can also be temporarily increased by equipping certain items.

- **Magic points**: A character's **magic points (MP)** represents how much magic power they have. Abilities consume some amount of MP, and if the player does not have enough MP for the ability, then that ability cannot be performed. MP can be replenished via items.

  It should be noted that enemies have effectively infinite MP, as their abilities do not cost them any MP.

- **Max magic**: This is the maximum amount of MP a character can have at any given time. Replenishing items only work up to this limit, never beyond. Max magic may increase as the character levels up, and can also be temporarily increased by equipping certain items.

- **Attack power**: A character's attack power represents how much damage they can do when they attack an enemy. Weapons have a separate attack power that is added to regular attacks. The exact formula used to deal with damage is as follows:

  max (player.ATK – enemy.DEF, 0) + player.weapon.ATK

  So firstly, enemy defense is subtracted from the player's attack power. If this value is less than zero, it is changed to zero. Then, the weapon's attack power is added to the result.

- **Defense**: A character's defense reduces the damage they take from an enemy attack.

  The exact formula is as given just previously (defense is subtracted from the enemy's base attack value and then the enemy's weapon attack power is added).

- **Luck**: A character's luck affects that character's chance of landing a critical hit, which will double the damage dealt to an enemy.

  Luck represents the percent chance of dealing with a critical hit. Luck ranges from 0 to 100, representing the range from 0% to 25%, so the formula is as follows:

  *isCriticalHit = random(0, 100) <= (player.Luck * 0.25)*

  So, if the player's luck is 10, given that the random number falls at the number 10 within its range of 0 to 100, then the chance of dealing a critical hit is 2.5%.

  The critical hit multiplier is applied after the damage is calculated, as follows:

  *2 * (max(player.ATK – enemy.DEF, 0) + player.weapon.ATK)*

Combat actions

Actions during combat are divided into three categories: attack and ability.

Attack

Every character has an attack ability that costs zero MP and, for player characters, is shown as the first option in the action menu during the decision phase of a round.

Generally, an attack takes a single enemy target and deals damage to that enemy. The damage formula is as given previously for the *attack power* stat.

Ability

Every character, as mentioned earlier, has a set of abilities they know. Excluding attack, abilities cost some amount of MP and have a variety of effects. Abilities can have different types of targets, as follows:

- A single enemy
- All enemies
- A single ally
- All allies

Abilities can heal targets, revive dead targets, remove some effects, summon temporary allies, temporarily increase a character's stats, and more. However, abilities never restore MP.

Abilities have a set MP cost. This is the amount of MP the character must have in order to perform that ability, and the amount of MP that will be consumed upon casting the ability.

After combat/victory

Once all enemy combatants have died, the player wins the fight. Upon winning the fight, the player is rewarded with random loot, and experience points are divided between party members.

Loot

Every enemy defines the loot that is received upon defeating the enemy. This includes how much gold is received to defeat this enemy.

Experience

Each enemy defines how much experience it is worth. After combat, the experience of every defeated enemy is summed up. Then, this value is evenly divided between all currently living players (any party member who has died does not receive any EXP) and rounded up to the nearest integer (for example, if the total experience is 100 and there are three party members, then *100/3 = 33.3333*, which is rounded up to 34).

Experience and leveling

As party members earn experience, they will level up.

The amount of experience required to go from one level to the next is given by the following formula:

$f(x) = (xa) + c$

Here, x is the current level, a is a positive value greater than one (affecting how steeply the curve increases), and c is the base offset, which is the amount of experience required to go from level 1 to level 2. This defines a simple exponential value increase. The a and c values are defined by the character's class.

To get the total amount of experience required to level up from the current level, the preceding formula is calculated and summed for each level up to the current level. For instance, if we want to know how much total EXP is required to get to level 31 (from level 30), we calculate it in the following way:

$f(1) + f(2) + f(3) + \ldots + f(30)$

When a player levels up, their stats increase and they may also learn a new ability. Stat increases and learned abilities are defined on the character class.

The maximum level of any character in the game is 50.

Stat increases

For a given character class, for every character stat, the class defines a starting value at level 1 and an ending value at 50. For example, using standard math library functions, the value of attack for any given level would be a simple linear interpolation between the starting value and the ending value, using the character's level (divided by max level) as the interpolation value (the result would then be rounded up to ensure it is a whole integer number).

So, for example, if a soldier's max HP starts at 100 at level 1 and ends at 1,000 at level 50, then at level 25 the soldier's max HP will be 550.

Learning abilities

Each character class defines a table of abilities. Each entry in the table references which ability will be learned and at what level that ability is learned. When the character levels up, any abilities in the table that has the given level will be added to that character's known abilities.

Any abilities *learned* at level 1 are automatically added to a character's skill set.

Game over

If all players have died, either during combat or in the field, then the game ends.

Choosing the right formula

In the preceding sections, the design of this sample game describes a small range of stats for characters in the game. It also outlines a variety of formulas for calculating damage, leveling up, and so on.

One thing to keep in mind is that these stats, values, and formulas are simply there to show you how to implement the core functionality of an RPG. These are not the be-all-end-all of stats or formulas. In fact, the design has intentionally used a limited set of stats and simple formulas to keep the scope simple.

With this in mind, when you're working on your own game, you will have to decide these things for yourself—what stats your characters use, how combat works, and what formulas the game will use to calculate the outcome of battle. So, how do you come up with all of these things on your own?

Unfortunately, the answer is "it depends". There's no silver bullet to balance your game and keep it fun. What stats you use depends on how your combat works (it makes no sense to have a "hit chance" stat if, for instance, your game takes place from a first-person perspective using guns).

Another thing to keep in mind is that the actual values and formulas you use don't matter. What does matter is that the end result is fun, fair, and balanced. It doesn't matter if it takes one, one hundred, or one million experience points to level up if the end result is still fun and feels fair.

Downloading the example code

You can download the example code files from your account at http://www.packtpub.com for all the Packt Publishing books you have purchased. If you purchased this book elsewhere, you can visit http://www.packtpub.com/support and register to have the files e-mailed directly to you.

Summary

In this chapter, we took a look at what tools are at your disposal to design the RPG of your dreams, how important it is to design your game before you begin developing, how to come up with a rough concept and design, and how to describe your game's mechanics. We've also seen an overview of the game that we will be developing over the course of this book.

In the next chapter, we'll start to dive into Unreal and learn about scripting gameplay elements and working with game data in Unreal Engine.

2
Scripting and Data in Unreal

Now that we've got a design to work from, we can begin to develop the game.

Before we can do that, however, we'll be exploring the variety of ways in which we can work with game code and game data in the Unreal game engine.

This chapter will walk you through the steps necessary to get Unreal and Visual Studio installed, and to create a new Unreal Engine project. Additionally, you will learn how to create new C++ game code, work with Blueprints and Blueprint graphs, and work with custom data for your game. In this chapter, we will cover the following topics:

- Downloading Unreal
- Setting up Visual Studio for use with Unreal
- Setting up a new Unreal project
- Creating new C++ classes
- Creating Blueprints and Blueprint graphs
- Using Data Tables to import spreadsheet data

Downloading Unreal

Before getting started, make sure that you have at least 18 GB of free disk space on your computer. You will need this disk space to hold the development environments for Unreal and also your project files.

We will now need to download Unreal. To do this, go to `https://www.unrealengine.com` and click on the **GET UNREAL** button.

Before you can download Unreal, you'll need to make an Epic Games account. The **GET UNREAL** button will redirect you to an account creation form, so fill it out and submit it.

After you've signed in, you'll see the **Download** button. This will download the installer for the Epic Games Launcher (from this launcher, you can download Unreal version 4.12).

Downloading Visual Studio

We will need to start programming soon, so if you haven't already, now is the time to download Visual Studio, which is the integrated development environment that we will need to program the framework for our engine and game logic in C++. Luckily, Microsoft provides Visual Studio Community for free.

To download Visual Studio Community, go to `https://www.visualstudio.com/` and download Community 2015. This will download the installer for Visual Studio. After it downloads, simply run the installer. Note that Visual Studio Community 2015 does not install C++ by default, so be sure that under **Features**, you are installing Visual C++, Common Tools for Visual C++ 2015, and Microsoft Foundation Classes for C++. If you do not have C++ installed, you will not be able to write or compile code written for UE4 in Visual Studio since UE4 is built on C++.

Setting up Visual Studio for Unreal

After you've installed Visual Studio, there are some steps you can take to make it easier to work with C++ code in Unreal. These steps are not at all necessary, and can be safely skipped.

Adding the Solution Platforms drop-down list

On the right-hand side of the toolbar is a drop-down arrow, as shown in the following screenshot:

Click on this button, hover over the **Add** or **Remove** buttons, and click on **Solution Platforms** to add the menu to the toolbar.

The **Solution Platforms** drop-down list allows you to switch the project between target platforms (for instance, Windows, Mac, and so on).

Disabling the Error List tab

The error list in Visual Studio shows you the errors that it detects in your code before you even compile the project. While normally this is incredibly useful, in Unreal, it can frequently detect false positives and become more annoying than helpful.

To disable the error list, first close the **Error List** tab (you can find this in the bottom pane, as shown in the following screenshot):

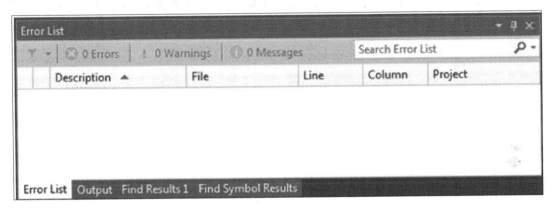

Then, navigate to **Tools | Options**, expand the **Projects and Solutions** group, and uncheck the **Always show Error List if build finishes with errors** option:

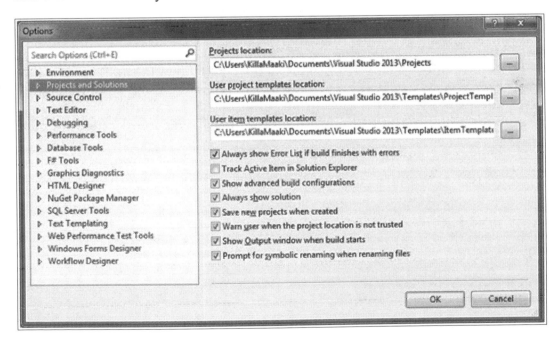

Setting up a new Unreal project

Now that you have both Unreal and Visual Studio downloaded and installed, we're going to create a project for our game.

Unreal comes with a variety of starter kits that you can use, but for our game, we'll be scripting everything from scratch.

After signing into Epic Games Launcher, you'll first want to download the Unreal Engine. This book uses version 4.12. You may use a later version, but depending on the version, some code and the navigation of the engine may slightly differ. The steps for creating a new project are as follows:

1. Firstly, in the **Unreal Engine** tab, select **Library**. Then, under **Engine Versions**, click on **Add Versions** and select the version you'd like to download.

2. After the engine has downloaded, click on the **Launch** button.

3. Once the Unreal Engine has launched, click on the **New Project** tab. Then, click on the **C++** tab and select **Basic Code**.

4. Finally, choose a location for your project and give it a name (in my case, I named the project RPG).

In my case, after the project was created, it automatically closed the engine and opened Visual Studio. At this point, I've found it best to close Visual Studio, go back to Epic Games Launcher, and relaunch the engine. Then, open your new project from here. Finally, after the editor has launched, go to **File | Open Visual Studio**.

The reason for this is because, while you can launch the editor by compiling your Visual Studio project, in some rare cases you may have to close the editor any time you want to compile a new change. If, on the other hand, you launch Visual Studio from the editor (rather than the other way around), you can make a change in Visual Studio and then compile the code from within the editor.

At this point, you have an empty Unreal project and Visual Studio that are ready to go.

Creating a new C++ class

We're now going to create a new C++ class with the following steps:

1. To do this, from the Unreal editor, click on **File | New C++ Class**. We'll be creating an Actor class, so select **Actor** as the base class. Actors are the objects that are placed in the scene (anything from meshes, to lights, to sounds, and more).

2. Next, enter a name for your new class, such as `MyNewActor`. Hit **Create Class**. After it adds the files to the project, open `MyNewActor.h` in Visual Studio. When you create a new class using this interface, it will generate both a header file and a source file for your class.

3. Let's just make our actor print a message to the output log when we start our game. To do this, we'll use the `BeginPlay` event. `BeginPlay` is called once the game has started (in a multiplayer game, this might be called after an initial countdown, but in our case, it will be called immediately).

4. The `MyNewActor.h` file (which should already be open at this point) should contain the following code after the `GENERATED_BODY()` line:

    ```
    public:    virtual void BeginPlay();
    ```

5. Then, in `MyNewActor.cpp`, add a log that prints **Hello, world!** in the `void AnyNewActor::BeginPlay()` function, which runs as soon as the game starts:

    ```
    void AnyNewActor::BeginPlay()
    {
        Super::BeginPlay();

        GEngine->AddOnScreenDebugMessage(-1, 15.0f, FColor::Yellow,
    TEXT("Hello World!"));
    }
    ```

6. Then, switch back to the editor and click on the **Compile** button in the main toolbar.

7. Now that your actor class has compiled, we need to add it to the scene. To do this, navigate to the **Content Browser** tab located at the bottom of the screen. Search for `MyNewActor` (there's a search bar to help you find it) and drag it into the scene view, which is the level viewport. It's invisible, so you won't see it or be able to click on it. However, if you scroll the **Scene/World Outliner** pane (on the right-hand side) to the bottom, you should see the **MyNewActor1** actor has been added to the scene:

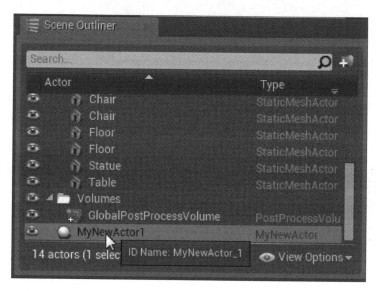

8. To test your new actor class, click on the **Play** button. You should see a yellow **Hello, world!** message printed to the console, as shown in the following screenshot. This can be seen in the **Output Log** tab on the right-hand side of the **Content Browser** tab at the bottom of the screen:

```
LogPlayLevel: PIE:    no Blueprints needed recompiling
PIE: New page: PIE session: Minimal_Default (Mar 15, 201
LogPlayLevel: PIE: StaticDuplicateObject took: (0.004481
LogPlayLevel: PIE: World Init took: (0.000706s)
LogPlayLevel: PIE: Created PIE world by copying editor w
LogWorld: Game class is 'DefaultRPGGameMode_C'
LogAIModule: Creating AISystem for world Minimal_Default
LogWorld: Bringing World /Game/StarterContent/UEDPIE_0_M
LogWorld: Bringing up level for play took: 0.000992
LogTemp:Warning: Hello, world!
PIE: Info Play in editor start time for /Game/StarterCon
LogParticles: Destroying 0 GPU particle simulations for
```

Congratulations, you have created your first actor class in Unreal.

Blueprints

Blueprints in Unreal is a C++ based visual scripting language built proprietary to Unreal. Blueprints will allow us to create code without the need to touch a line of text in an IDE such as Visual Studio. Instead, Blueprints allows us to create code through the use of drag and drop visual nodes, and connect them together to create nearly any kind of functionality you desire. Those of you who have come from UDK may find some similarity between Kismet and Blueprints, but unlike Kismet, Blueprints allows you to have full control over the creation and modification of functions and variables. It also compiles, which is something Kismet did not do.

Blueprints can inherit from C++ classes, or from other Blueprints. So, for instance, you might have an `Enemy` class. An enemy might have a **Health** field, a **Speed** field, an **Attack** field, and a **Mesh** field. You can then create multiple enemy templates by creating Blueprints that inherit from your `Enemy` class and changing each type of enemy's Health, Speed, Attack, and Mesh.

You can also expose parts of your C++ code to Blueprint graphs so that your Blueprint graphs and your core game code can communicate and work with each other. As an example, your inventory code may be implemented in C++, and it might expose functions to Blueprints so that a Blueprint graph can give items to the player.

Creating a new Blueprint

The steps to create a new Blueprint are as follows:

1. In the **Content Browser** pane, create a new Blueprint folder by clicking on the **Add New** drop-down list and selecting **New Folder**, then renaming the folder `Blueprint`. Inside this folder, right-click and select **Blueprints | Blueprint Class**. Select **Actor** as the parent class for the Blueprint.

2. Next, give a name to your new Blueprint, such as MyNewBlueprint. To edit this Blueprint, double-click on its icon in the **Content Browser** tab.

3. Next, switch to the **Event Graph** tab.

4. If **Event Begin Play** is not already there, right-click on the graph and expand **Add Event**; then, click on **Event Begin Play**. If you ever need to move around nodes such as **Event Begin Play**, you can simply left-click on the node and drag it anywhere on the graph you want. You can also navigate through the graph by holding down the right-click mouse button and dragging across the screen:

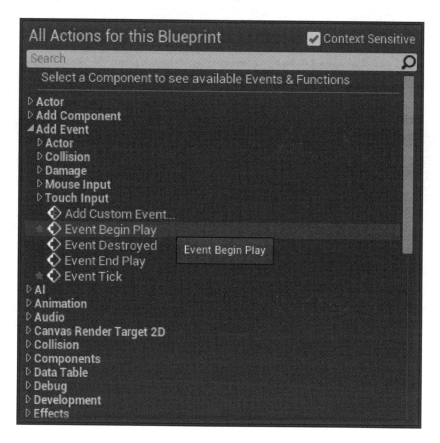

This will add a new event node to the graph.

5. Next, right-click and begin typing print into the search bar. You should see the **Print String** option in the list. Click on it to add a new **Print String** node to your graph.

6. Next, we want to have this node triggered when the **Event Begin Play** node is triggered. To do this, drag from the output arrow of the **Event Begin Play** node to the input arrow of the **Print String** node:

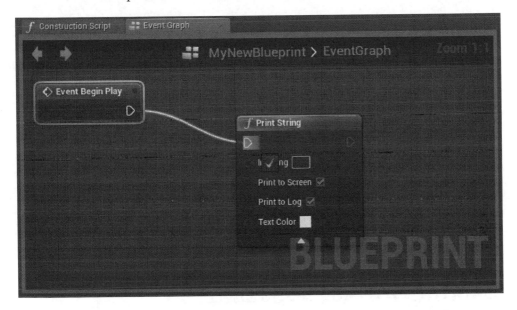

7. Now, the **Print String** node will be triggered when the game begins. However, let's take this one step further and add a variable to our Blueprint.

8. On the left-hand side in the **My Blueprint** pane, click on the **Variable** button. Give a name to your variable (such as `MyPrintString`) and change the **Variable Type** drop-down list to **String**.

9. To feed the value of this variable into our **Print String** node, right-click and search for `MyPrintString`. You should see a **Get My Print String** node available in the list. Click on this to add the node to your graph:

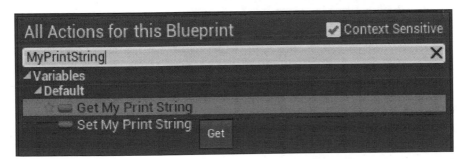

10. Next, just as you did to connect **Event Begin Play** and **Print String** together, drag from the output arrow of the **Get My Print String** node to the input pin of the **Print String** node that is right next to the **In String** label.

11. Finally, switch over to the **Defaults** tab. At the very top, under the **Defaults** section, there should be a text field for editing the value of the MyPrintString variable. Enter whatever text you'd like into this field. Then, to save your Blueprint, first press the **Compile** button in the **Blueprint** window and then click on the **Save** button next to it.

Adding a Blueprint to the scene

Now that you've created the Blueprint, simply drag it from the **Content Browser** tab into the scene. Just as with our custom actor class, it will be invisible, but if you scroll **Scene Outliner** to the bottom, you'll see the **MyNewBlueprint** item in the list.

To test our new Blueprint, press the **Play** button. You should see that the text you entered is briefly printed to the screen (it will also show up in the **Output Log**, but it may be difficult to spot amidst the other output messages).

Blueprints for Actor classes

You can choose other classes for a Blueprint to inherit from. For instance, let's create a new Blueprint to inherit from the custom MyNewActor class we created earlier:

1. To do this, start creating a new Blueprint as before. Then, when choosing a parent class, search for MyNewActor. Click on the **MyNewActor** entry in the list:

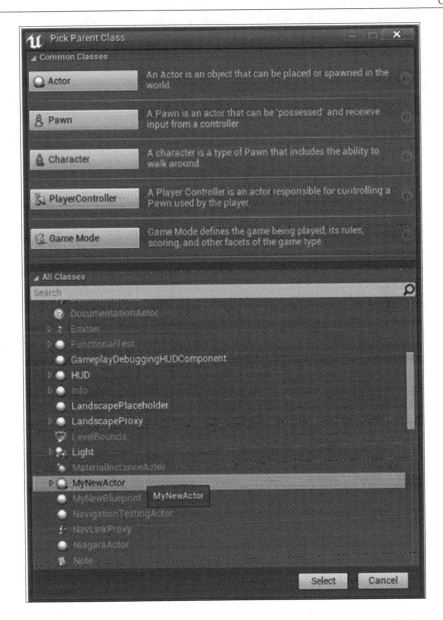

2. You can name this Actor whatever you want. Next, open the Blueprint and click on **Save**. Now, add the Blueprint to your scene and run the game. You should now have two **Hello, world!** messages logged to the console (one from our placed actor and the other from our new Blueprint).

Using Data Tables to import spreadsheet data

In Unreal, **Data Tables** are a method of importing and using custom game data exported from a spreadsheet application. To do this, you first ensure that your spreadsheet follows some guidelines for format; additionally, you write a C++ struct that contains the data for one row of the spreadsheet. Then, you export a CSV file and select your C++ struct as the data type for that file.

The spreadsheet format

Your spreadsheet must follow some simple rules in order to correctly export to Unreal.

The very first cell must remain blank. After this, the first row will contain the names of the fields. These will be the same as the variable names in your C++ struct later, so do not use spaces or other special characters.

The first column will contain the **lookup key** for each entry. That is, if the first cell of the first item in this spreadsheet is 1, then in Unreal, you would use 1 to find that entry. This must be unique for every row.

Then, the following columns contain the values for each variable.

A sample spreadsheet

Let's create a simple spreadsheet to import into Unreal. It should look like this:

	A	B	C
1		SomeNumber	SomeString
2	1	10	Hello, world
3	2	15	Hello, again
4	3	30	Hello!

As mentioned in the previous section:

- Column **A** contains the lookup keys for each row. The first cell is empty and the following cells have the lookup keys for each row.
- Column **B** contains the values for the SomeNumber field. The first cell contains the field name (SomeNumber) and the following cells contain the values for that field.
- Column **C** contains the values for the SomeString field. Just as with column **B**, the first cell contains the name of the field (SomeString) and the following cells contain the values for that field.

I'm using Google Spreadsheets—with this, you would click on **File | Download as | Comma-separated values (.csv, current sheet)** to export this to CSV. Most spreadsheet applications have the ability to export to the CSV format.

At this point, you have a CSV file that can be imported into Unreal. However, do not import it yet. Before we do that, we'll need to create the C++ struct for it.

The Data Table struct

Just as you created the actor class earlier, let's create a new class. Choose Actor as the parent class and give it a name such as TestCustomData. Our class won't actually inherit from Actor (and, for that matter, it won't be a class), but doing this allows Unreal to generate some code in the background for us.

Next, open the TestCustomData.h file and replace the entire file with the following code:

```
#pragma once

#include "TestCustomData.generated.h"

USTRUCT(BlueprintType)
struct FTestCustomData : public FTableRowBase
{
  GENERATED_USTRUCT_BODY()

  UPROPERTY( BlueprintReadOnly, Category = "TestCustomData" )
  int32 SomeNumber;

  UPROPERTY( BlueprintReadOnly, Category = "TestCustomData" )
  FString SomeString;
};
```

Notice how the variable names are exactly the same as the header cells in the spreadsheet—this is important, as it shows how Unreal matches columns in the spreadsheet to the fields of this struct.

Next, remove everything from the `TestCustomData.cpp` file, with the exception of the `#include` statements.

Now, switch back to the editor and click on **Compile**. It should compile without any issues.

Now that you've created the struct, it's time to import your custom spreadsheet.

Importing the spreadsheet

Next, simply drag your CSV file into the **Content Browser** tab. This will show a pop-up window, asking you to pick how you want to import the data and also what type of data it is. Leave the first drop-down list to **Data Table** and expand the second drop-down list to pick **TestCustomData** (the struct you just created).

Click on **OK** and it will import the CSV file. If you double-click the asset in the **Content Browser** tab, you'll see a list of the items that were in the spreadsheet:

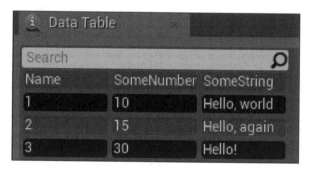

Querying the spreadsheet

You can query the spreadsheet in order to find particular rows by name.

We'll add this to our custom actor class, `MyNewActor`. The first thing we need to do is expose a field to a Blueprint, allowing us to assign a Data Table for our actor to use.

Firstly, add the following code just after the `GENERATED_BODY` line:

```
public:
    UPROPERTY( BlueprintReadWrite, EditAnywhere, Category = "My New
        Actor")
    UDataTable* DataTable;
```

The preceding code will expose the Data Table to Blueprint and allow it to be edited within Blueprint. Next, we'll fetch the first row and log its `SomeString` field. In the `MyNewActor.cpp` file, add this code to the end of the `BeginPlay` function:

```
if( DataTable != NULL )
{
  FTestCustomData* row = DataTable->FindRow<FTestCustomData>(
    TEXT( "2" ), TEXT(" LookupTestCustomData" ) );
  FString someString = row->SomeString;
  UE_LOG( LogTemp, Warning, TEXT( "%s" ), *someString );
}
```

You will also need to add `#include TestCustomData.h` at the top of your `MyNewActor.cpp` file so that you can see the Data Table properties in it.

Compile the code in the editor. Next, open up the Blueprint you created from this actor class. Switch to the **Class Defaults** tab and find the **My New Actor** group (this should be at the very top). This should show a **Data Table** field that you can expand to pick the CSV file you imported.

Compile and save the Blueprint and then press **Play**. You should see the value of `SomeString` for the entry 2 logged to the console.

Summary

In this chapter, we set up Unreal and Visual Studio and created a new project. Additionally, we learned how to create new actor classes in C++, what a Blueprint is, and how to create and use Blueprint graphs for visual scripting. Finally, we learned how to import custom data from spreadsheet applications and query them from the game code.

In the next chapter, we'll start diving into some actual gameplay code and start prototyping our game.

3
Exploration and Combat

We have a design for our game and an Unreal project set up for our game. It's now time to dive into the actual game code.

In this chapter, we'll be making a game character that moves around the world, defining our game data, and prototyping a basic combat system for the game. We will cover the following topics in this chapter:

- Creating the player pawn
- Defining characters, classes, and enemies
- Keeping track of active party members
- Creating a basic turn-based combat engine
- Triggering a game over screen

This particular chapter is the most C++ heavy portion of the book, and provides the basic framework that the rest of the book is going to use. Because this chapter provides much of the backend of our game, the code in this chapter must work to completion before moving on to the rest of the content in the book. If you bought this book because you are a programmer looking for more background in creating a framework for an RPG, this chapter is for you! If you bought this book because you are a designer, and care more about building upon the framework rather than programming it from scratch, you will probably be more into the upcoming chapters because those chapters contain less C++ and more UMG and Blueprints. No matter who you are, it is a good idea to download the source code provided through the directions located in the preface of the book in case you get stuck or would like to skip chapters based on your interests.

Creating the player pawn

The very first thing we are going to do is create a new Pawn class. In Unreal, the *Pawn* is the representation of a character. It handles the movement, physics, and rendering of a character.

Here's how our character pawn is going to work. The player is divided into two parts: there's the Pawn that, as mentioned earlier, is responsible for handling the movement, physics, and rendering. Then there's the Player Controller, responsible for translating the player's input into making the Pawn perform what the player wants.

The Pawn

Now, let's create the actual pawn.

Create a new C++ class and select `Character` as the parent class for it. We will be deriving this class from the `Character` class because `Character` has a lot of built-in move functions that we can use for our field player. Name the class `RPGCharacter`. Open `RPGCharacter.h` and change the class definition using the following code:

```
UCLASS(config = Game)
class ARPGCharacter : public ACharacter
{
  GENERATED_BODY()

  /** Camera boom positioning the camera behind the character */
  UPROPERTY(VisibleAnywhere, BlueprintReadOnly, Category = Camera, meta =
  (AllowPrivateAccess = "true")) class USpringArmComponent* CameraBoom;

  /** Follow camera */
  UPROPERTY(VisibleAnywhere, BlueprintReadOnly, Category = Camera, meta =
  (AllowPrivateAccess = "true")) class UCameraComponent* FollowCamera;
public:
  ARPGCharacter();

  /**Base turn rate, in deg/sec. Other scaling may affect final turn rate.*/
  UPROPERTY(VisibleAnywhere, BlueprintReadOnly, Category = Camera)
    float BaseTurnRate;

protected:
```

```
  /** Called for forwards/backward input */
  void MoveForward(float Value);

  /** Called for side to side input */
  void MoveRight(float Value);

  /**
  * Called via input to turn at a given rate.
  * @param Rate  This is a normalized rate, i.e. 1.0 means 100% of desired turn rate
  */
  void TurnAtRate(float Rate);

protected:
  // APawn interface
virtual void SetupPlayerInputComponent
(class UInputComponent* InputComponent) override;
  // End of APawn interface

public:
  /** Returns CameraBoom subobject **/
FORCEINLINE class USpringArmComponent* GetCameraBoom() const {
return CameraBoom; }
  /** Returns FollowCamera subobject **/
FORCEINLINE class UCameraComponent* GetFollowCamera() const {
return FollowCamera; }
};
```

Next, open RPGCharacter.cpp and replace it with the following code:

```
#include "RPG.h"
#include "RPGCharacter.h"

ARPGCharacter::ARPGCharacter()
{
  // Set size for collision capsule
  GetCapsuleComponent()->InitCapsuleSize(42.f, 96.0f);

  // set our turn rates for input
  BaseTurnRate = 45.f;

// Don't rotate when the controller rotates.
//Let that just affect the camera.
  bUseControllerRotationPitch = false;
  bUseControllerRotationYaw = false;
```

```
bUseControllerRotationRoll = false;

  // Configure character movement
// Character moves in the direction of input...
GetCharacterMovement()->bOrientRotationToMovement = true;
// ...at this rotation rate
GetCharacterMovement()->RotationRate = FRotator(0.0f, 540.0f, 0.0f);


  // Create a camera boom
CameraBoom =
CreateDefaultSubobject<USpringArmComponent>(TEXT("CameraBoom"));
  CameraBoom->SetupAttachment(RootComponent);
// The camera follows at this distance behind the character
CameraBoom->TargetArmLength = 300.0f;
CameraBoom->RelativeLocation = FVector(0.f, 0.f, 500.f);
// Rotate the arm based on the controller
CameraBoom->bUsePawnControlRotation = true;

  // Create a follow camera
FollowCamera =
CreateDefaultSubobject<UCameraComponent>(TEXT("FollowCamera"));
FollowCamera->SetupAttachment(CameraBoom,
USpringArmComponent::SocketName);
// Camera does not rotate relative to arm
FollowCamera->bUsePawnControlRotation = false;
FollowCamera->RelativeRotation = FRotator(-45.f, 0.f, 0.f);

/* Note: The skeletal mesh and anim blueprint references on the Mesh
component (inherited from Character) are set in the derived blueprint
asset named MyCharacter (to avoid direct content references in C++)*/
}


//////////////////////////////////////////////////////////////
// Input

void ARPGCharacter::SetupPlayerInputComponent(class UInputComponent*
InputComponent)
{
  // Set up gameplay key bindings
  check(InputComponent);

InputComponent->BindAxis("MoveForward", this,
&ARPGCharacter::MoveForward);
```

```
InputComponent->BindAxis("MoveRight", this,
&ARPGCharacter::MoveRight);

/* We have 2 versions of the rotation bindings to handle different
kinds of devices differently "turn" handles devices that provide an
absolute delta, such as a mouse. "turnrate" is for devices that we
choose to treat as a rate of change, such as an analog joystick*/
InputComponent->BindAxis("Turn", this, &APawn::AddControllerYawInput);
InputComponent->BindAxis("TurnRate", this,
&ARPGCharacter::TurnAtRate);
}


void ARPGCharacter::TurnAtRate(float Rate)
{
  // calculate delta for this frame from the rate information
AddControllerYawInput(Rate * BaseTurnRate *
GetWorld()->GetDeltaSeconds());
}

void ARPGCharacter::MoveForward(float Value)
{
  if ((Controller != NULL) && (Value != 0.0f))
  {
    // find out which way is forward
    const FRotator Rotation = Controller->GetControlRotation();
    const FRotator YawRotation(0, Rotation.Yaw, 0);

    // get forward vector
    const FVector Direction =
    FRotationMatrix(YawRotation).GetUnitAxis(EAxis::X);
    AddMovementInput(Direction, Value);
  }
}

void ARPGCharacter::MoveRight(float Value)
{
  if ((Controller != NULL) && (Value != 0.0f))
  {
    // find out which way is right
    const FRotator Rotation = Controller->GetControlRotation();
    const FRotator YawRotation(0, Rotation.Yaw, 0);
```

```
    // get right vector
    const FVector Direction =
    FRotationMatrix(YawRotation).GetUnitAxis(EAxis::Y);
    // add movement in that direction
    AddMovementInput(Direction, Value);
  }
}
```

If you have ever created and worked with the C++ **ThirdPerson** game template, you will notice that we are not reinventing the wheel here. The RPGCharacter class should look familiar because it is a modified version of the ThirdPerson Character class code given to us when we create a C++ ThirdPerson template, provided for us to use by Epic Games.

Since we are not creating a fast-paced action game and are simply using the Pawn as an RPG character to maneuver out in the field, we eliminated mechanics that are often associated with action games, such as jumping. But we kept in the code that is important to us, which is the ability to move forward, backward, left, and right; rotational behaviors of the pawn; a camera that will follow the character around in an isometric view; a collision capsule for the character to be able to collide with collidable objects; configuration for character movement; and a camera boom, which will allow the camera to move closer to the character in case it runs into collisions such as a wall or other meshes, important for not blocking a player's view. If you want to edit the character mechanics, feel free to do so by following the comments in the code to change the values of some specific mechanics such as TargetArmLength to change the distance of the camera from the player, or adding jumping, which can be seen in the ThirdPerson character template that came with the Engine.

Because we derived the RPGCharacter class from the Character class, its default camera is not rotated for an isometric view; instead, the camera rotations and locations are zeroed out by default to the pawn's location. So what we did was add a CameraBoom relative location in RPGCharacter.cpp (CameraBoom->RelativeLocation = FVector(0.f, 0.f, 500.f);); this offsets the camera 500 units up on the *z* axis. Along with rotating the camera that follows the player -45 units on the pitch (FollowCamera->RelativeRotation = FRotator(-45.f, 0.f, 0.f);), we get a traditional isometric view. If you would like to edit these values to customize your camera even more, it is suggested; for instance, if you still think your camera is too close to the player, you can simply change the relative location of CameraBoom on the *z* axis to a value higher than 500 units, and/or adjust TargetArmLength to something larger than 300.

Lastly, if you take a look at the `MoveForward` and `MoveRight` movement functions, you will notice that no movement is being added to the pawn unless the value that is passed to `MoveForward` or `MoveRight` is not equal to 0. Later on in this chapter, we will bind keys *W*, *A*, *S*, and *D* to these functions and set each one of these inputs to pass a scalar of 1 or -1 to the corresponding movement function as values. This 1 or -1 value is then used as a multiplier to the direction of the pawn, which will then allow the player to move in a specific direction based on its walk speed. For instance, if we set *W* as a keybind to `MoveForward` with a scalar of 1, and *S* as a keybind to `MoveFoward` with a scalar of -1, when the player presses *W*, the value in the `MoveFoward` function will be equal to 1 and cause the pawn to move in the positive forward direction as a result. Alternatively, if the player presses the *S* key, -1 is then passed into the value used by the `MoveForward` function, which will cause the pawn to move in the negative forward direction (in other words, backwards). Similar logic can be said about the `MoveRight` function, which is why we don't have a `MoveLeft` function—simply because pressing the *A* key would cause the player to move in the negative right direction, which is in fact left.

The GameMode class

Now, in order to use this pawn as a player character, we need to set up a new game mode class. This game mode will then specify the default pawn and player controller classes to use. We'll also be able to make a Blueprint of the game mode and override these defaults.

Create a new class and choose `GameMode` as the parent class. Name this new class `RPGGameMode` (if `RPGGameMode` already exists in your project, simply navigate to your C++ source directory and proceed to open up `RPGGameMode.h`, as listed in the next step).

Open `RPGGameMode.h` and change the class definition using the following code:

```
UCLASS()
class RPG_API ARPGGameMode : public AGameMode
{
    GENERATED_BODY()

    ARPGGameMode( const class FObjectInitializer& ObjectInitializer );
};
```

Just as we've done before, we're just defining a constructor for the CPP file to implement.

We're going to implement that constructor now in RPGGameMode.cpp:

```cpp
#include "RPGCharacter.h"

ARPGGameMode::ARPGGameMode( const class FObjectInitializer& ObjectInitializer )
    : Super( ObjectInitializer )
{

   DefaultPawnClass = ARPGCharacter::StaticClass();
}
```

Here, we include the RPGCharacter.h file so that we can reference these classes. Then, in the constructor, we set the class as the default class to use for the Pawn.

Now, if you compile this code, you should be able to assign your new game mode class as the default game mode. To do this, go to **Edit | Project Settings**, find the **Default Modes** box, expand the **Default GameMode** drop-down menu, and select **RPGGameMode**.

However, we don't necessarily want to use this class directly. Instead, if we make a Blueprint, we can expose the properties of the game mode that can be modified in the Blueprint.

So, let's make a new Blueprint Class in **Content | Blueprints**, pick RPGGameMode as its parent class, and call it DefaultRPGGameMode:

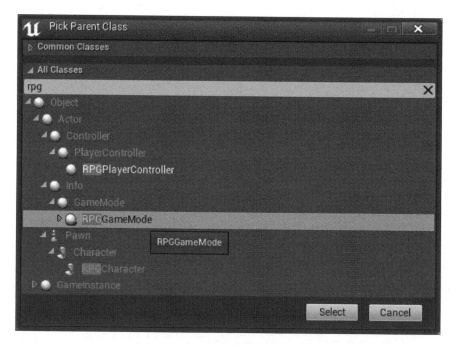

If you open the Blueprint and navigate to the **Defaults** tab, you can modify the settings for the game mode for **Default Pawn Class**, **HUD Class**, **Player Controller Class**, and more settings:

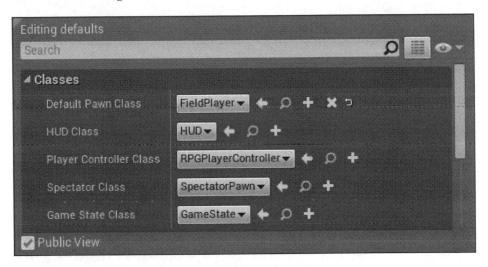

However, we still have one extra step before we can test our new Pawn. If you run the game, you will not see the Pawn at all. In fact, it will appear as if nothing is happening. We need to give our Pawn a skinned mesh and also make the camera follow the pawn.

Adding the skinned mesh

For now, we're just going to import the prototype character that comes with the ThirdPerson sample. To do this, make a new project based on the ThirdPerson sample. Locate the `ThirdPersonCharacter` Blueprint class in **Content | ThirdPersonCPP | Blueprints** and migrate it to the `Content` folder of your RPG project by right-clicking on the `ThirdPersonCharacter` Blueprint class and navigating to **Asset Actions | Migrate…**. This action should copy `ThirdPersonCharacter` with all its assets into your RPG project:

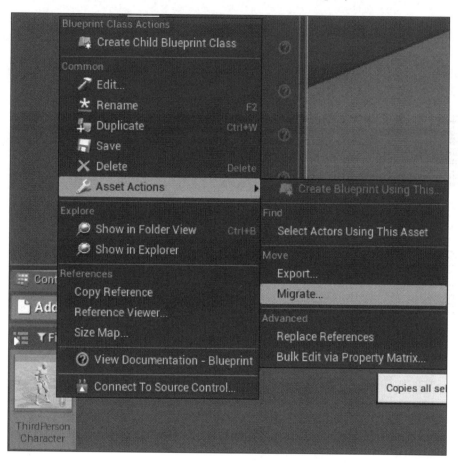

Now, let's create a new Blueprint for our Pawn. Create a new Blueprint class and select **RPGCharacter** as the parent class. Name it **FieldPlayer**.

Expand **Mesh** located in the **Details** tab when selecting the **Mesh** component from the **Components** tab and choose **SK_Mannequin** as the skeletal mesh for the pawn. Next, expand **Animation** and choose **ThirdPerson_AnimBP** as the animation Blueprint to use. You will most likely need to move your character's mesh down the z axis so that the bottom of the character's feet meet the bottom of the collision capsule. Also be sure that the character mesh is facing the same direction that the blue arrow in the component is facing. You may need to rotate the character on the z axis as well to ensure that the character is facing the right direction:

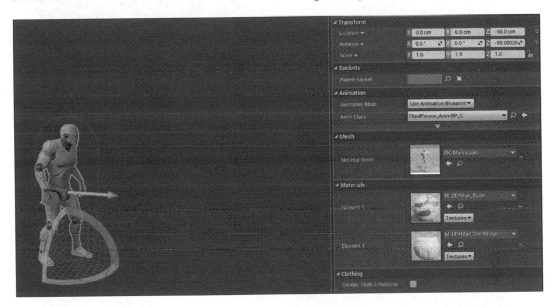

Finally, open your game mode Blueprint and change the pawn to your new **FieldPlayer** Blueprint.

Now, our character will be visible, but we may not be able to move it yet because we have not bound keys to any of our movement variables. To do so, go into **Project Settings** and locate **Input**. Expand **Bindings** and then expand **Axis Mappings**. Add an axis mapping by pressing the **+** button. Call the first axis mapping **MoveRight**, which should match the `MoveRight` movement variable you created earlier in this chapter. Add two key bindings for **MoveRight** by pressing the **+** button. Let one of those keys be *A* with a scale of -1 and other be *D* with a scale of 1. Add another axis mapping for **MoveForward**; only this time, have a *W* key binding with a scale of 1 and an *S* key binding with a scale of -1:

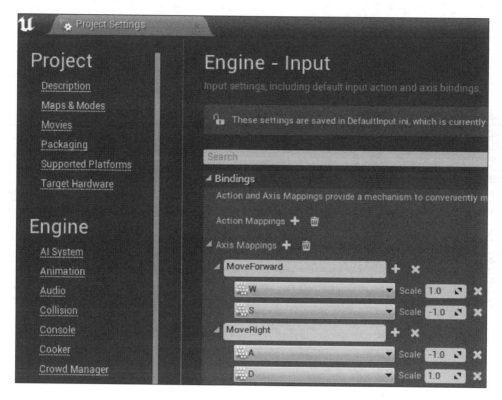

Once you play test, you should see your character moving and animating using the *W*, *A*, *S*, and *D* keys you bound to the player.

When you run the game, the camera should track the player in an overhead view. Now that we have a character that can explore the game world, let's take a look at defining characters and party members.

Defining characters and enemies

In the last chapter, we covered how to use Data Tables to import custom data. Before that, we decided on what stats would play into combat and how. Now we're going to combine those to define our game's characters, classes, and enemy encounters.

Classes

Remember that in *Chapter 1, Getting Started with RPG Design in Unreal*, we established that our characters have the following stats:

- Health
- Max health
- Magic
- Max magic
- Attack power
- Defense
- Luck

Of these, we can discard health and magic because they vary during the game, while the other values are predefined based on the character class. The remaining stats are what we will define in the Data Table. As mentioned in *Chapter 1, Getting Started with RPG Design in Unreal*, we also need to store what the value should be at level 50 (the maximum level). Characters will also have some abilities they start out with, and some they learn as they level up.

We'll define these in the character class spreadsheet, along with the name of the class. So our character class schema will look something like the following:

- Class name (string)
- Starting max HP (integer)
- Max HP at level 50 (integer)
- Starting max MP (integer)
- Max MP at level 50 (integer)
- Starting attack (integer)
- Attack at level 50 (integer)
- Starting defense (integer)

- Defense at level 50 (integer)
- Starting luck (integer)
- Luck at level 50 (integer)
- Starting abilities (string array)
- Learned abilities (string array)
- Learned ability levels (integer array)

The ability string arrays will contain the ID of the ability (the value of the reserved name field in UE4). Additionally, there are two separate cells for learned abilities—one that contains the ability IDs, another that contains the levels at which those abilities are learned.

In a production game, one thing you might consider is writing a custom tool to help manage this data and reduce human error. However, writing such a tool is outside the scope of this book.

Now, instead of creating a spreadsheet for this, we're actually going to first create the class and then the Data Table inside Unreal. The reason for this is that at the time of writing, the proper syntax to specify arrays in a cell of a Data Table is not well documented. However, arrays can still be edited from inside the Unreal editor, so we'll simply create the table there and use Unreal's array editor.

Firstly, as usual, create a new class. The class will be used as an object that you can call from, so choose Object as the parent class. Name this class FCharacterClassInfo and, for organization purposes, path your new class to your Source/RPG/Data folder.

Open FCharacterClassInfo.h and replace the class definition with the following code:

```
USTRUCT( BlueprintType )
struct FCharacterClassInfo : public FTableRowBase
{
  GENERATED_USTRUCT_BODY()

  UPROPERTY( BlueprintReadWrite, EditAnywhere, Category =
    "ClassInfo" )
    FString Class_Name;

  UPROPERTY( BlueprintReadWrite, EditAnywhere, Category =
    "ClassInfo" )
    int32 StartMHP;
```

```
UPROPERTY( BlueprintReadWrite, EditAnywhere, Category =
  "ClassInfo" )
  int32 StartMMP;

UPROPERTY( BlueprintReadWrite, EditAnywhere, Category =
  "ClassInfo" )
  int32 StartATK;

UPROPERTY( BlueprintReadWrite, EditAnywhere, Category =
  "ClassInfo" )
  int32 StartDEF;

UPROPERTY( BlueprintReadWrite, EditAnywhere, Category =
  "ClassInfo" )
  int32 StartLuck;

UPROPERTY( BlueprintReadWrite, EditAnywhere, Category =
  "ClassInfo" )
  int32 EndMHP;

UPROPERTY( BlueprintReadWrite, EditAnywhere, Category =
  "ClassInfo" )
  int32 EndMMP;

UPROPERTY( BlueprintReadWrite, EditAnywhere, Category =
  "ClassInfo" )
  int32 EndATK;

UPROPERTY( BlueprintReadWrite, EditAnywhere, Category =
  "ClassInfo" )
  int32 EndDEF;

UPROPERTY( BlueprintReadWrite, EditAnywhere, Category =
  "ClassInfo" )
  int32 EndLuck;

UPROPERTY( BlueprintReadWrite, EditAnywhere, Category =
  "ClassInfo" )
  TArray<FString> StartingAbilities;

UPROPERTY( BlueprintReadWrite, EditAnywhere, Category =
  "ClassInfo" )
  TArray<FString> LearnedAbilities;

UPROPERTY( BlueprintReadWrite, EditAnywhere, Category =
  "ClassInfo" )
  TArray<int32> LearnedAbilityLevels;
};
```

Most of this code should be familiar to you already; however, you may not recognize the last three fields. These are all of the `TArray` type, which is a dynamic array type provided by Unreal. Essentially, a `TArray` can have elements dynamically added to it and removed from it, unlike a standard C++ array.

Upon compiling this code, create a new folder called `Data` within your `Content` folder so that you can stay organized by keeping Data Tables that you create within the `Data` folder. Navigate to **Content | Data** in the Content Browser and create a new Data Table by right-clicking on **Content Browser** and choosing **Miscellaneous | Data Table**. Then, select **Character Class Info** from the drop-down list. Name your Data Table **CharacterClasses** and then double-click to open it.

To add a new entry, hit the **+** button. Then, give a name to the new entry by entering something in the **Row Name** field and pressing *Enter*.

After an entry has been added, you can select the entry in the **Data Table** pane and edit its properties in the **Row Editor** pane.

Let's add a Soldier class to the list. We will it give the name `S1` (which we'll use to refer to the character class from other Data Tables) and it will have the following properties:

- **Class Name**: Soldier
- **Start MHP**: 100
- **Start MMP**: 100
- **Start ATK**: 5
- **Start DEF**: 0
- **Start Luck**: 0
- **End MHP**: 800
- **End MMP**: 500
- **End ATK**: 20
- **End DEF**: 20
- **End Luck**: 10
- **Starting Abilities**: (leave empty for now)
- **Learned Abilities**: (leave empty for now)
- **Learned Ability Levels**: (leave empty for now)

When you are finished, your Data Table should look like this:

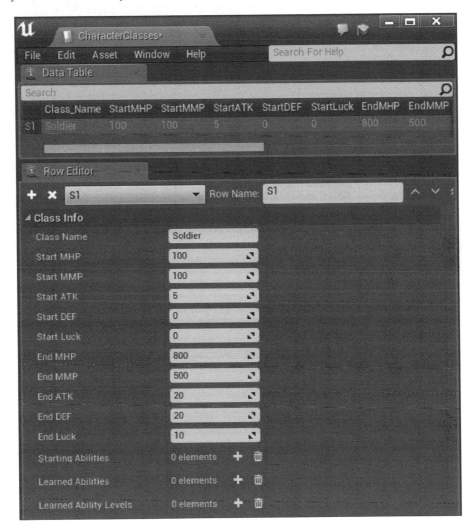

If you have more character classes that you would like to define, continue to add them to your Data Table.

Characters

With classes defined, let's take a look at characters. Since most of the important combat-related data is already defined as part of a character's class, the character itself is going to be quite a bit simpler. In fact, for now, our characters will be defined by just two things: the name of the character and the character's class.

Firstly, create a new C++ class called `FCharacterInfo` whose parent is `Object`, and path it to the `Source/RPG/Data` folder. Now, replace the class definition in `FCharacterInfo.h` with this:

```
USTRUCT(BlueprintType)
struct FCharacterInfo : public FTableRowBase
{
  GENERATED_USTRUCT_BODY()

  UPROPERTY( BlueprintReadWrite, EditAnywhere, Category =
    "CharacterInfo" )
  FString Character_Name;

  UPROPERTY( BlueprintReadOnly, EditAnywhere, Category =
    "CharacterInfo" )
  FString Class_ID;
};
```

As we did earlier, we're just defining the two fields for the character (character name and class ID).

After compiling, create a new Data Table in your `Data` folder that you created earlier from within the Content Browser and select **CharacterInfo** as the class; call it `Characters`. Add a new entry with the name `S1`. You can name this character whatever you like (we named our character soldier **Kumo**), but for class ID, enter `S1` (as this is the name of the Soldier class we defined earlier).

Enemies

As for enemies, rather than defining a separate character and class information, we'll create a simplified combined table for these two pieces of information. An enemy generally does not have to deal with experience and leveling up, so we can omit any data related to this. Additionally, enemies do not consume MP as players do, so we can omit this data as well.

Therefore, our enemy data will have the following properties:

- Enemy name (string array)
- MHP (integer)
- ATK (integer)
- DEF (integer)
- Luck (integer)
- Abilities (string array)

Much like the previous Data Class creations, we create a new C++ class that derives from `Object`, but this time we will call it `FEnemyInfo` and place it with the rest of our data in the `Source/RPG/Data` directory.

At this point, you should have an understanding of how to construct the class for this data, but let's take a look at the struct header anyway. In `FEnemyInfo.h`, replace your class definition with the following:

```
USTRUCT( BlueprintType )
struct FEnemyInfo : public FTableRowBase
{
  GENERATED_USTRUCT_BODY()

  UPROPERTY( BlueprintReadWrite, EditAnywhere, Category =
    "EnemyInfo" )
    FString EnemyName;

  UPROPERTY( BlueprintReadOnly, EditAnywhere, Category =
    "EnemyInfo" )
    int32 MHP;

  UPROPERTY( BlueprintReadOnly, EditAnywhere, Category =
    "EnemyInfo" )
    int32 ATK;

  UPROPERTY( BlueprintReadOnly, EditAnywhere, Category =
    "EnemyInfo" )
    int32 DEF;

  UPROPERTY( BlueprintReadOnly, EditAnywhere, Category =
    "EnemyInfo" )
    int32 Luck;
```

```
UPROPERTY( BlueprintReadOnly, EditAnywhere, Category =
  "EnemyInfo" )
  TArray<FString> Abilities;
};
```

After compiling, create a new Data Table, select `EnemyInfo` as the class, and call the Data Table `Enemies`. Add a new entry with the name `S1` and the following properties:

- **Enemy Name**: Goblin
- **MHP**: 20
- **ATK**: 5
- **DEF**: 0
- **Luck**: 0
- **Abilities**: (leave empty for now)

At this point, we've got the data for a character, the character's class, and a single enemy for the character to fight. Next, let's start keeping track of which characters are in the active party and what their current stats are.

Party members

Before we can keep track of party members, we'll need a way to track a character's current state, such as how much HP the character has or what it has equipped.

To do this, we'll create a new class named `GameCharacter`. As usual, create a new class and pick `Object` as the parent class.

The header for this class looks like the following code snippet:

```
#pragma once

#include "Data/FCharacterInfo.h"
#include "Data/FCharacterClassInfo.h"

#include "GameCharacter.generated.h"

UCLASS( BlueprintType )
class RPG_API UGameCharacter : public UObject
{
  GENERATED_BODY()
```

```
public:
  FCharacterClassInfo* ClassInfo;

  UPROPERTY( EditAnywhere, BlueprintReadWrite, Category =
    CharacterInfo )
  FString CharacterName;

  UPROPERTY( EditAnywhere, BlueprintReadWrite, Category =
    CharacterInfo )
  int32 MHP;

  UPROPERTY( EditAnywhere, BlueprintReadWrite, Category =
    CharacterInfo )
  int32 MMP;

  UPROPERTY( EditAnywhere, BlueprintReadWrite, Category =
    CharacterInfo )
  int32 HP;

  UPROPERTY( EditAnywhere, BlueprintReadWrite, Category =
    CharacterInfo )
  int32 MP;

  UPROPERTY( EditAnywhere, BlueprintReadWrite, Category =
    CharacterInfo )
  int32 ATK;

  UPROPERTY( EditAnywhere, BlueprintReadWrite, Category =
    CharacterInfo )
  int32 DEF;

  UPROPERTY( EditAnywhere, BlueprintReadWrite, Category =
    CharacterInfo )
  int32 LUCK;

public:
  static UGameCharacter* CreateGameCharacter( FCharacterInfo*
    characterInfo, UObject* outer );

public:
  void BeginDestroy() override;
};
```

For now, we're keeping track of the character's name, character's source class information, and character's current stats. Later, we will use the UCLASS and UPROPERTY macros to expose information to the Blueprint. We'll add other information later as we work on the combat system.

As for the .cpp file, it will look like this:

```cpp
#include "RPG.h"
#include "GameCharacter.h"

UGameCharacter* UGameCharacter::CreateGameCharacter(
  FCharacterInfo* characterInfo, UObject* outer )
{
  UGameCharacter* character = NewObject<UGameCharacter>( outer );

  // locate character classes asset
  UDataTable* characterClasses = Cast<UDataTable>(
    StaticLoadObject( UDataTable::StaticClass(), NULL, TEXT(
    "DataTable'/Game/Data/CharacterClasses.CharacterClasses'" ) )
    );

  if( characterClasses == NULL )
  {
    UE_LOG( LogTemp, Error, TEXT( "Character classes datatable not found!" ) );
  }
  else
  {
    character->CharacterName = characterInfo->Character_Name;
    FCharacterClassInfo* row = characterClasses->FindRow
      <FCharacterClassInfo>( *( characterInfo->Class_ID ), TEXT(
      "LookupCharacterClass" ) );
    character->ClassInfo = row;

    character->MHP = character->ClassInfo->StartMHP;
    character->MMP = character->ClassInfo->StartMMP;
    character->HP = character->MHP;
    character->MP = character->MMP;

    character->ATK = character->ClassInfo->StartATK;
    character->DEF = character->ClassInfo->StartDEF;
    character->LUCK = character->ClassInfo->StartLuck;
  }
```

```
    return character;
  }

  void UGameCharacter::BeginDestroy()
  {
    Super::BeginDestroy();
  }
```

The `CreateGameCharacter` factory for our `UGameCharacter` class takes a pointer to an `FCharacterInfo` struct, which is returned from a Data Table, and also an `Outer` object, which is passed to the `NewObject` function. It then attempts to find the character class Data Table from a path, and if the result is not null, it locates the proper row in the Data Table, stores the result, and also initializes the stats and the `CharacterName` field. In the preceding code, you can see the path where the character class Data Table is located. You can get this path by right-clicking on your Data Table from the Content Browser, selecting **Copy Reference**, and then pasting the result into your code.

While this is currently a very basic bare-bones representation of a character, it will work for now. Next, we're going to store a list of these characters as the current party.

The GameInstance class

We have already created a `GameMode` class, and this might seem like the perfect place to keep track of information such as party members and inventory, right?

However, `GameMode` does not persist between level loads! This means that unless you save some information to disk, you lose all of that data whenever you load a new area.

The `GameInstance` class was introduced to deal with just this sort of problem. A `GameInstance` class persists through the whole game, regardless of level loads, unlike `GameMode`. We're going to create a new `GameInstance` class to keep track of our persistent data, such as party members and inventory.

Create a new class, and this time, select `GameInstance` as the parent class (you'll have to search for it). Name it `RPGGameInstance`.

In the header file, we're going to add a TArray of the UGameCharacter pointers, a flag to know whether the game has been initialized, and an Init function. Your RPGGameInstance.h file should look like this:

```
#pragma once

#include "Engine/GameInstance.h"
#include "GameCharacter.h"
#include "RPGGameInstance.generated.h"
UCLASS()
class RPG_API URPGGameInstance : public UGameInstance
{
  GENERATED_BODY()

  URPGGameInstance( const class FObjectInitializer&
    ObjectInitializer );

public:
  TArray<UGameCharacter*> PartyMembers;

protected:
  bool isInitialized;

public:
  void Init();
};
```

In the Init function for the game instance, we'll add a single default party member and then set the isInitialized flag to true. Your RPGGameInstance.cpp should look like this:

```
#include "RPG.h"
#include "RPGGameInstance.h"
URPGGameInstance::URPGGameInstance(const class FObjectInitializer&
ObjectInitializer)
: Super(ObjectInitializer)
{
  isInitialized = false;
}

void URPGGameInstance::Init()
{
  if( this->isInitialized ) return;
```

```
    this->isInitialized = true;

    // locate characters asset
    UDataTable* characters = Cast<UDataTable>( StaticLoadObject(
      UDataTable::StaticClass(), NULL,
TEXT( "DataTable'/Game/Data/Characters.Characters'" ) ) );
        if( characters == NULL )
    {
      UE_LOG( LogTemp, Error, TEXT( "Characters data table not found!" ) );

      return;
    }

    // locate character
    FCharacterInfo* row = characters->FindRow<FCharacterInfo>( TEXT(
      "S1" ), TEXT( "LookupCharacterClass" ) );

    if( row == NULL )
    {
      UE_LOG( LogTemp, Error, TEXT( "Character ID 'S1' not found!" ) );
      return;
    }

    // add character to party
    this->PartyMembers.Add( UGameCharacter::CreateGameCharacter(
      row, this ) );
  }
```

You may run into a linker error at this point if you try to compile. It is recommended that before you move on, save and close everything. Then restart your project. After you do that, compile the project.

To set this class as your `GameInstance` class, in Unreal, open **Edit | Project Settings**, go to **Maps & Modes**, scroll down to the **Game Instance** box, and pick **RPGGameInstance** from the drop-down list. Finally, from the game mode, we override `BeginPlay` to call this `Init` function.

Open `RPGGameMode.h` and add `virtual void BeginPlay() override;` at the end of your class so that your header will now look like this:

```
#pragma once

#include "GameFramework/GameMode.h"
```

```
#include "RPGGameMode.generated.h"

UCLASS()
class RPG_API ARPGGameMode : public AGameMode
{
  GENERATED_BODY()

  ARPGGameMode(const class FObjectInitializer& ObjectInitializer);
  virtual void BeginPlay() override;
};
```

And in `RPGGameMode.cpp`, cast `RPGGameInstance` at `BeginPlay` so that `RPGGameMode.cpp` now looks like this:

```
#include "RPG.h"
#include "RPGGameMode.h"
#include "RPGCharacter.h"
#include "RPGGameInstance.h"

ARPGGameMode::ARPGGameMode(const class FObjectInitializer&
ObjectInitializer)
: Super(ObjectInitializer)
{
  DefaultPawnClass = ARPGCharacter::StaticClass();
    }

void ARPGGameMode::BeginPlay()
{
  Cast<URPGGameInstance>(GetGameInstance())->Init();
}
```

Once you compile the code, you now have a list of active party members. It's time to start prototyping the combat engine.

Turn-based combat

So, as mentioned in *Chapter 1, Getting Started with RPG Design in Unreal,* combat is turn-based. All characters first choose an action to perform; then, the actions are executed in order.

Combat will be split into two main phases: **Decision**, in which all characters decide on their course of action; and **Action**, in which all characters execute their chosen course of action.

Let's create a class with an empty parent to handle combat for us, which we'll call `CombatEngine`, and path it to a new directory located in `Source/RPG/Combat`, where we can organize all of our combat-related classes. Formulate the header file to look like this:

```
#pragma once
#include "RPG.h"
#include "GameCharacter.h"

enum class CombatPhase : uint8
{
  CPHASE_Decision,
  CPHASE_Action,
  CPHASE_Victory,
  CPHASE_GameOver,
};

class RPG_API CombatEngine
{
public:
  TArray<UGameCharacter*> combatantOrder;
  TArray<UGameCharacter*> playerParty;
  TArray<UGameCharacter*> enemyParty;

  CombatPhase phase;

protected:
  UGameCharacter* currentTickTarget;
  int tickTargetIndex;

public:
  CombatEngine( TArray<UGameCharacter*> playerParty,
    TArray<UGameCharacter*> enemyParty );
  ~CombatEngine();

  bool Tick( float DeltaSeconds );

protected:
  void SetPhase( CombatPhase phase );
  void SelectNextCharacter();
};
```

There's a lot going on here, so I'll explain.

Firstly, our combat engine is designed to be allocated when an encounter starts and deleted when combat is over.

An instance of `CombatEngine` keeps three `TArray`: one for combat order (a list of all participants in combat, in the order they will take turns in), another for a list of players, and the third one for a list of enemies. It also keeps track of `CombatPhase`. There are two main phases of combat: `Decision` and `Action`. Each round starts in `Decision`; in this phase, all characters are allowed to choose their course of action. Then, combat transitions to the `Action` phase; in this phase, all characters perform their previously chosen course of action.

The `GameOver` and `Victory` phases will be transitioned to when all enemies are dead or all players are dead, respectively (which is why the player and enemy lists are kept separate).

The `CombatEngine` class defines a `Tick` function. This will be called by the game mode of every frame as long as combat is not over, and it returns `true` when combat has finished (or `false` otherwise). It takes the duration of the last frame in seconds as a parameter.

There's also the `currentTickTarget` and `tickTargetIndex`. During the `Decision` and `Action` phases, we'll keep a pointer to a single character. For instance, during the `Decision` phase, this pointer starts with the first character in the combat order. At every frame, the character will be asked to make a decision—which will be a function that returns `true` if the character has made a decision, or `false` otherwise. If the function returns `true`, the pointer will advance to the next character and so on until all characters have decided at which point the combat transitions to the `Action` phase.

The CPP for this file is fairly big, so let's take it in small chunks. Firstly, the constructor and destructor are as follows:

```
CombatEngine::CombatEngine( TArray<UGameCharacter*> playerParty,
  TArray<UGameCharacter*> enemyParty )
{
  this->playerParty = playerParty;
  this->enemyParty = enemyParty;

  // first add all players to combat order
  for( int i = 0; i < playerParty.Num(); i++ )
  {
    this->combatantOrder.Add( playerParty[i] );
  }
```

```
    // next add all enemies to combat order
    for( int i = 0; i < enemyParty.Num(); i++ )
    {
        this->combatantOrder.Add( enemyParty[i] );
    }

    this->tickTargetIndex = 0;
    this->SetPhase( CombatPhase::CPHASE_Decision );
}


CombatEngine::~CombatEngine()
{
}
```

The constructor first assigns the player party and enemy party fields and then adds all players followed by all enemies to the combat order list. Finally, it sets the `tick` target index to 0 (the first character in the combat order) and the combat phase to `Decision`.

Next, the `Tick` function is as follows:

```
bool CombatEngine::Tick( float DeltaSeconds )
{
    switch( phase )
    {
        case CombatPhase::CPHASE_Decision:
            // todo: ask current character to make decision

            // todo: if decision made
            SelectNextCharacter();

            // no next character, switch to action phase
            if( this->tickTargetIndex == -1 )
            {
                this->SetPhase( CombatPhase::CPHASE_Action );
            }
            break;
        case CombatPhase::CPHASE_Action:
            // todo: ask current character to execute decision

            // todo: when action executed
            SelectNextCharacter();
```

```cpp
      // no next character, loop back to decision phase
      if( this->tickTargetIndex == -1 )
      {
        this->SetPhase( CombatPhase::CPHASE_Decision );
      }
      break;
    // in case of victory or combat, return true (combat is finished)
    case CombatPhase::CPHASE_GameOver:
    case CombatPhase::CPHASE_Victory:
      return true;
      break;
  }


  // check for game over
  int deadCount = 0;
  for( int i = 0; i < this->playerParty.Num(); i++ )
  {
    if( this->playerParty[ i ]->HP <= 0 ) deadCount++;
  }


  // all players have died, switch to game over phase
  if( deadCount == this->playerParty.Num() )
  {
    this->SetPhase( CombatPhase::CPHASE_GameOver );
    return false;
  }


  // check for victory
  deadCount = 0;
  for( int i = 0; i < this->enemyParty.Num(); i++ )
  {
    if( this->enemyParty[ i ]->HP <= 0 ) deadCount++;
  }


  // all enemies have died, switch to victory phase
  if( deadCount == this->enemyParty.Num() )
  {
    this->SetPhase( CombatPhase::CPHASE_Victory );
    return false;
  }


  // if execution reaches here, combat has not finished - return false
  return false;
}
```

Firstly, we switch on the current combat phase. In the case of `Decision`, it currently just selects the next character or, if there is no next character, switches to the `Action` phase. It is the same for `Action` — except that if there is no next character, it loops back to the `Decision` phase.

Later, this will be modified to call functions on the character in order to make and execute decisions (and additionally, the "select next character" code will only be called once the character has finished deciding or executing).

In the case of `GameOver` or `Victory`, `Tick` returning `true` means combat is over. Otherwise, it first checks whether all players are dead (in this case, it is game over) or whether all enemies are dead (in this case, players win combat). In both cases, the function will return `true` as combat is finished.

The very end of the function returns `false`, which means combat has not yet finished.

Next, we have the `SetPhase` function:

```
void CombatEngine::SetPhase( CombatPhase phase )
{
  this->phase = phase;

  switch( phase )
  {
    case CombatPhase::CPHASE_Action:
    case CombatPhase::CPHASE_Decision:
      // set the active target to the first character in the combat order
      this->tickTargetIndex = 0;
      this->SelectNextCharacter();
      break;
    case CombatPhase::CPHASE_Victory:
      // todo: handle victory
      break;
    case CombatPhase::CPHASE_GameOver:
      // todo: handle game over
      break;
  }
}
```

This function sets the combat phase, and in the case of `Action` or `Decision`, it sets the `tick` target to the first character in the combat order. Both `Victory` and `GameOver` have stubs to handle the respective states.

Finally, we have the `SelectNextCharacter` function:

```cpp
void CombatEngine::SelectNextCharacter()
{
  for( int i = this->tickTargetIndex; i < this->combatantOrder.
    Num(); i++ )
  {
    GameCharacter* character = this->combatantOrder[ i ];

    if( character->HP > 0 )
    {
      this->tickTargetIndex = i + 1;
      this->currentTickTarget = character;
      return;
    }
  }

  this->tickTargetIndex = -1;
  this->currentTickTarget = nullptr;
}
```

This function starts at the current `tickTargetIndex` and, from there, finds the first non-dead character in the combat order. If one is found, it sets the `tick` target index to the next index and the `tick` target to the found character. Otherwise, it sets the `tick` target index to -1 and the `tick` target to a null pointer (which is interpreted to mean no remaining characters in combat order).

There's a very important thing missing at this point: characters cannot yet make or execute decisions.

Let's add this to the `GameCharacter` class. For now, they will just be stubs.

Firstly, we'll add the `testDelayTimer` field to `GameCharacter.h`. This will just be for testing purposes:

```cpp
protected:
    float testDelayTimer;
```

Next, we add several public functions to the class:

```cpp
public:
  void BeginMakeDecision();
  bool MakeDecision( float DeltaSeconds );

  void BeginExecuteAction();
  bool ExecuteAction( float DeltaSeconds );
```

We split `Decision` and `Action` into two functions each—the first function tells the character to begin making a decision or executing an action, the second function essentially queries the character until the decision is made or action is finished.

The implementation for these two functions in `GameCharacter.cpp` will, for now, just log a message and a delay for 1 second:

```
void UGameCharacter::BeginMakeDecision()
{
  UE_LOG( LogTemp, Log, TEXT( "Character %s making decision" ),
    *this->CharacterName );
  this->testDelayTimer = 1;
}


bool UGameCharacter::MakeDecision( float DeltaSeconds )
{
  this->testDelayTimer -= DeltaSeconds;
  return this->testDelayTimer <= 0;
}


void UGameCharacter::BeginExecuteAction()
{
  UE_LOG( LogTemp, Log, TEXT( "Character %s executing action" ),
    *this->CharacterName );
  this->testDelayTimer = 1;
}


bool UGameCharacter::ExecuteAction( float DeltaSeconds )
{
  this->testDelayTimer -= DeltaSeconds;
  return this->testDelayTimer <= 0;
}
```

We're also going to add a pointer to the combat instance. Since the combat engine references characters, having characters reference the combat engine would produce a circular dependency. To solve this, we're going to add a forward declaration at the top of `GameCharacter.h` directly after our includes:

```
class CombatEngine;
```

Then, the `include` statement for the combat engine will actually be placed in `GameCharacter.cpp` rather than in the header file:

```
#include "Combat/CombatEngine.h"
```

Next, we'll make the combat engine call the `Decision` and `Action` functions. Firstly, we'll add a protected variable to `CombatEngine.h`:

```
bool waitingForCharacter;
```

This will be used to switch between, for example, `BeginMakeDecision` and `MakeDecision`.

Next, we'll modify the `Decision` and `Action` phases in the `Tick` function. Firstly, we'll modify the `Decision` switch case:

```
case CombatPhase::CPHASE_Decision:
{
  if( !this->waitingForCharacter )
  {
    this->currentTickTarget->BeginMakeDecision();
    this->waitingForCharacter = true;
  }

  bool decisionMade = this->currentTickTarget->MakeDecision(
    DeltaSeconds );

  if( decisionMade )
  {
    SelectNextCharacter();

    // no next character, switch to action phase
    if( this->tickTargetIndex == -1 )
    {
      this->SetPhase( CombatPhase::CPHASE_Action );
    }
  }
}
break;
```

If `waitingForCharacter` is `false`, it calls `BeginMakeDecision` and sets `waitingForCharacter` to `true`.

Keep note of the brackets enclosing the whole case statement—if you do not add these brackets, you will get compile errors about the `decisionMade` initialization being skipped by the case statement.

Next, it calls `MakeDecision` and passes the frame time. If this function returns `true`, it selects the next character, or failing that, switches to the `Action` phase.

The `Action` phase looks identical to the following:

```
case CombatPhase::CPHASE_Action:
{
  if( !this->waitingForCharacter )
  {
    this->currentTickTarget->BeginExecuteAction();
    this->waitingForCharacter = true;
  }

  bool actionFinished = this->currentTickTarget->ExecuteAction(
    DeltaSeconds );

  if( actionFinished )
  {
    SelectNextCharacter();

    // no next character, switch to action phase
    if( this->tickTargetIndex == -1 )
    {
      this->SetPhase( CombatPhase::CPHASE_Decision );
    }
  }
}
break;
```

Next, we'll modify `SelectNextCharacter` so that it sets `waitingForCharacter` to `false`:

```
void CombatEngine::SelectNextCharacter()
{
  this->waitingForCharacter = false;
  for (int i = this->tickTargetIndex; i < this->combatantOrder.
    Num(); i++)
  {
    UGameCharacter* character = this->combatantOrder[i];

    if (character->HP > 0)
    {
      this->tickTargetIndex = i + 1;
      this->currentTickTarget = character;
      return;
    }
  }
}
```

```
        this->tickTargetIndex = -1;
        this->currentTickTarget = nullptr;
    }
```

Finally, a few remaining details: our combat engine should set the `CombatInstance` pointer of all characters to point to itself, which we'll do in the constructor; then we'll clear the pointer in the destructor and also release enemy pointers. So first, create a pointer to `combatInstance` in `GameCharacter.h` right after your `UProperty` declarations and before your protected variables:

```
    CombatEngine* combatInstance;
```

Then, in `CombatEngine.cpp`, replace your constructor and deconstructor with this:

```
    CombatEngine::CombatEngine( TArray<UGameCharacter*> playerParty,
        TArray<UGameCharacter*> enemyParty )
    {
        this->playerParty = playerParty;
        this->enemyParty = enemyParty;

        // first add all players to combat order
        for (int i = 0; i < playerParty.Num(); i++)
        {
            this->combatantOrder.Add(playerParty[i]);
        }

        // next add all enemies to combat order
        for (int i = 0; i < enemyParty.Num(); i++)
        {
            this->combatantOrder.Add(enemyParty[i]);
        }

        this->tickTargetIndex = 0;
        this->SetPhase(CombatPhase::CPHASE_Decision);

        for( int i = 0; i < this->combatantOrder.Num(); i++ )
        {
            this->combatantOrder[i]->combatInstance = this;
        }

        this->tickTargetIndex = 0;
        this->SetPhase( CombatPhase::CPHASE_Decision );
    }
```

```
CombatEngine::~CombatEngine()
{
  // free enemies
  for( int i = 0; i < this->enemyParty.Num(); i++ )
  {
    this->enemyParty[i] = nullptr;
  }

  for( int i = 0; i < this->combatantOrder.Num(); i++ )
  {
    this->combatantOrder[i]->combatInstance = nullptr;
  }
}
```

The combat engine itself is almost fully functional at this point. We still need to hook it up to the rest of the game, but with a way to trigger combat and update it from the game mode.

So, firstly in our `RPGGameMode` class, we will add a pointer to the current combat instance and also override the `Tick` function; additionally, keep track of a list of enemy characters (decorated with UPROPERTY so that enemies can be garbage-collected):

```
#pragma once
#include "GameFramework/GameMode.h"
#include "GameCharacter.h"
#include "Combat/CombatEngine.h"
#include "RPGGameMode.generated.h"

UCLASS()
class RPG_API ARPGGameMode : public AGameMode
{
  GENERATED_BODY()

  ARPGGameMode( const class FObjectInitializer& ObjectInitializer
    );
  virtual void BeginPlay() override;
  virtual void Tick( float DeltaTime ) override;

public:
  CombatEngine* currentCombatInstance;
  TArray<UGameCharacter*> enemyParty;
};
```

Next, in the `.cpp` file, we implement the `Tick` function:

```cpp
void ARPGGameMode::Tick( float DeltaTime )
{
  if( this->currentCombatInstance != nullptr )
  {
    bool combatOver = this->currentCombatInstance->Tick( DeltaTime
      );
    if( combatOver )
    {
      if( this->currentCombatInstance->phase == CombatPhase::
        CPHASE_GameOver )
      {
        UE_LOG( LogTemp, Log, TEXT( "Player loses combat, game over" ) );
              }
      else if( this->currentCombatInstance->phase == CombatPhase::
        CPHASE_Victory )
      {
        UE_LOG( LogTemp, Log, TEXT( "Player wins combat" ) );
      }

      // enable player actor
      UGameplayStatics::GetPlayerController( GetWorld(), 0 )->
        SetActorTickEnabled( true );

      delete( this->currentCombatInstance );
      this->currentCombatInstance = nullptr;
      this->enemyParty.Empty();
    }
  }
}
```

For now, this simply checks whether there is currently an instance of combat; if so, it calls that instance's `Tick` function. If it returns `true`, the game mode checks for either `Victory` or `GameOver` (for now, it just logs a message to the console). Then, it deletes the combat instance, sets the pointer to null, and clears the enemy party list (which will make the enemies eligible for garbage collection since the list was decorated with the UPROPERTY macro). It also enables the tick of the player actor (we're going to disable the tick when combat begins so that the player actor freezes in place for the duration of combat).

However, we aren't ready to start combat encounters just yet! There are no enemies for players to fight.

We have a table of enemies defined, but our `GameCharacter` class does not support being initialized from `EnemyInfo`.

To support this, we will add a new factory to the `GameCharacter` class (be sure you add the `include` statement for the `EnemyInfo` class as well):

```
static UGameCharacter* CreateGameCharacter( FEnemyInfo* enemyInfo,
  UObject* outer );
```

Also, the implementation of this constructor overload in `GameCharacter.cpp` would be as follows:

```
UGameCharacter* UGameCharacter::CreateGameCharacter( FEnemyInfo*
enemyInfo, UObject* outer )
{
  UGameCharacter* character = NewObject<UGameCharacter>( outer );

  character->CharacterName = enemyInfo->EnemyName;
  character->ClassInfo = nullptr;

  character->MHP = enemyInfo->MHP;
  character->MMP = 0;
  character->HP = enemyInfo->MHP;
  character->MP = 0;

  character->ATK = enemyInfo->ATK;
  character->DEF = enemyInfo->DEF;
  character->LUCK = enemyInfo->Luck;

  return character;
}
```

It's very simple by comparison; simply assign the name and null for `ClassInfo` (as enemies do not have classes associated with them) and other stats (both MMP and MP are set to zero, as enemy abilities will not consume MP).

To test our combat system, we will create a function in `RPGGameMode.h` that can be called from the Unreal console:

```
UFUNCTION(exec)
void TestCombat();
```

The `UFUNCTION(exec)` macro is what allows this function to be called as a console command.

The implementation of this function is placed in RPGGameMode.cpp, as follows:

```cpp
void ARPGGameMode::TestCombat()
{
  // locate enemies asset
  UDataTable* enemyTable = Cast<UDataTable>( StaticLoadObject(
    UDataTable::StaticClass(), NULL,
TEXT( "DataTable'/Game/Data/Enemies.Enemies'" ) ) );


  if( enemyTable == NULL )
  {
    UE_LOG( LogTemp, Error, TEXT( "Enemies data table not found!" ) );
    return;
  }

  // locate enemy
  FEnemyInfo* row = enemyTable->FindRow<FEnemyInfo>( TEXT( "S1" ),
    TEXT( "LookupEnemyInfo" ) );

  if( row == NULL )
  {
    UE_LOG( LogTemp, Error, TEXT( "Enemy ID 'S1' not found!" ) );
    return;
  }

  // disable player actor
  UGameplayStatics::GetPlayerController( GetWorld(), 0 )->
    SetActorTickEnabled( false );

  // add character to enemy party
  UGameCharacter* enemy = UGameCharacter::CreateGameCharacter(
    row, this );
  this->enemyParty.Add( enemy );

  URPGGameInstance* gameInstance = Cast<URPGGameInstance>(
    GetGameInstance() );

  this->currentCombatInstance = new CombatEngine( gameInstance->
    PartyMembers, this->enemyParty );

  UE_LOG( LogTemp, Log, TEXT( "Combat started" ) );
}
```

It locates the enemy Data Table, picks the enemy with ID S1, constructs a new `GameCharacter`, constructs a list of enemies, adds the new enemy character, and then creates a new instance of `CombatEngine`, passing the player party and the enemy list. It also disables the tick of the player actor so that the player stops updating when combat begins.

Finally, you should be able to test the combat engine. Start the game and press the tilde (~) key to bring up the console command textbox. Enter `TestCombat` and press *Enter*.

Take a look at the output window and you should see something like the following:

```
LogTemp: Combat started
LogTemp: Character Kumo making decision
LogTemp: Character Goblin making decision
LogTemp: Character Kumo executing action
LogTemp: Character Goblin executing action
LogTemp: Character Kumo making decision
LogTemp: Character Goblin making decision
LogTemp: Character Kumo executing action
LogTemp: Character Goblin executing action
LogTemp: Character Kumo making decision
LogTemp: Character Goblin making decision
LogTemp: Character Kumo executing action
LogTemp: Character Goblin executing action
LogTemp: Character Kumo making decision
```

This shows that the combat engine is working as intended—firstly, all characters make a decision, execute their decisions, then they make a decision again, and so on. Since nobody is actually doing anything (much less dealing any damage), combat just goes on forever at the moment.

There are two issues with this: firstly, the aforementioned problem that nobody actually does anything yet. Additionally, player characters need to have a different way of making decisions than enemies (player characters will need a UI to pick actions, whereas enemies should pick actions automatically).

We'll solve the first issue before tackling decision making.

Performing actions

In order to allow characters to perform actions, we will boil all combat actions down to a single common interface. A good place to start is for this interface to map to what we already have — that is, the character's BeginExecuteAction and ExecuteAction functions.

Let's create a new ICombatAction interface for this, which can start off as a class that is not parented to anything and in a new path called Source/RPG/Combat/Actions; the ICombatAction.h file should look like this:

```
#pragma once

#include "GameCharacter.h"

class UGameCharacter;

class ICombatAction
{
public:
  virtual void BeginExecuteAction( UGameCharacter* character ) =
    0;
  virtual bool ExecuteAction( float DeltaSeconds ) = 0;
};
```

BeginExecuteAction takes a pointer to the character that this action is executing for. ExecuteAction, as before, takes the duration of the previous frame in seconds.

In ICombatAction.cpp, remove the default constructor and deconstructor so that the file looks like this:

```
#include "RPG.h"
#include "ICombatAction.h"
```

Next, we can create a new empty C++ class to implement this interface. Just as a test, we'll replicate the functionality that the characters are already doing (that is, absolutely nothing) in a new class called TestCombatAction to be pathed to the Source/RPG/Combat/Actions folder.

Firstly, the header will be as follows:

```
#pragma once

#include "ICombatAction.h"

class TestCombatAction : public ICombatAction
{
```

```
protected:
  float delayTimer;

public:
  virtual void BeginExecuteAction( UGameCharacter* character )
    override;
  virtual bool ExecuteAction( float DeltaSeconds ) override;
};
```

The `.cpp` file will be as follows:

```
#include "RPG.h"
#include "TestCombatAction.h"

void TestCombatAction::BeginExecuteAction( UGameCharacter*
  character )
{
  UE_LOG( LogTemp, Log, TEXT( "%s does nothing" ), *character->
    CharacterName );
  this->delayTimer = 1.0f;
}

bool TestCombatAction::ExecuteAction( float DeltaSeconds )
{
  this->delayTimer -= DeltaSeconds;
  return this->delayTimer <= 0.0f;
}
```

Next, we'll change the character so that it can store and execute actions.

Firstly, let's replace the test delay timer field with a combat action pointer. Later, we'll make it public for when we create a decision making system in `GameCharacter.h`:

```
public:
  ICombatAction* combatAction;
```

Also remember to include `ICombatAction` at the top of `GameCharacter.h`, followed by a class declaration for `ICombatAction`:

```
#pragma once

#include "Data/FCharacterInfo.h"
#include "Data/FEnemyInfo.h"
#include "Data/FCharacterClassInfo.h"
#include "Combat/Actions/ICombatAction.h"
```

```
#include "GameCharacter.generated.h"

class CombatEngine;
class ICombatAction;
```

Next, we need to change our decision functions to assign a combat action, and the action functions to execute this action in GameCharacter.cpp:

```
void UGameCharacter::BeginMakeDecision()
{
  UE_LOG( LogTemp, Log, TEXT( "Character %s making decision" ), *(
    this->CharacterName ) );
  this->combatAction = new TestCombatAction();
}


bool UGameCharacter::MakeDecision( float DeltaSeconds )
{
  return true;
}


void UGameCharacter::BeginExecuteAction()
{
  this->combatAction->BeginExecuteAction( this );
}


bool UGameCharacter::ExecuteAction( float DeltaSeconds )
{
  bool finishedAction = this->combatAction->ExecuteAction(
    DeltaSeconds );
  if( finishedAction )
  {
    delete( this->combatAction );
    return true;
  }

  return false;
}
```

Also remember to use include TestCombatAction at the top of GameCharacter.cpp:

```
#include "Combat/Actions/TestCombatAction.h"
```

`BeginMakeDecision` now assigns a new instance of `TestCombatAction`.
`MakeDecision` just returns `true`. `BeginExecuteAction` calls the function of the
same name on the stored combat action, passing the character as the pointer. Finally,
`ExecuteAction` calls the function of the same name, and if the result is `true`, it
deletes the pointer and returns `true`; otherwise it returns `false`.

By running this and testing combat, you should get nearly identical output, but now
it says `does nothing` instead of `executing action`.

Now that we have a way for characters to store and execute actions, we can work on
a decision making system for characters.

Making decisions

As we did with actions, we're going to create an interface for decision making that
follows a similar pattern to the `BeginMakeDecision` and `MakeDecision` functions.
Similar to the `ICombatAction` class, we will create an empty `IDecisionMaker` class
and we will path it to a new directory, `Source/RPG/Combat/DecisionMakers`. The
following will be `IDecisionMaker.h`:

```
#pragma once

#include "GameCharacter.h"

class UGameCharacter;

class IDecisionMaker
{
public:
  virtual void BeginMakeDecision( UGameCharacter* character ) = 0;
  virtual bool MakeDecision( float DeltaSeconds ) = 0;
};
```

Also, remove the constructor and deconstructor to `IDecisionMaker.cpp`, so that it
looks like this:

```
#include "RPG.h"
#include "IDecisionMaker.h"
```

Now, we can create the `TestDecisionMaker` C++ class and path it to `Source/RPG/`
`Combat/DecisionMakers` as well. Then, program `TestDecisionMaker.h` as follows:

```
#pragma once
#include "IDecisionMaker.h"
```

```
class RPG_API TestDecisionMaker : public IDecisionMaker
{
public:
  virtual void BeginMakeDecision( UGameCharacter* character )
    override;
  virtual bool MakeDecision( float DeltaSeconds ) override;
};
```

Then, program `TestDecisionMaker.cpp` as follows:

```
#include "RPG.h"
#include "TestDecisionMaker.h"

#include "../Actions/TestCombatAction.h"

void TestDecisionMaker::BeginMakeDecision( UGameCharacter*
  character )
{
  character->combatAction = new TestCombatAction();
}

bool TestDecisionMaker::MakeDecision( float DeltaSeconds )
{
  return true;
}
```

Next, we'll add a pointer to `IDecisionMaker` to the game character class and modify the `BeginMakeDecision` and `MakeDecision` functions to use the decision maker in `GameCharacter.h`:

```
public:
  IDecisionMaker* decisionMaker;
```

Also remember to include `ICombatAction` at the top of `GameCharacter.h` followed by a class declaration for `ICombatAction`:

```
#pragma once

#include "Data/FCharacterInfo.h"
#include "Data/FEnemyInfo.h"
#include "Data/FCharacterClassInfo.h"
#include "Combat/Actions/ICombatAction.h"
#include "Combat/DecisionMakers/IDecisionMaker.h"
#include "GameCharacter.generated.h"
```

```
class CombatEngine;
class ICombatAction;
class IDecisionMaker;
```

Next, replace the `BeginDestroy`, `BeginMakeDecision`, and `MakeDecision` functions in `GameCharacter.cpp` with this:

```
void UGameCharacter::BeginDestroy()
{
  Super::BeginDestroy();
  delete( this->decisionMaker );
}

void UGameCharacter::BeginMakeDecision()
{
  this->decisionMaker->BeginMakeDecision( this );}

bool UGameCharacter::MakeDecision( float DeltaSeconds )
{
  return this->decisionMaker->MakeDecision( DeltaSeconds );
}
```

Note that we delete the decision maker in the destructor. The decision maker will be assigned when the character is created, and should therefore be deleted when the character is released.

We will then include `TestDecisionMaker` implementations to allow each party to make combat decisions, so include `TestDecisionMaker` at the top of the class:

```
#include "Combat/DecisionMakers/TestDecisionMaker.h"
```

The final step here is to assign a decision maker in the constructors for the character. To both constructor overloads, add the following line of code: `character->decisionMaker = new TestDecisionMaker();`. When you are finished, the player and enemy character constructors should look like this:

```
UGameCharacter* UGameCharacter::CreateGameCharacter(
  FCharacterInfo* characterInfo, UObject* outer)
{
  UGameCharacter* character = NewObject<UGameCharacter>(outer);

  // locate character classes asset
  UDataTable* characterClasses = Cast<UDataTable>(
    StaticLoadObject(UDataTable::StaticClass(), NULL, TEXT(
```

```
              "DataTable'/Game/Data/CharacterClasses.CharacterClasses'"))
        );

    if (characterClasses == NULL)
    {
      UE_LOG(LogTemp, Error,
TEXT("Character classes datatable not found!" ) );
    }
    else
    {
      character->CharacterName = characterInfo->Character_Name;
      FCharacterClassInfo* row =
characterClasses->FindRow<FCharacterClassInfo>
(*(characterInfo->Class_ID), TEXT("LookupCharacterClass"));
      character->ClassInfo = row;

      character->MHP = character->ClassInfo->StartMHP;
      character->MMP = character->ClassInfo->StartMMP;
      character->HP = character->MHP;
      character->MP = character->MMP;

      character->ATK = character->ClassInfo->StartATK;
      character->DEF = character->ClassInfo->StartDEF;
      character->LUCK = character->ClassInfo->StartLuck;

      character->decisionMaker = new TestDecisionMaker();
    }

    return character;
}

UGameCharacter* UGameCharacter::CreateGameCharacter(FEnemyInfo*
enemyInfo, UObject* outer)
{
  UGameCharacter* character = NewObject<UGameCharacter>(outer);

  character->CharacterName = enemyInfo->EnemyName;
  character->ClassInfo = nullptr;

  character->MHP = enemyInfo->MHP;
  character->MMP = 0;
  character->HP = enemyInfo->MHP;
  character->MP = 0;
```

```
    character->ATK = enemyInfo->ATK;
    character->DEF = enemyInfo->DEF;
    character->LUCK = enemyInfo->Luck;

    character->decisionMaker = new TestDecisionMaker();

    return character;
}
```

Run the game and test combat again, and you should get very similar output to what was already there. However, the big difference is that it's now possible to assign different implementations of a decision maker to different characters, and those decision makers have an easy way to assign combat actions to be executed. For instance, it will now be easy to make our test combat action deal with the damage of a target. However, before we do this, let's make a small change to the GameCharacter class.

Target selection

We're going to add a field to GameCharacter that identifies a character as either a player or an enemy. Additionally, we'll add a SelectTarget function that selects the first live character from either the current combat instance's enemyParty or playerParty, depending on whether this character is a player or an enemy.

Firstly, in GameCharacter.h, we'll add a public isPlayer field:

```
bool isPlayer;
```

Then, we'll add a SelectTarget function, as follows:

```
UGameCharacter* SelectTarget();
```

In GameCharacter.cpp, we'll assign the isPlayer field in the constructors (this is easy enough, as we have separate constructors for players and enemies):

```
UGameCharacter* UGameCharacter::CreateGameCharacter(
    FCharacterInfo* characterInfo, UObject* outer)
{
    UGameCharacter* character = NewObject<UGameCharacter>(outer);

    // locate character classes asset
    UDataTable* characterClasses = Cast<UDataTable>(
        StaticLoadObject(UDataTable::StaticClass(), NULL, TEXT(
            "DataTable'/Game/Data/CharacterClasses.CharacterClasses'"))
        );
```

```cpp
    if (characterClasses == NULL)
    {
      UE_LOG(LogTemp, Error,
        TEXT("Character classes datatable not found!"));
    }
    else
    {
      character->CharacterName = characterInfo->Character_Name;
      FCharacterClassInfo* row =
        characterClasses->FindRow<FCharacterClassInfo>
  (*(characterInfo->Class_ID), TEXT("LookupCharacterClass"));
      character->ClassInfo = row;

      character->MHP = character->ClassInfo->StartMHP;
      character->MMP = character->ClassInfo->StartMMP;
      character->HP = character->MHP;
      character->MP = character->MMP;

      character->ATK = character->ClassInfo->StartATK;
      character->DEF = character->ClassInfo->StartDEF;
      character->LUCK = character->ClassInfo->StartLuck;

      character->decisionMaker = new TestDecisionMaker();
    }
    character->isPlayer = true;
    return character;
}

UGameCharacter* UGameCharacter::CreateGameCharacter(FEnemyInfo*
enemyInfo, UObject* outer)
{
  UGameCharacter* character = NewObject<UGameCharacter>(outer);

  character->CharacterName = enemyInfo->EnemyName;
  character->ClassInfo = nullptr;

  character->MHP = enemyInfo->MHP;
  character->MMP = 0;
  character->HP = enemyInfo->MHP;
  character->MP = 0;

  character->ATK = enemyInfo->ATK;
  character->DEF = enemyInfo->DEF;
```

```
        character->LUCK = enemyInfo->Luck;

        character->decisionMaker = new TestDecisionMaker();
        character->isPlayer = false;
        return character;
    }
```

Finally, the `SelectTarget` function is as follows:

```
    UGameCharacter* UGameCharacter::SelectTarget()
    {
        UGameCharacter* target = nullptr;

        TArray<UGameCharacter*> targetList = this->combatInstance->
          enemyParty;
        if( !this->isPlayer )
        {
            targetList = this->combatInstance->playerParty;
        }

        for( int i = 0; i < targetList.Num(); i++ )
        {
          if( targetList[ i ]->HP > 0 )
          {
            target = targetList[i];
            break;
          }
        }

        if( target->HP <= 0 )
        {
          return nullptr;
        }

        return target;
    }
```

This first figures out which list (enemies or players) to use as potential targets and then goes through that list to find the first non-dead target. If there is no target, this function returns a null pointer.

Dealing damage

Now that there's an easy way to select targets, let's make our `TestCombatAction` class finally deal some damage!

We'll add a couple of fields to maintain references to the character and the target, and also a constructor that takes the target as a parameter:

```
protected:
  UGameCharacter* character;
  UGameCharacter* target;

public:
  TestCombatAction( UGameCharacter* target );
```

Also, the implementation is by creating and updating the `BeginExecuteAction` function in `TestCombatAction.cpp`, as follows:

```
void TestCombatAction::BeginExecuteAction( UGameCharacter*
  character )
{
  this->character = character;

  // target is dead, select another target
  if( this->target->HP <= 0 )
  {
    this->target = this->character->SelectTarget();
  }

  // no target, just return
  if( this->target == nullptr )
  {
    return;
  }

  UE_LOG( LogTemp, Log, TEXT( "%s attacks %s" ), *character->
    CharacterName, *target->CharacterName );

  target->HP -= 10;

  this->delayTimer = 1.0f;
}
```

And then have the constructor of the class set the target:

```
TestCombatAction::TestCombatAction(UGameCharacter* target)
{
    this->target = target;
}
```

Firstly, the constructor assigns the target pointer. Then, the `BeginExecuteAction` function assigns the character reference and checks to see whether the target is alive. If the target is dead, it picks a new target via the `SelectTarget` function we just created. If the target pointer is now null, there is no target and this function just returns null. Otherwise, it logs a message of the form *[character] attacks [target]*, subtracts some HP from the target, and sets the delay timer as before.

The next step is to change our `TestDecisionMaker` to pick a target and pass this target to the `TestCombatAction` constructor. This is a relatively simple change in `TestDecisionMaker.cpp`:

```
void TestDecisionMaker::BeginMakeDecision( UGameCharacter*
    character )
{
    // pick a target
    UGameCharacter* target = character->SelectTarget();
    character->combatAction = new TestCombatAction( target );
}
```

At this point, you should be able to run the game, start a test encounter, and also see an output similar to the following:

```
LogTemp: Combat started
LogTemp: Kumo attacks Goblin
LogTemp: Goblin attacks Kumo
LogTemp: Kumo attacks Goblin
LogTemp: Player wins combat
```

Finally, we have a combat system in which our two parties can attack each other and one or the other can win.

Next, we'll begin hooking this up to a user interface.

Combat UI with UMG

To get started, we'll need to set up our project to properly import UMG and Slate-related classes.

First, open `RPG.Build.cs` (or `[ProjectName].Build.cs`) and change the first line of the constructor to the following code:

```
PublicDependencyModuleNames.AddRange( new string[] { "Core",
   "CoreUObject", "Engine", "InputCore", "UMG", "Slate",
   "SlateCore" } );
```

This adds the `UMG`, `Slate`, and `SlateCore` strings to the existing string array.

Next, open `RPG.h` and make sure the following lines of code are there:

```
#include "Runtime/UMG/Public/UMG.h"
#include "Runtime/UMG/Public/UMGStyle.h"
#include "Runtime/UMG/Public/Slate/SObjectWidget.h"
#include "Runtime/UMG/Public/IUMGModule.h"
#include "Runtime/UMG/Public/Blueprint/UserWidget.h"
```

Now compile the project. This may take a while.

Next, we're going to create a base class for the combat UI. Basically, we'll use this base class to allow our C++ game code to communicate with Blueprint UMG code by defining Blueprint-implementable functions in the header, which are functions that can be implemented by Blueprint and called from C++.

Create a new class named `CombatUIWidget` and select `UserWidget` as the parent class; then path it to `Source/RPG/UI`. Replace the contents of `CombatUIWidget.h` with the following code:

```
#pragma once
#include "GameCharacter.h"

#include "Blueprint/UserWidget.h"
#include "CombatUIWidget.generated.h"

UCLASS()
class RPG_API UCombatUIWidget : public UUserWidget
{
   GENERATED_BODY()

public:
   UFUNCTION( BlueprintImplementableEvent, Category = "Combat UI" )
   void AddPlayerCharacterPanel( UGameCharacter* target );
```

```
    UFUNCTION( BlueprintImplementableEvent, Category = "Combat UI" )
    void AddEnemyCharacterPanel( UGameCharacter* target );
};
```

For the most part, we're just defining a couple of functions. The `AddPlayerCharacterPanel` and `AddEnemyCharacterPanel` functions will be responsible for taking a character pointer and spawning a widget for that character (to display the character's current status).

Next, after compiling the code, back in the editor, create a new folder in the `Contents/Blueprints` directory called `UI`. In the `Content/Blueprints/UI` directory, create a new Widget Blueprint named `CombatUI`. After you've created and opened the Blueprint, go to **File | Reparent Blueprint** and select **CombatUIWidget** as the parent class.

In the **Designer** interface, create two Horizontal Box widgets and name them `enemyPartyStatus` and `playerPartyStatus`. These will hold child widgets for enemies and players respectively, to display the status of each character. For both of these, be sure to enable the **Is Variable** checkbox so that they will be available as variables to Blueprint. Save and compile the Blueprint.

We will position the `enemyPartyStatus` Horizontal Box at the top of the Canvas Panel. It will help to first set a top horizontal anchor.

Then set the values for the Horizontal Box as follows, **Offset Left**: 10, **Position Y**: 10, **Offset Right**: 10, **Size Y**: 200.

Proceed to position the `playerPartyStatus` Horizontal Box in a similar way; the only major difference is that we will anchor the box to the bottom of the Canvas Panel and position it so it spans the bottom of the screen:

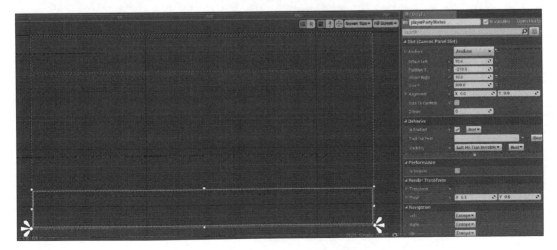

Next, we'll create widgets to display player and enemy character statuses. Firstly, we'll make a base widget that each will inherit from.

Create a new Widget Blueprint and name it `BaseCharacterCombatPanel`. In this Blueprint, navigate to the graph, then add a new variable from the **MyBlueprint** tab, **CharacterTarget**, and select the **Game Character** variable type from the **Object Reference** category.

Next, we'll make separate widgets for the enemies and players.

Create a new Widget Blueprint and name it `PlayerCharacterCombatPanel`. Set the new Blueprint's parent to `BaseCharacterCombatPanel`.

In the **Designer** interface, add three text widgets. One label will be for the character's name, another for the character's HP, and third one for the character's MP. Position each Text Block so that they are anchored to the bottom left of the screen, and well within the 200 high pixels of the `playerPartyStatus` box size that we created in the `CombatUI` widget:

Also be sure to check **Size to Content** located in the **Details** panel of each Text Block so that the Text Block can resize if the content does not fit within the Text Block parameters.

Create a new binding for each of these by selecting the widget and clicking on **Bind** next to the **Text** input in the **Details** panel:

This will create a new Blueprint function that will be responsible for generating the Text Block.

To bind the HP Text Block, for example, you can execute the following steps:

1. Right-click in an open area in the grid, search for **Get Character Target**, and then select it.

2. Drag the output pin of this node and select **Get HP** under **Variables | Character Info**.

3. Create a new **Format Text** node. Set the text to **HP: {HP}** and then connect the output of **Get HP** to the **HP** input of the **Format Text** node.

4. Finally, connect the output of the **Format Text** node to the **Return** value of the **Return** node.

You can repeat similar steps for the character name and MP Text Blocks.

After you've created `PlayerCharacterCombatPanel`, you can repeat the same steps to create `EnemyCharacterCombatPanel`, except without the MP Text Block (as mentioned before, enemies do not consume MP). The only major difference is that the Text Blocks in `EnemyCharacterCombatPanel` need to be placed at the top of the screen to match the positioning of the `enemyPartyStatus` Horizontal Box from the `CombatUI` widget.

The resulting graph for displaying the MP will look something like the following screenshot:

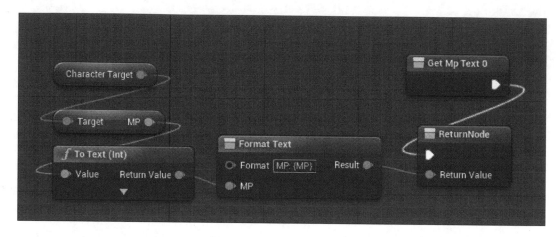

Now that we have widgets for players and enemies, let's implement the `AddPlayerCharacterPanel` and `AddEnemyCharacterPanel` functions in the `CombatUI` Blueprint.

Firstly, we'll create a helper Blueprint function to spawn character status widgets. Name this new function `SpawnCharacterWidget` and add the following parameters to the input:

- **Target Character** (of type Game Character Reference)
- **Target Panel** (of type Panel Widget Reference)
- **Class** (of type Base Character Combat Panel Class)

This function will perform the following steps:

1. Create a new widget of the given class using **Create Widget**.
2. Cast the new widget to the `BaseCharacterCombatPanel` type.
3. Set the **Character Target** of the result to the **TargetCharacter** input.
4. Add the new widget as a child of the **TargetPanel** input.

And that looks like this in Blueprint:

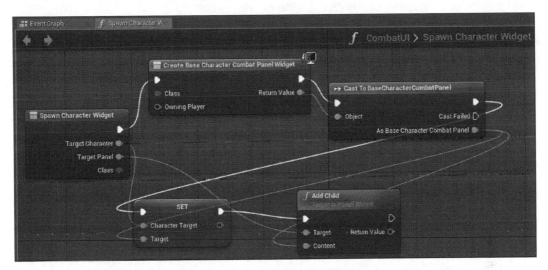

Next, in the event graph for the CombatUI Blueprint, right-click and add the EventAddPlayerCharacterPanel and EventAddEnemyCharacterPanel events. Hook each of these up to a SpawnCharacterWidget node, connecting the **Target** output to the **Target Character** input and the appropriate panel variable to the **Target Panel** input, as follows:

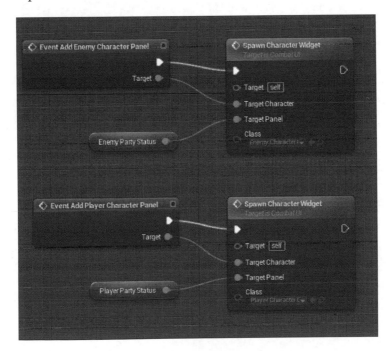

Finally, we can spawn this UI from our game mode at the beginning of combat and destroy it at the end of combat. In the header of RPGGameMode, add a pointer to UCombatUIWidget and also a class to spawn for the combat UI (so we can select a Widget Blueprint that inherits from our CombatUIWidget class); these should be public:

```
UPROPERTY()
UCombatUIWidget* CombatUIInstance;

UPROPERTY( EditDefaultsOnly, BlueprintReadOnly, Category = "UI" )
TSubclassOf<class UCombatUIWidget> CombatUIClass;
```

Also make sure that RPGGameMode.h includes the CombatWidget; at this point, your list of includes at the top of RPGGameMode.h should look like this:

```
#include "GameFramework/GameMode.h"
#include "GameCharacter.h"
#include "Combat/CombatEngine.h"
#include "UI/CombatUIWidget.h"
#include "RPGGameMode.generated.h"
```

At the end of the TestCombat function in RPGGameMode.cpp, we'll spawn a new instance of this widget, as follows:

```
this->CombatUIInstance = CreateWidget<UCombatUIWidget>(
  GetGameInstance(), this->CombatUIClass );
this->CombatUIInstance->AddToViewport();

UGameplayStatics::GetPlayerController(GetWorld(), 0)
->bShowMouseCursor = true;

for( int i = 0; i < gameInstance->PartyMembers.Num(); i++ )
  this->CombatUIInstance->AddPlayerCharacterPanel( gameInstance->
    PartyMembers[i] );

for( int i = 0; i < this->enemyParty.Num(); i++ )
  this->CombatUIInstance->AddEnemyCharacterPanel( this->
    enemyParty[i] );
```

This creates the widget, adds the viewport to it, adds a mouse cursor, and then calls its AddPlayerCharacterPanel and AddEnemyCharacterPanel functions for all players and enemies respectively.

After combat is over, we'll remove the widget from the viewport and set the reference to null so it can be garbage-collected; your `Tick` function should now look like this:

```
void ARPGGameMode::Tick(float DeltaTime)
{
  if (this->currentCombatInstance != nullptr)
  {
    bool combatOver = this->currentCombatInstance->Tick(DeltaTime
    );
    if (combatOver)
    {
      if (this->currentCombatInstance->phase == CombatPhase::
        CPHASE_GameOver)
      {
        UE_LOG(LogTemp, Log,
        TEXT("Player loses combat, game over" ) );
      }
      else if
      (this->currentCombatInstance->phase ==
      CombatPhase::  CPHASE_Victory)
      {
        UE_LOG(LogTemp, Log, TEXT("Player wins combat"));
      }
      UGameplayStatics::GetPlayerController(GetWorld(),0)
      ->bShowMouseCursor = false;

      // enable player actor
      UGameplayStatics::GetPlayerController(GetWorld(), 0)->
        SetActorTickEnabled(true);

      this->CombatUIInstance->RemoveFromViewport();
      this->CombatUIInstance = nullptr;

      delete(this->currentCombatInstance);
      this->currentCombatInstance = nullptr;
      this->enemyParty.Empty();
    }
  }
}
```

At this point, you can compile, but the game will crash if you test the combat. That is because you need to set `DefaultRPGGameMode` class defaults to use `CombatUI` as the `CombatUIClass` that you created in `RPGGameMode.h`. Otherwise, the system will not know that the `CombatUIClass` variable is to be pointing to `CombatUI`, which is a widget, and therefore won't be able to create the widget. Note that the editor may crash the first time you do this step.

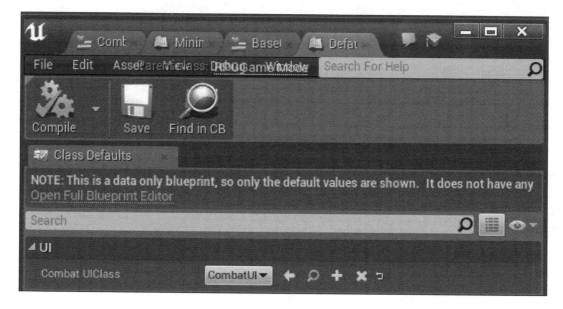

Now, if you run the game and start combat, you should see the status of the goblin and the status of the player. Both should have their HP reducing until the goblin's health reaches zero; at this point, the UI disappears (as combat is over).

Next, we're going to change things so that instead of the player characters automatically making decisions, the player gets to choose their actions via the UI.

UI-driven decision making

One idea is to change how the decision maker is assigned to the player—rather than assigning one when the player is first created, we could make our `CombatUIWidget` class implement the decision maker and just assign it when combat starts (and clear the pointer when combat ends).

We're going to have to make a couple of changes to `GameCharacter.cpp`. First, in the player overload of `CreateGameCharacter`, remove the following line of code:

```
character->decisionMaker = new TestDecisionMaker();
```

Then, in the `BeginDestroy` function, we'll wrap the `delete` line in an `if` statement:

```
if( !this->isPlayer )
  delete( this->decisionMaker );
```

The reason for this is that the decision maker for players will be the UI—and we do not want to delete the UI manually (doing so would crash Unreal). Instead, the UI will be garbage-collected automatically as long as there are no UPROPERY decorated pointers to it.

Next, in `CombatUIWidget.h`, we'll make the class implement the `IDecisionMaker` interface and add `BeginMakeDecision` and `MakeDecision` as public functions:

```
#pragma once
#include "GameCharacter.h"
#include "Blueprint/UserWidget.h"
#include "CombatUIWidget.generated.h"

UCLASS()
class RPG_API UCombatUIWidget : public UUserWidget, public IDecisionMaker
{
  GENERATED_BODY()

public:
  UFUNCTION(BlueprintImplementableEvent, Category = "Combat UI")
    void AddPlayerCharacterPanel(UGameCharacter* target);

  UFUNCTION(BlueprintImplementableEvent, Category = "Combat UI")
    void AddEnemyCharacterPanel(UGameCharacter* target);

  void BeginMakeDecision(UGameCharacter* target);
  bool MakeDecision(float DeltaSeconds);
};
```

We're also going to add a couple of helper functions that can be called by our UI Blueprint graph:

```
public:
  UFUNCTION( BlueprintCallable, Category = "Combat UI" )
  TArray<UGameCharacter*> GetCharacterTargets();

  UFUNCTION( BlueprintCallable, Category = "Combat UI" )
  void AttackTarget( UGameCharacter* target );
```

The first function retrieves a list of potential targets for the current character. The second function will give the character a new `TestCombatAction` with the given target.

Additionally, we'll add a function to be implemented in the Blueprint that will show a set of actions for the current character:

```
UFUNCTION( BlueprintImplementableEvent, Category = "Combat UI" )
void ShowActionsPanel( UGameCharacter* target );
```

We're also going to add a flag and a definition for `currentTarget`, as follows:

```
protected:
  UGameCharacter* currentTarget;
   bool finishedDecision;
```

This will be used to signal that a decision has been made (and that `MakeDecision` should return `true`).

The implementations of these four functions are fairly straightforward in `CombatUIWidget.cpp`:

```cpp
#include "RPG.h"
#include "CombatUIWidget.h"
#include "../Combat/CombatEngine.h"
#include "../Combat/Actions/TestCombatAction.h"

void UCombatUIWidget::BeginMakeDecision( UGameCharacter* target )
{
  this->currentTarget = target;
  this->finishedDecision = false;

  ShowActionsPanel( target );
}


bool UCombatUIWidget::MakeDecision( float DeltaSeconds )
{
  return this->finishedDecision;
}


void UCombatUIWidget::AttackTarget( UGameCharacter* target )
{
  TestCombatAction* action = new TestCombatAction( target );
  this->currentTarget->combatAction = action;
```

```
      this->finishedDecision = true;
   }

   TArray<UGameCharacter*> UCombatUIWidget::GetCharacterTargets()
   {
     if( this->currentTarget->isPlayer )
     {
       return this->currentTarget->combatInstance->enemyParty;
     }
     else
     {
       return this->currentTarget->combatInstance->playerParty;
     }
   }
```

BeginMakeDecision sets the current target, sets the finishedDecision flag to false, and then calls ShowActionsPanel (which will be handled in our UI Blueprint graph).

MakeDecision simply returns the value of the finishedDecision flag.

AttackTarget assigns a new TestCombatAction to the character and then sets finishedDecision to true to signal that a decision has been made.

Finally, GetCharacterTargets returns an array of this character's possible opponents.

Since the UI now implements the IDecisionMaker interface, we can assign it as the decision maker for the player characters. Firstly, in the TestCombat function of RPGGameMode.cpp, we'll change the loop that iterates over the characters so that it assigns the UI as the decision maker:

```
for( int i = 0; i < gameInstance->PartyMembers.Num(); i++ )
{
   this->CombatUIInstance->AddPlayerCharacterPanel( gameInstance->
     PartyMembers[i] );
   gameInstance->PartyMembers[i]->decisionMaker = this->
     CombatUIInstance;
}.
```

Then, we'll set the players' decision makers to null when combat is over:

```
for( int i = 0; i < this->currentCombatInstance->
  playerParty.Num(); i++ )
{
   this->currentCombatInstance->playerParty[i]->decisionMaker =
     nullptr;
}
```

Now, player characters will use the UI to make decisions. However, the UI currently does nothing. We'll need to work in Blueprint to add this functionality.

Firstly, we'll create a widget for the attack target options. Name it `AttackTargetOption`, add a button, and put a Text Block in the button. Check **Size to Content** so that the button will dynamically resize to any Text Block that is in the button. Then position it at the top-left corner of the Canvas Panel.

In the Graph, add two new variables. One is the `targetUI` of the Combat UI Reference type. The other is the `target` of the Game Character Reference type. From the **Designer** view, click on your button, then scroll down the **Details** panel and click on **OnClicked** to create an event for the button. The button will use the `targetUI` reference to call the **Attack Target** function and the `target` reference (which is the target this button represents) to pass to the **Attack Target** function.

The graph for the button-click event is fairly simple; just route the execution to the **Attack Target** function of the assigned `targetUI` and pass the `target` reference as a parameter:

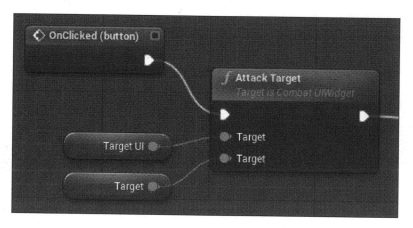

Next, we'll add a panel for character actions to the main combat UI. This is a Canvas Panel with a single button child for **Attack** and a Vertical Box for the target list:

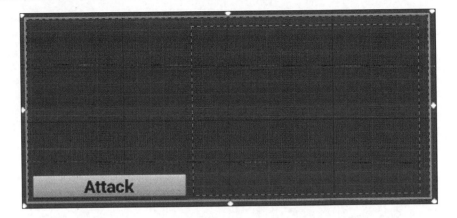

Name the **Attack** button `attackButton`. Name the Vertical Box `targets`. And name the Canvas Panel encapsulating these items as `characterActions`. These should have **Is Variable** enabled so that they are visible to Blueprint.

Then, in the Blueprint graph, we'll implement the **Show Actions Panel** event. This will first route execution to a **Set Visibility** node, which will enable the **Actions** panel and then route execution to another **Set Visibility** node that hides the target list:

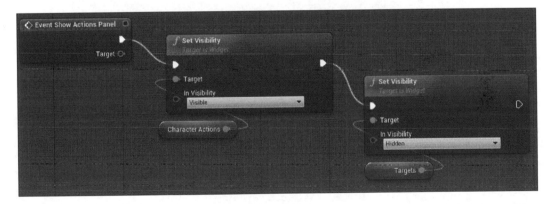

The Blueprint graph for when the **Attack** button is clicked is fairly large, so we'll take a look at it in small chunks.

Firstly, create an `OnClicked` event for your `attackButton` by selecting the button in the **Designer** view and clicking on **OnClicked** in the **Events** portion of the **Details** panel. In the graph, we then use a **Clear Children** node when the button is clicked to clear out any target options that may have been previously added:

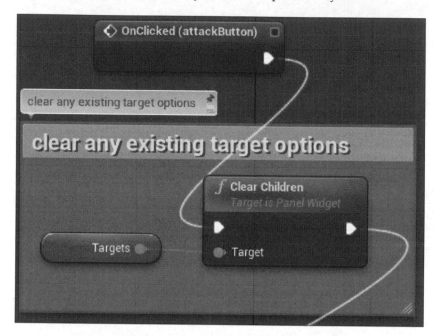

Then, we use a **ForEachLoop** coupled with a **CompareInt** node to iterate over all characters returned by **Get Character Targets** that have HP > 0 (not dead):

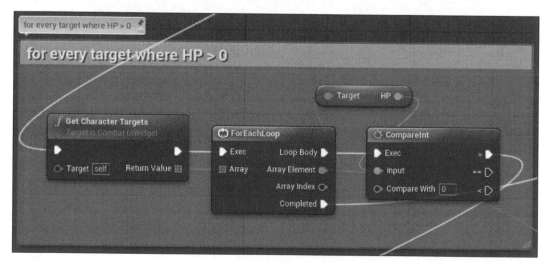

From the **>** (greater than) pin of the **CompareInt** node, we create a new instance of the **AttackTargetOption** widget and add it to the attack target list Vertical Box:

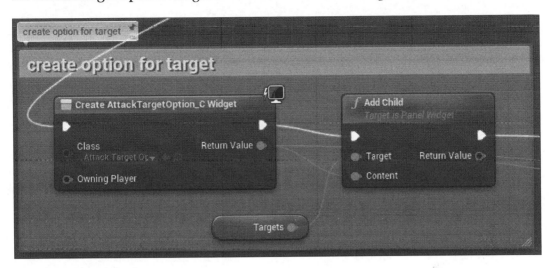

Then, for the widget we just added, we connect a **Self** node to set its `targetUI` variable and pass the **Array Element** pin of the **ForEachLoop** to set its `target` variable:

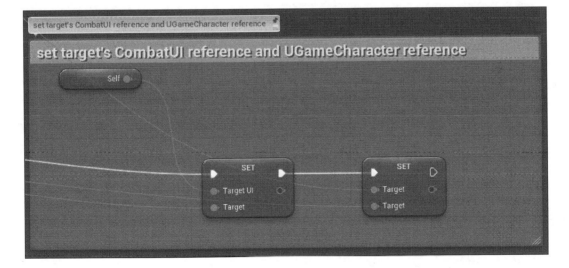

Finally, from the **Completed** pin of the **ForEachLoop**, we set the visibility of the target option list to **Visible**:

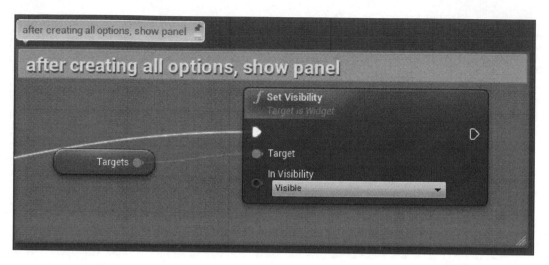

After all this is done, we still need to hide the **Actions** panel when an action is chosen. We'll add a new function to the CombatUI called **Hide Action Panel**. This function is very simple; it just sets the visibility of the action panel to **Hidden**:

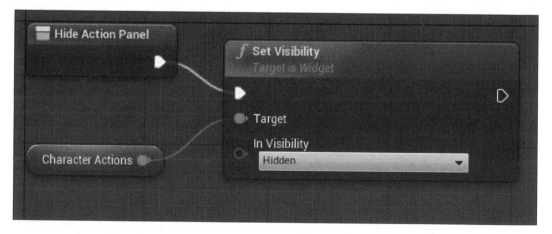

Also, in the click handler in the **AttackTargetOption** graph, we connect the execution pin of the **Attack Target** node to this **Hide Action Panel** function:

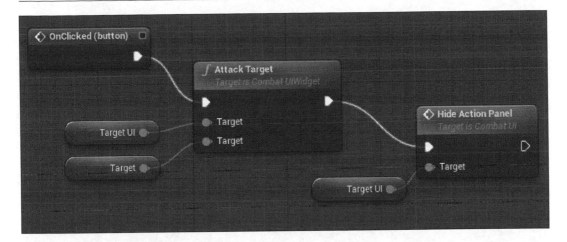

Lastly, you will need to bind the Text Block that was in the button located in the **AttackTargetOption** widget. So go into the **Designer** view and create a bind for the text just like you have done with previous Text Blocks in this chapter. Now in the graph, link **target** to the **Character Name**, and adjust the format of the text to show the CharacterName variable, and link it to the **return** node of your text. This Blueprint should show the current target's character name on the button:

After all this, you should be able to run the game and start a test encounter, and on the player's turn, you'll see an **Attack** button that allows you to pick the goblin to attack.

Our combat engine is now fully functional. The final step of this chapter will be to create a game over screen so that when all party members have died, the player will see a **Game Over** message.

Creating the game over screen

The first step is to create the screen itself. Create a new Widget Blueprint called **GameOverScreen**. We'll just add an image to which we can do a full-screen anchor, and zero out the offsets in the **Details** panel. You can also set the color to black. Also add a Text Block with the text **Game Over**, and a button with a child Text Block **Restart**:

Create an `OnClicked` event for the **Restart** button. In the Blueprint graph, link the event for the button to Restart Game whose target is **Get Game Mode** (you may have to uncheck **Context Sensitive** to find this node):

You will also need to show the mouse cursor here. The best way to do this is from **Event Construct**; link **Set Show Mouse Cursor**, whose target is **Get Player Controller**. Be sure to check the **Show Mouse Cursor** box. Between **Event Construct** and **Set Show Mouse Cursor**, put a 0.2-second delay so that you are assured that the mouse re-appears after you removed it when combat ended:

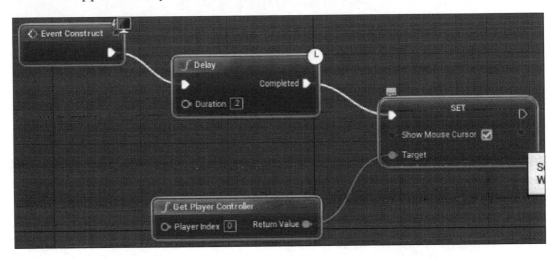

Next, in RPGGameMode.h, we add a public property for the widget type to be used for game over:

```
UPROPERTY( EditDefaultsOnly, BlueprintReadOnly, Category = "UI" )
TSubclassOf<class UUserWidget> GameOverUIClass;
```

In the case of game over, we create the widget and add it to the viewport, which we can add as a condition nested in the if(combatOver) condition within void ARPGGameMode::Tick(float DeltaTime) in RPGGameMode.cpp:

```
if( this->currentCombatInstance->phase == CombatPhase::
  CPHASE_GameOver )
{
  UE_LOG( LogTemp, Log, TEXT( "Player loses combat, game over" ) );

  Cast<URPGGameInstance>( GetGameInstance() )->PrepareReset();

  UUserWidget* GameOverUIInstance = CreateWidget<UUserWidget>(
    GetGameInstance(), this->GameOverUIClass );
  GameOverUIInstance->AddToViewport();
}
```

As you can see, we're also calling a `PrepareReset` function on the game instance. This function isn't defined yet, so we'll create it now in `RPGGameInstance.h` as a public function:

```
public:
  void PrepareReset();
```

Then implement it in `RPGGameInstance.cpp`:

```
cpp.void URPGGameInstance::PrepareReset()
{
  this->isInitialized = false;
  this->PartyMembers.Empty();
}
```

In this case, the purpose of `PrepareReset` is to set `isInitialized` to `false` so that the next time `Init` is called, the party members are reloaded. We are also emptying the `partyMembers` array so that when party members are added back into the array, we don't append them to instances of party members from our last playthrough (we don't want to reset the game with dead party members).

At this point, you can compile. But before we can test this, we need to set the **Game Over UIClass** that we created and set it to **GameOverScreen** as a class default in **DefaultRPGGameMode**:

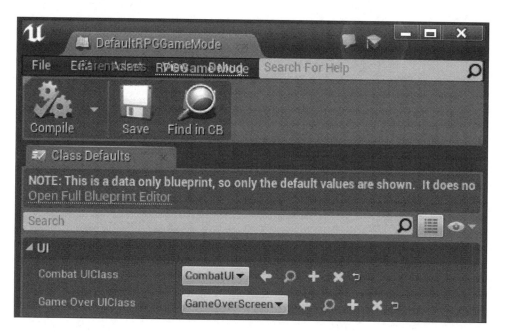

Much like the last time you did this, the editor may crash, but when you come back to **DefaultRPGGameMode**, you should see that **GameOverScreen** is set correctly.

In order to test this, we'll need to give the goblin more health than the player. Open the enemies table and give the goblin anything over 100 HP (for instance, 200 would do). Then, start an encounter and play until the main party member runs out of health. You should then see a **Game Over** screen pop up, and by clicking on **Restart**, you will restart the level and the main party member will be back up to 100 HP.

Summary

In this chapter, we created a foundation for the core gameplay of an RPG. We have a character that can explore the overworld, a system for keeping track of party members, a turn-based combat engine, and a game over condition.

In the next chapters, we'll expand this by adding an inventory system, allowing the player to consume items, and give their party members equipment to boost their stats.

4

Pause Menu Framework

At this point, we have created a basic combat engine for our game. We can now dive into out-of-combat operations such as the creation of a pause menu screen, where we will be able to view player stats and edit inventory.

In this chapter, we will create the first part of our menu system, which is to design and create a framework for a pause menu. We will cover the following topics in this chapter:

- UMG pause screen initial setup
- UMG background color
- UMG text
- UMG buttons
- UMG inventory submenu
- UMG equipment submenu
- Key binding
- Button programming

UMG pause screen initial setup

For our pause screen, we will need to think about quite a few things regarding the design. As listed in the earlier chapter, the pause screen will give the ability to the player to view party members, equip and unequip equipment, use items, and so on. So we must design our pause screen with that sort of functionality in mind.

To design the pause screen, we will be using **Unreal Motion Graphics (UMG)**, which is a separate portion of UE4 that allows us to design virtual user interfaces without the need for programs such as Adobe Flash. UMG is very intuitive and does not require programming knowledge in order to use it.

To start with, we will navigate to our already created **Blueprints | UI** folder and create a Widget Blueprint for our pause menu. To do this, right-click on your **UI** folder and then navigate to **User Interface | Widget Blueprint**:

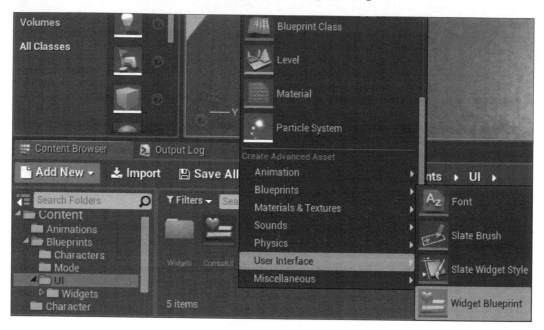

Name the Widget Blueprint as `Pause`:

The Widget Blueprint will allow you to use UMG to design any user interface; we will be using this widget to design our own UI for the pause menu.

To start designing the pause menu, open the **Pause** Widget Blueprint by double-clicking on it from within **Content Browser**. You should see the **Designer** screen that looks like the following screenshot:

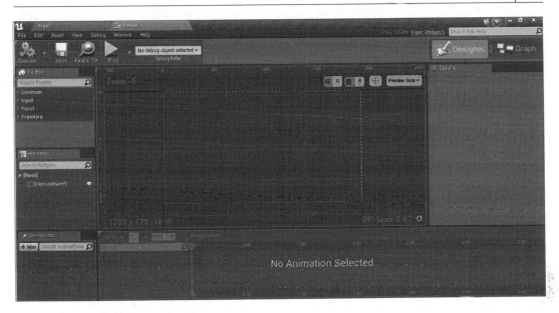

We are first going to create an area for our first screen where we want the pause menu to be. We will first be adding a Canvas Panel that acts as a container to allow several widgets to be laid out within it. This is a great place to start because we will need to feature several navigation points, which we will design in the form of buttons within our pause screen. To add a Canvas Panel, navigate to **Palette | Panel | Canvas Panel**. Then, drag the Canvas Panel into your **Designer** viewport (note that if you already have a Canvas Panel in your **Hierarchy** tab by default, you can skip this step):

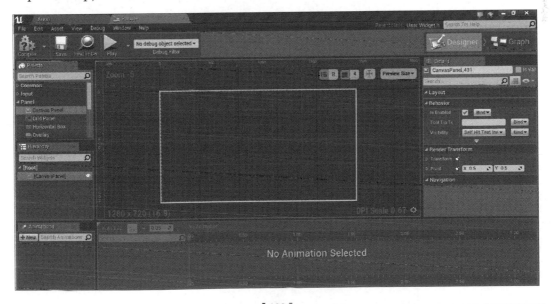

You should see a few new things in your pause menu. Firstly, you will see that under the **Hierarchy** tab, there is now **CanvasPanel** in **Root**. This means that in the root of the pause screen is the Canvas Panel that we just added. You will also notice that your Canvas Panel, while selected, contains details that can be seen in the **Details** tab. The **Details** tab will allow you to edit properties of any selected item. We will be using these areas of Widget Blueprint frequently throughout our development process.

We now need to think about what sorts of navigation points and information we need on our screen when the player presses the pause button. Based on the functionality, the following are the items we will need to lay out on our first screen:

- Characters along with their stats (level, HP, MP, and experience/next level)
- The **Inventory** button
- The **Equipment** button
- The **Exit** button
- Gold

UMG background color

Before we begin creating texts and buttons for our menu, we should first make a background color that will be laid behind the texts and buttons of the pause screen. To do this, navigate to **Palette** | **Common** | **Image**. Then, drag and drop the image onto the Canvas Panel so that the image is within the Canvas Panel. From here, locate the **Anchors** drop-down menu under **Details** | **Slots**. Select the **Anchors** option that creates anchors on all the four corners of the canvas.

This is an icon that looks like a large square covering the entire canvas located on the bottom-right of the **Anchors** drop-down menu:

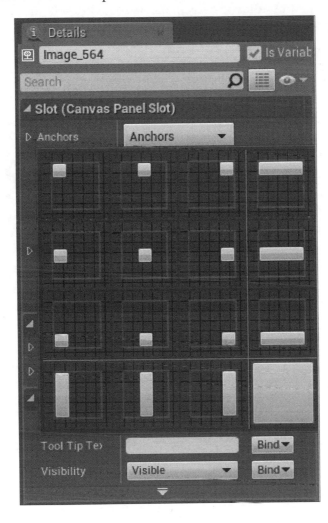

Once this is done, set the **Offset Right** and **Offset Bottom** values to 0. This will ensure that, just like the left and the top of the image, the right and the bottom of the image will start at 0, thus, allowing the image to stretch to all our anchor points that are positioned at all four corners of our canvas:

To make the background image a little easier on the eyes, we should make it a bit more of a dull color. To adjust the color, navigate to **Details | Appearance | Color and Opacity** and then click on the rectangular box next to it. This will open a **Color Picker** box where we can pick any color we want. In our example, we will use a dull blue:

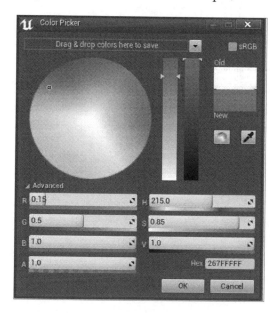

Press **OK** once you are finished. You will notice that your image name is something like **Image_###**; we should adjust this so that it is more descriptive. To rename the image, simply navigate to **Details** and change the name. We will change the name to **BG_Color**. Lastly, change the **ZOrder** value in **Details | Slot** to **-1**. This will ensure that the background is drawn behind other widgets:

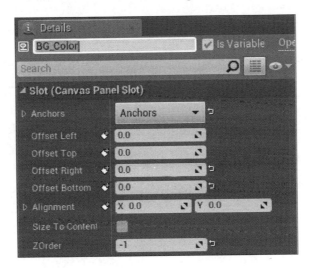

UMG text

Now that we have finished creating a background for our menu, it is time to lay out our text and navigation. We will add text by navigating to **Common | Text**. Then, we will drag and drop the text into the Canvas Panel located in the **Hierarchy** tab:

Note down a few important details. Firstly, you will see that in the **Hierarchy** tab, the Text Block is located within the Canvas Panel. This means that the Canvas Panel is acting as a container for the text; thus, it can only be seen if the player is navigating through the Canvas Panel. You will also notice that the **Details** tab has changed in order to include specific properties for the text. Some really important details are listed here, such as position, size, text, and anchors. Lastly, you should see that the selected text is in the form of a movable and resizable text box, which means we can place and edit this however we choose to. For now, we won't worry about making the pause screen look pretty, we just need to focus on the layout and functionality. A common layout will be one that navigates the eyes left to right and top to bottom. Since we are starting with the characters, we will make our first text be the character names. Also, we will have them start at the top-left corner of the pause menu.

Firstly, we will add the text necessary for the character names or classes. While selecting the text, navigate to **Details** | **Content** | **Text** and type the name of the first class — Soldier. You will notice that the text that you wrote in the **Content** tab is now written in your Text Block in the **Designer** view. However, it is small, which makes the text hard to see. Change its size by navigating to **Details** | **Appearance** | **Font**. Here, you can change the size to something larger such as **48**:

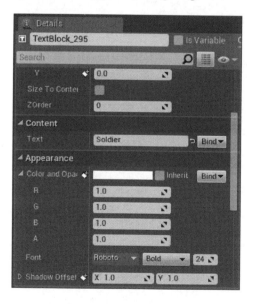

Position the text by navigating to **Details | Slot** and moving the text so that it is located on the top-left corner, but give it some padding. In our example, we will set **Position X** to **100** and **Position Y** to **100** so that there is a 100-pixel padding for **Soldier**. Lastly, we will rename the text as **Header_Soldier**:

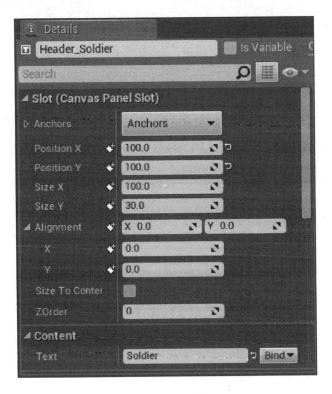

You will notice that the font size does not change and this is because you must press **Compile** at the top-left corner of the window. You will need to press **Compile** whenever you make technical changes such as these in your **Design** view. Once compiled, you should see that your font is resized. However, the text is too large for the Text Block. You can fix this by simply checking **Size to Content**, which is located in **Details | Slot**:

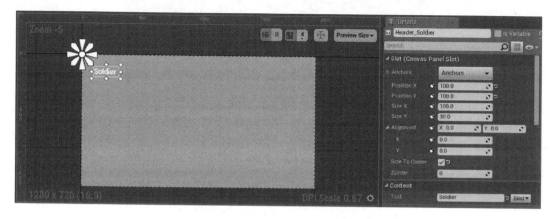

Now that we have created the header for our first character, we can continue to create more texts for its stats. We will start by creating a font for HP. To do so, you will need another Text Block on your canvas:

From here, you can position your Text Block so that it is somewhere below the **Header_Soldier** text. In this example, we will place it at a **Position X** value of **200** and a **Position Y** value of **200**:

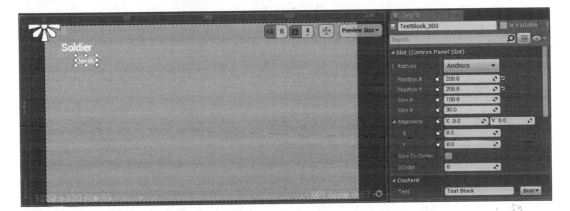

We will then write content for the text; in this case, the content will be **HP**. Here, we will give a font size of **32** to the text and compile it; then, we will check **Size to Content**:

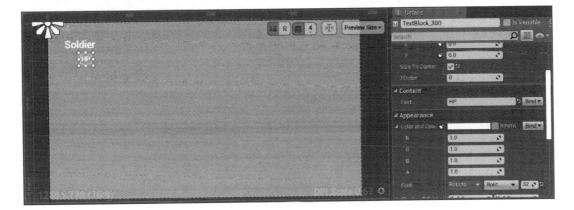

Lastly, we will name this widget **Menu_HP**:

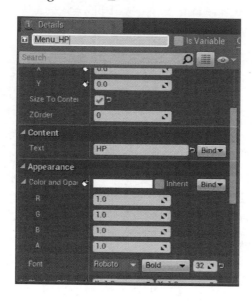

As you can see, all we did was added text that says **HP** in the menu; however, you will also need actual numbers for the HP displayed on the screen. For now, we are simply going to make a blank Text Block on the right-hand side of the HP text. Later on in this chapter, we will tie this in with the code we created for the character HP in the previous chapter. So for now, drag and drop a Text Block as a child of your Canvas Panel:

Rename it as **Editable_Soldier_HP**. Then, position it so that it is to the right of **Menu_HP**. In this case, we can set the **Position X** value as **300** and the **Position Y** value as **200**:

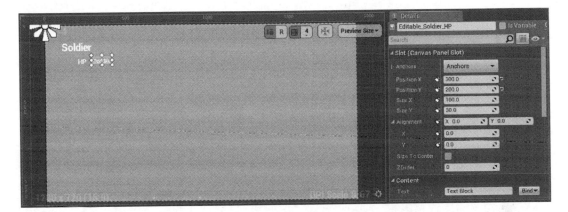

Lastly, we can change the font style to **Regular**, the font size to **32**, check **Size to Content**, and compile:

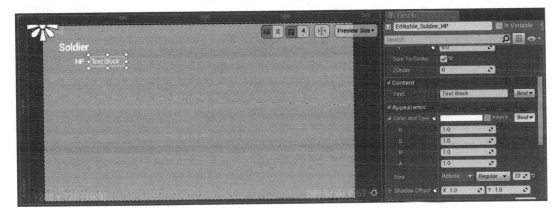

Now that you know what the layout is like and how we can create text blocks for characters and their stats, you can proceed to create the other necessary stats for your character such as level, MP, and experience/next level. After you have finished laying out characters and their stats, your final result should look something like the following:

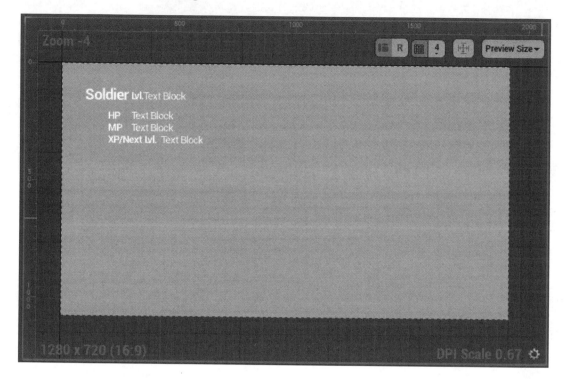

At this point, you may also move on to creating more characters. For instance, if you wanted to create a Healer, you could have easily copied most of the content we created for the Soldier and its layout in our pause screen. Your pause screen with placeholders for both Soldier and Healer stats may look something like the following:

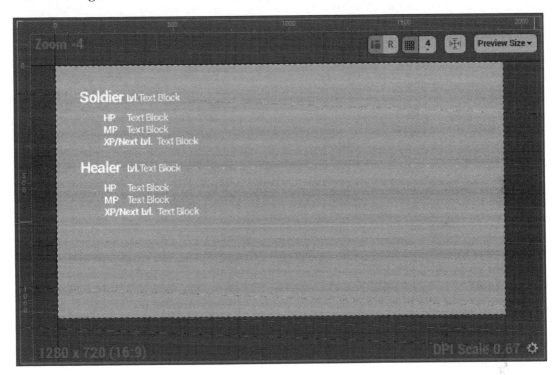

The last placeholder we need to make on this screen is for gold that is collected by the player. Just like we did for the party stats, create a Text Block and make sure the content of the text is **Gold**. Place this somewhere away from the character stats, for example, in the bottom-left corner of the pause screen. Then, rename the Text Block as **Menu_Gold**. Finally, create a second Text Block, place it to the right of **Menu_ Gold**, and call it **Editable_Gold**:

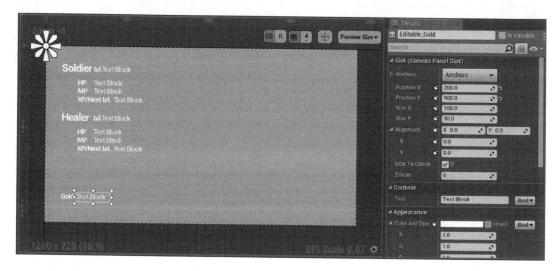

Like the empty text boxes in the character stats, we will link **Editable_Gold** with the gold accumulated in the game later on.

We can now move on to creating buttons for our menu, which will eventually navigate to submenus.

UMG buttons

So far, we have created the first screen of our pause menu that includes all of our characters and placeholders for their stats and gold. The next thing we need to design is buttons, which will be the last portion of our first pause screen. Much like buttons in other software packages, they are typically used to trigger events built around mouse clicks. A programmer can simply have their button listen to a press from a mouse button and cause an action or series of actions to occur based around that button click. The buttons we are creating will be used as navigation to submenus since we need a way of navigating through the inventory and equipment screens. Therefore, on our main screen, we will need a button for both inventory and equipment. We will also need a button to go to the pause menu and resume playing the game as well.

Let us start by creating our first button. Navigate to **Palette** | **Common** | **Button** and place it in your Canvas Panel under the **Hierarchy** tab:

For organization purposes, we will lay our first button on the top-right of the menu. So the best thing to do is navigate to **Details** | **Slot** | **Anchors** and anchor the button at the top-right. This will ensure that as the screen or objects resize, the button aligns to the right-hand side:

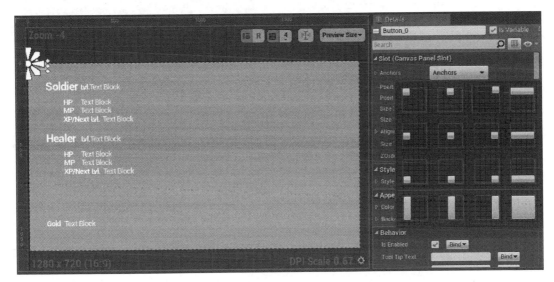

You should notice that the anchor icon on your screen moves to the top-right of the screen. You will also notice that the **Position X** value changes to a negative number that reflects the size of your screen, since the origin of the button position is placed at the opposite end of the screen; the values of **Position X** of this particular button are now flipped. This concept may be confusing at first, but it will make the math for the placement of each button much easier in the long run:

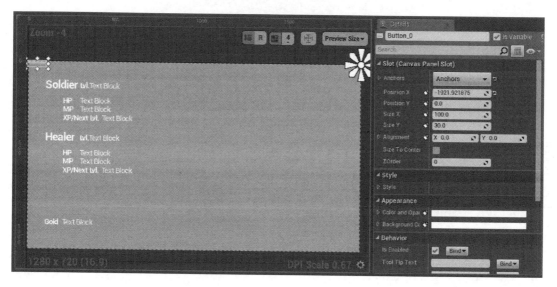

Change the **Position X** value to **-200** (since **Position X** of the button is now **-1920** to be positioned from the left and **-100** to be positioned to the right, to add **100** pixels of padding would be **-200**) and **Position Y** value to **100**. Name this button **Button_Inventory**:

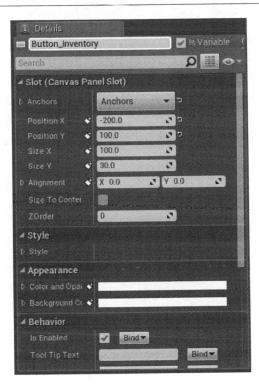

We will now add text to the button. So select **Text** under **Palette | Common | Text** and drag it into the button. You will notice that the text is within the button in both the **Hierarchy** tab and the **Designer** view:

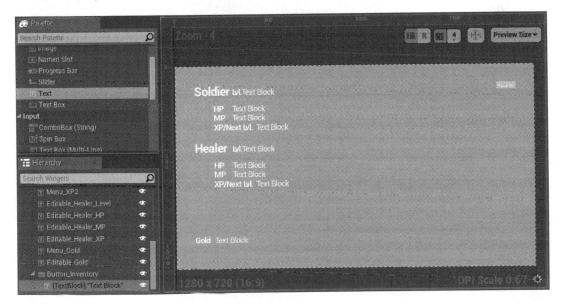

You may also notice that the text is not sized to our liking and it does not fit into the button. Rather than resizing the button right away, let us resize the text to our liking first and then resize the button around the text so that the text is readable. Navigate to **Details** | **Appearance** | **Font** and change the font size to **48**:

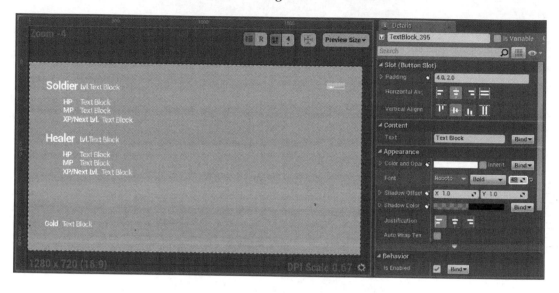

Then, under **Details** | **Content** | **Text**, change the text to **Inventory** and the name of the Text widget to **Menu_Inventory**:

Click on **Button_Inventory**. You may be thinking that checking **Size to Content** would be the right idea here, but it isn't in our circumstances because you will be creating multiple buttons, each with a different text in it. Therefore, if they were all sized to the content (content being the text within the button), all your buttons would be sized differently, which is very unattractive. Instead, you should pick a button size that will easily fit all the text, even for your longest worded text. For this button, we will change the **Size X** value to **350** and **Size Y** value to **100**:

You will notice that the button is drawn off the screen and this is because the button, like every other object, is still drawn from the top-left of the object, so we will need to adjust our **Position X** value again; however, the math is easy since we are anchored at the top-right. All we need to do is take the horizontal sizes of our button, 350, and then subtract it from where the button thinks the right edge of our screen is due to the anchor, which is 0. So this gives us *0 - 350 = -350*. Then, we take -350 and subtract the 100 pixels of padding that we want, which gives us *-350 - 100 = -450*, which is the value we should change our **Position X** to:

Now that we have a button perfectly placed, we can place more buttons. We will use the same steps to create an **Equipment** button below the **Inventory** button. Once you have completed creating the **Equipment** button, it can be placed just below the **Inventory** button:

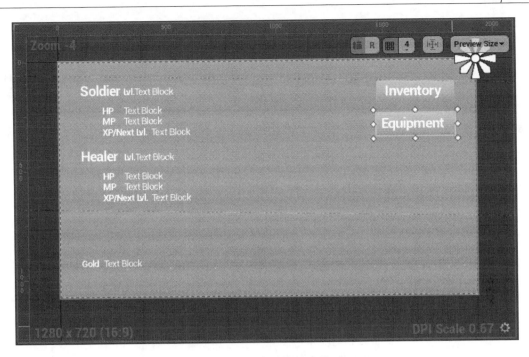

We can also create an **Exit** button, which we will place at the bottom-right of the screen:

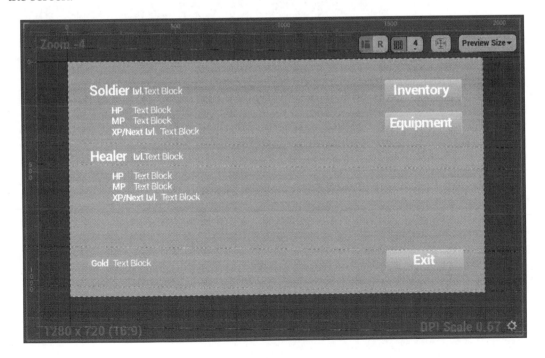

There you have it—we have finished designing the first screen of our pause menu. You will notice that we have not yet programmed the buttons to do anything, and this is because we do not have screens for the buttons to navigate to, so it won't make sense to program the buttons just yet. The next steps will be to design our submenus.

The UMG inventory submenu

As mentioned earlier, we need to create submenus for our buttons to navigate to. Using UMG, there are several ways to create submenus, but the most straightforward way is to create a new Widget Blueprint for each submenu and then bind the Widget Blueprints together.

Since we will need many of the same items in our submenus such as the character names and most of their stats, we can save a lot of time by carefully making a copy of our main pause menu, renaming it, and then editing it to fit whatever submenus we need. Since we have initially saved the main pause menu as **Pause**, we may want to first rename it so that it is more descriptive. So head back into your **Content Browser**, locate where you saved your pause menu, and rename it by right-clicking on the pause menu widget and selecting **Rename**. Rename this file as **Pause_Main**:

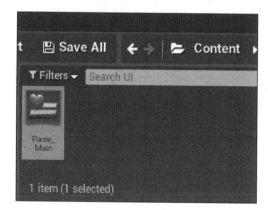

Next, make a duplicate of **Pause_Main** by right clicking on the file and selecting **Duplicate**:

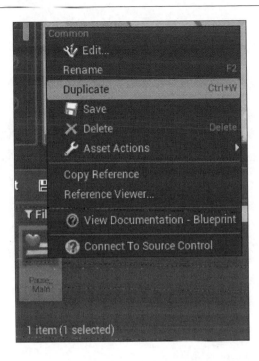

Rename this as **Pause_Inventory**:

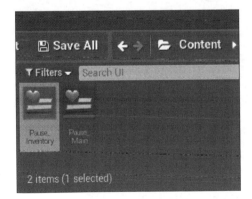

We will now be able to design an **Inventory** screen. Open up your newly created **Pause_Inventory** Widget Blueprint. You will notice that it is an exact duplicate of **Pause_Main**. From here, we can edit out what is not needed. First of all, we are not planning to have any items that affect XP, so we can remove XP Text Blocks from our characters:

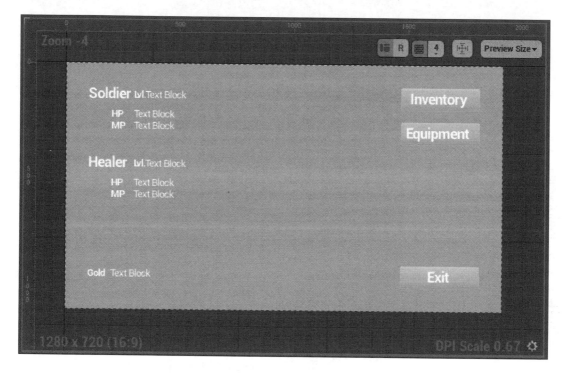

Also, we will not need to keep a track of gold in our **Inventory** screen either. So, we can remove gold.

For ease of creation, we will also make the navigation around the main pause screen and its submenus "old school", by using **Pause_Main** as a central hub to all submenus, such as **Pause_Inventory** and **Pause_Equipment**, and only allowing the player to enter the **Equipment** screen if they are backed out to **Pause_Main** and they press the **Equipment** button from there. Based on the idea behind this design, we may also remove the **Inventory** and **Equipment** buttons from this screen:

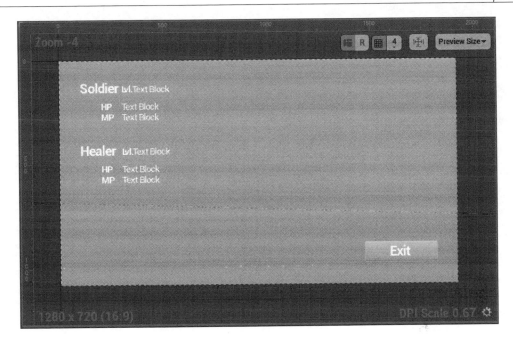

We can, however, keep the **Exit** button, but based on our ideas behind the screen navigation, we should rename this button and its Text Block to reflect backing out of the screen and going to **Pause_Main** when pressed. So we can select **Button_Exit** and rename it as **Button_Back**:

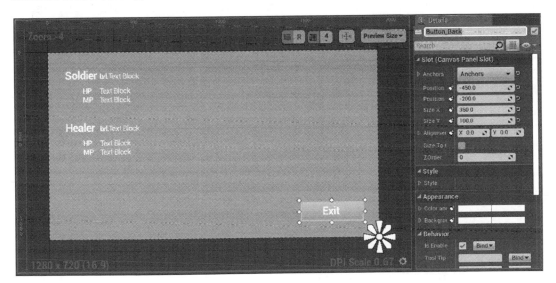

Then, select the Text Block within the **Exit** button, rename it as **Menu_Back**, and change the text to **Back**:

In the previous chapter, we defined more stats than just HP and MP; we also defined attack power, defense, and luck. While health and magic potions don't typically affect any stats other than HP or MP, you may later on want to create items that are usable and effect things such as luck, defense, or attack power. In preparation of this, we will create placeholders for these three other stats for each character in the same way you created the HP and MP Text Blocks. We will be positioning these stats below the HP and MP stats. Note that, if you run out of room for these stats, you may need to play around with spacing. Also, remember to name all Text Blocks you make with something very descriptive so that you can identify them when the time comes to reference them.

When you are finished adding stats, your Text Blocks should look something like the following screenshot:

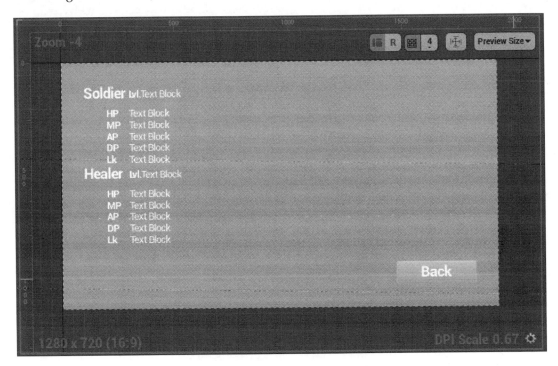

We now need a place that will populate our inventory. Since we are unsure about how many items the player in the game will carry, it will be safest to create a Scroll Box that will be populated with our inventory. We will also want to create a Scroll Box that is wide enough in case we have items that have very long names. If you designed your screen like I have, you should have plenty of room for a Scroll Box. To create a Scroll Box, navigate to **Palette** | **Panel** | **Scroll Box**:

Then, drag it into your Canvas Panel under the **Hierarchy** tab:

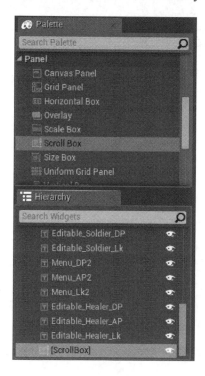

For now, rename the Scroll Box as **ScrollBox_Inventory**. Then, change the position so that it is placed in the middle of the screen while neatly taking up a wide amount space on the screen. I will change my **Position X** value to **700**, **Position Y** value to **200**, **Size X** value to 600, and **Size Y** value to **600**. When you are finished, your Scroll Box should look something like the following screenshot:

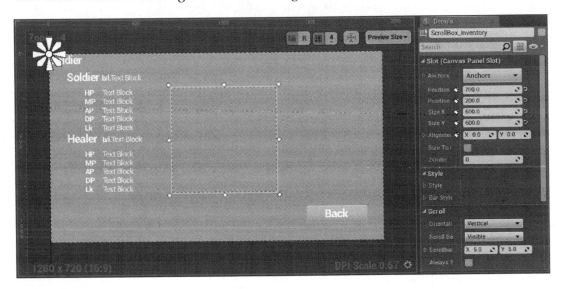

In a later chapter, we will be dynamically inserting items into the Scroll Box and creating logic to apply the effects of the items to each character.

To finish off this screen, you should notify the player about which screen they are currently viewing. So create another Text Block and size the font to something large, such as 48 pixels. Pick an anchor for your Text Block that is at the center-top. This will make it such that your Text Block recognizes the 0 *X* position as the middle of the screen and the *0* Y position as the top of the screen. So you can now put **0** as the **Position X** value and pad the **Position Y** value:

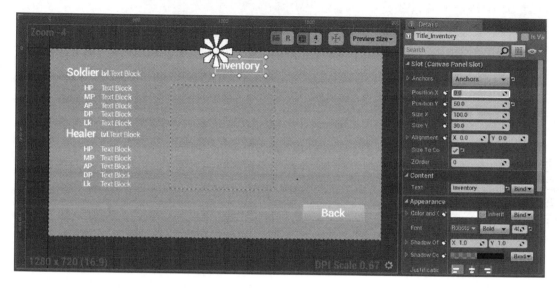

You will notice that the inventory is not quite written at the middle of the screen, so adjust the **Position X** value until it is. I changed my **Position X** value to half of the size of the Text Block, which came out to be -135:

At this point, you can save and compile your **Inventory** screen. We are done for now.

The UMG equipment submenu

The last submenu we need to design is the equipment submenu. Since our submenu for equipment will be very similar to the submenu for inventory, the easiest way to start would be to navigate back to **Content Browser**, duplicate **Pause_Inventory**, and rename it as **Pause_Equipment** so that **Pause_Equipment** is a direct copy of **Pause_Inventory**. Next, open up **Pause_Equipment**.

We will be designing this screen in a similar way to the **Inventory** screen. We will still be using the Scroll Box to populate items (in this case, equipment). We will be mostly keeping the same stats for each character; we will continue utilizing the Back button that will eventually navigate back to the pause screen. Let us edit the differences. First, change the title of the screen from **Inventory** to **Equipment** and reposition it so that it is horizontally aligned to the middle of the screen:

Next, we will need to edit the character stats. We may have equipment in this game that when equipped, will change the AP, DP, and Lk stats. However, we will most likely not have equipment that will have an effect on HP and MP. We also know that we will need weapons and armor for each character. Therefore, we can easily edit the text of HP and MP out with weapon and armor (which I will call **Weap** and **Arm** to save space). In terms of details, I will change the name of the **Menu_HP** text block to **Menu_Weapon** and the text of the Text Block to **Weap**. We will do something similar to **Menu_MP** by changing it to an armor slot:

Follow similar naming conventions when switching out any other character's HP and MP with weapon and armor placeholders. When you are finished, your screen should look like the following screenshot:

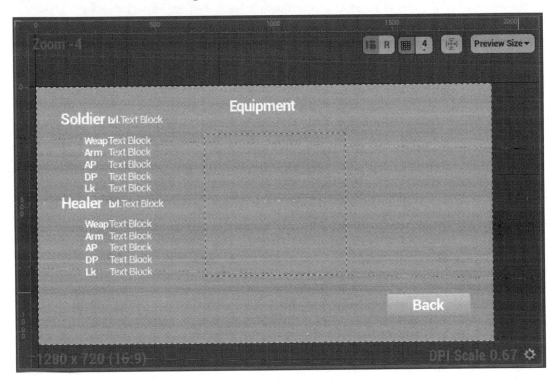

Since our characters will be equipping weapons and armor, we will need placeholders for these slots. Eventually, we will allow the player to select equipment that they want to equip, and the equipment will appear in the appropriate weapon or armor slot. The type of widget that would be most appropriate is **Border**. This will contain a Text Block that will change when a weapon or armor is equipped. To do this, select **Border** from **Palette | Common | Border**. Drag the Border into the Canvas Panel:

Then, position the Canvas Panel so that it is in the same position as the Text Block that is placed to the right of the soldier's **Menu_Weapon**. At this point, you may delete the Text Block that is to the right of **Menu_Weapon**. It was originally used as the text for HP, and we will no longer need it:

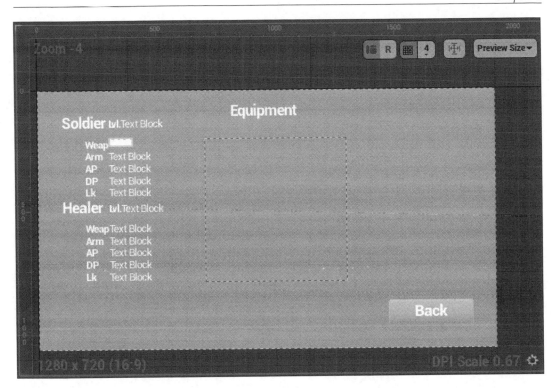

We will still need text in the border, so drop text from **Palette | Common | Text** into your Border:

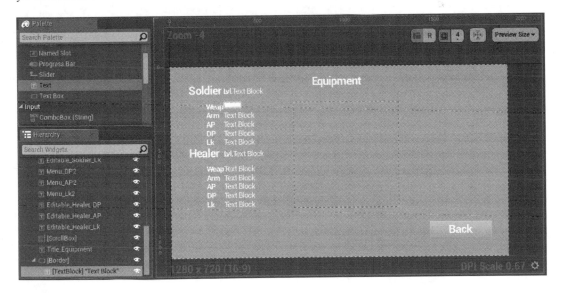

You can keep the defaults of the Text Block for now, except you will notice that the border did not resize and everything is still white. Navigate back to your Border and check **Size to Content**. Under **Appearance | Brush Color**, change the **A** value to **0**. The **A** value is alpha. When the alpha is 0, the color is completely transparent, and when the alpha is 1, the color is completely opaque; anywhere in between is only slightly transparent. We don't really care about seeing the color of the block, we want it to be invisible to the player:

Lastly, change the Border name to something descriptive such as **Border_Weapon**:

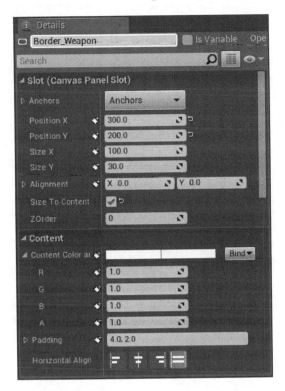

Navigate back to the Text Block within the border. Name the Text Block
Text_Weapon, and change the font to a regular style at 32 pixels to match the
rest of the Text Blocks:

Now that you know how to design borders and Text Blocks for the soldier's weapon, you can design Borders and Text Blocks for the soldier's armor and any other character's weapon and armor. When you are finished, you should have something that looks like the following screenshot:

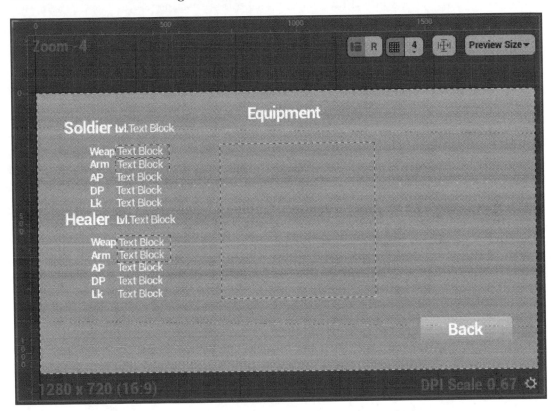

At this point, we are finished designing all our screens that appear when the player presses the pause button. The next steps will be to program the functionality of these screens.

Key binding

We are now going to bind a key to open up the pause menu, and only allow this to happen when the player is not in battle (in other words, the player is out in the field). Since we already have a **FieldPlayer** set up from the previous chapter, we can easily create actions within our **FieldPlayer** Blueprint class that will control our pause menu. To start, navigate to **Blueprints | Open Blueprint Class… | FieldPlayer**:

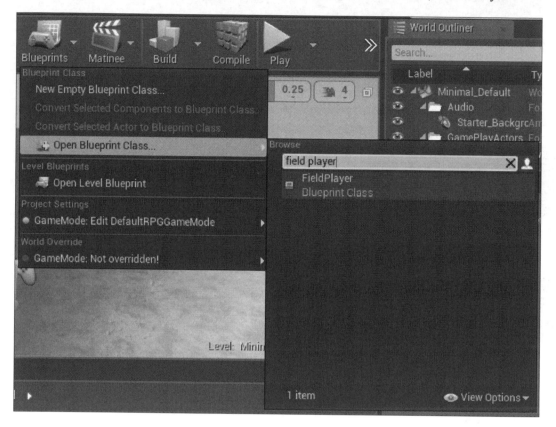

At this point, we are going to want to have the pause screen pop up when the player presses a key; in this case, we will use *P* for pause. To do this, we will first need to create a key event that will fire off a set of actions of our choice after a specific key is pressed. To start this key event, right-click on your Event Graph, which will open up all actions that can be associated with this Blueprint, and then navigate to **Input | KeyEvents | P**:

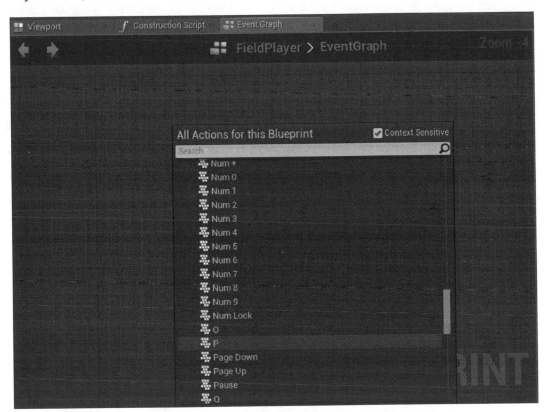

Once done, this will create a key event for the press and release of *P*. You will notice that this event has pressed and released executables that work as they are described, an action can occur when the player presses *P* or when the player releases *P*. For our actions regarding the pausing of the game and the pop up of the pause menu, we will use the released executable, because in order for the released executable to be called, it would mean that the player has gone through the act of pressing and releasing the key. It is often the best practice for a player to commit to a button press just like a player commits to a move in Chess by letting go of a piece. Before we pop up the pause menu, let us pause the game by creating a call to the **Set Game Paused** function that can be found by right-clicking in the Event Graph and navigating to **Game | Set Game Paused**:

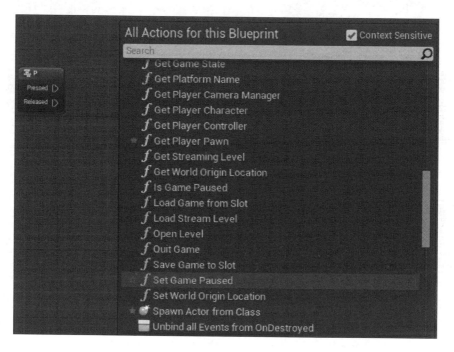

Within the **Set Game Paused** node, check **Paused** so that it is set to true, and link the **Released** executable of the key event **P** to the in pin of the **Set Game Paused**. Your game should now pause whenever the player presses and releases *P*:

From here, we will pop up the pause menu. To do so, upon the game being paused, we will create the main pause screen by right-clicking on the Event Graph and navigating to **User Interface | Create Widget**. This allows us to create instances of any widget that we made. We can create our **Pause_Main** here by pressing the **Select Class** drop-down menu within **Create Widget** and selecting **Pause_Main**:

Next, we can link the out pin of **Set Game Paused** to the in pin of the **Create Pause_MainWidget**:

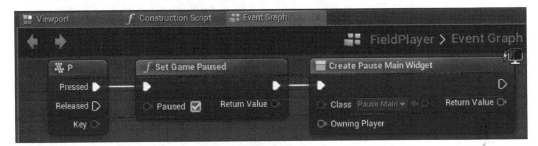

This will make it such that after the game is paused, **Pause_Main** will be created. Although we are creating **Pause_Main**, this will still not pop up on screen until we tell it to draw on screen. To do so, we will need to create a call to the **Add to Viewport** function that can add any graphic to a viewport. To do this, left-click and drag out the **Return Value** pin from the **Create Pause_Main** widget node, and select **User Interface | Viewport | Add to Viewport**. This will create a new **Add to Viewport** node:

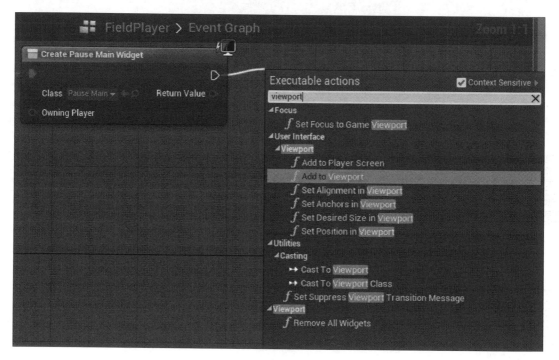

If you test this, you will notice that the game pauses and the pause menu pops up, but it is missing a mouse cursor. To add the mouse cursor, we will first need to get the player controller by right-clicking on the Event Graph and navigating to **Game | Get Player Controller | Get Player Controller**:

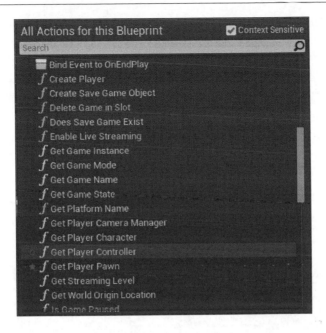

From here, simply left-click and drag out the **Return Value** pin from the **Get Player Controller** node, then select **Variables | Mouse Interface | Set Show Mouse Cursor**:

Once done, link the out pin of the **Add to Viewport** node to the in pin of **Set Show Mouse Cursor**. What this will do is set the **Show Mouse Cursor** variable (which is a Boolean) to either true or false after the pause menu has been displayed in the viewport. The **Set Show Mouse Cursor** variable needs to also get the player controller because the player controller holds the mouse input information.

If you playtest this now, you will notice that the mouse cursor still does not show up; this is because **Show Mouse Cursor** within **Set Show Mouse Cursor** is unchecked, meaning that **Show Mouse Cursor** is set to false, so check the box whenever you want to show the mouse cursor.

At this point, your menu should pop up perfectly after pressing *P* and the mouse should be completely visible and controllable. Your level blueprint should now look like the following screenshot:

You will notice that none of the buttons work in the actual menu so we cannot exit the pause menu or view any of the submenus. This is because we have not programmed any of the menu buttons yet. We will now focus on programming those buttons.

Button programming

Now that we have completed player access to the pause menu, we will now focus on navigation within the main pause menu and its submenus. At this point, head back into your **Pause_Main** widget. Let us first create the navigation to **Pause_Inventory**. To do this, click on the **Inventory** button:

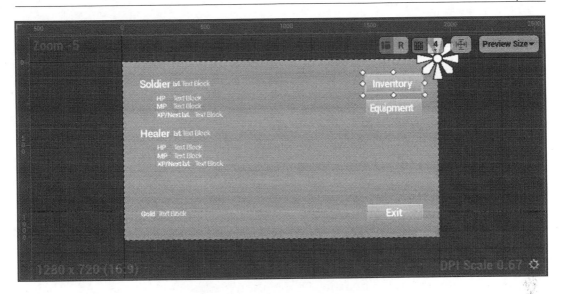

Navigate to **Details** | **Events** | **OnClicked** and then press the **+** button:

Clicking on the + button will automatically open the Event Graph of **Pause_Main** and also create an **OnClicked** event:

The **OnClicked** event will work similar to our key bind in the previous section where we created something that allows us to press a key, which triggers an event that can then trigger a series of actions. Only this time, the **OnClicked** event is bound to our **Inventory** button and will only trigger when the user has left-clicked on the **Inventory** button. What we will want to do is, when we click on the **Inventory** button, have it create a **Pause_Inventory** widget that gets displayed on the screen. This should sound very familiar because we just did something like this with **Pause_Main**. So firstly, create a widget and attach it to the **OnClicked** event. Next, you will notice that the **Class** pin in the widget is empty so we need to select a class. You will be selecting **Pause_Inventory** since we want to create the inventory widget when the button is pressed:

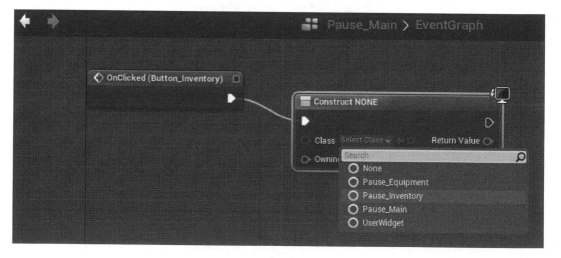

Lastly, just add this widget to the viewport so the user can see the inventory being displayed. In the end, your Blueprint should look like the following screenshot:

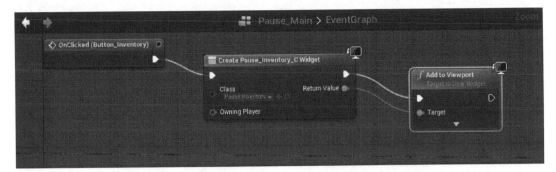

If you test your pause screen now, you should notice that you are able to navigate to your inventory screen, but you are not able to navigate back to your main pause screen. This is easily fixable. Simply open your **Pause_Inventory** widget, press the **Back** button, navigate to **Details** | **Events** | **OnClicked**, and then press the **+** button:

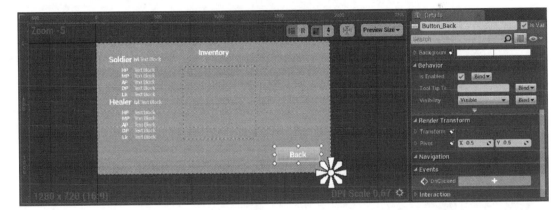

Just like our last button, the Event Graph will automatically open up and an **OnClicked** event for our button will be created; only this time, the event is bound to our **Back** button:

From here, you will set the screen to remove itself by linking the **OnClicked** event to **Remove from Parent**.

When you are finished creating the Blueprint for your **Back** button, it should look like the following screenshot:

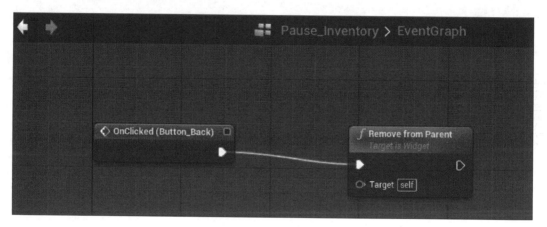

You can now create the same setup for navigation from **Pause_Equipment** by making sure that when we click on the **Equipment** button, we create a **Pause_Equipment** widget and display it; when we click on the **Back** button in the **Pause_Equipment**, we navigate back to the **Pause_Main** removing the **Pause_Inventory** screen.

The next step is to allow the player to exit when they click on the **Exit** button. To do this, you must first create an **OnClicked** event on the **Exit** button within **Pause_Main**. Again, when you press the **+** button of **OnClicked** within the **Design** view, an **OnClicked** button for the **Exit** button will be created in the Event Graph:

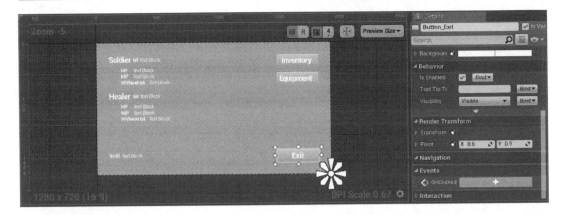

From here, you will set the screen to remove itself by linking the **OnClicked** event to **Remove from Parent**:

Your screens should now navigate perfectly, but we are not done yet. The last thing you will notice is that the game is still paused when the pause menu is exited. We will need to unpause the game. This fix is very simple. Within the **Pause_Main** Blueprint, simply link **Set Game Paused** to **Remove from Parent** so that when the widget is removed, the game unpauses:

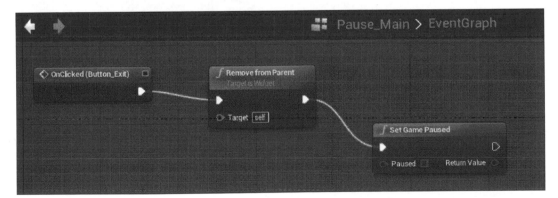

You may notice that when leaving the pause menu, the mouse cursor is still present. You can remove the mouse cursor by simply creating a **Set Show Mouse Cursor** node and having it connected to your **OnClicked Button_Exit** event after you unpause the game, which would be similar to how you added a mouse cursor in the first place, this time making sure the checkbox within the **Set Show Mouse Cursor** node is unchecked meaning that **Set Show Mouse Cursor** is set to false, and attaching a **Get Player Controller** to it.

There you have it. We are now finished with the navigation of our pause menu and its submenus.

Summary

In this chapter, we completed pause menu placeholders for other important aspects of our game such as the **Inventory** and **Equipment** Scroll Boxes that will hold the inventory/equipment that we acquire in the game. We will continue to add to this pause menu in the next few chapters by covering the tracking of stats, gold, items, and equipment.

5
Bridging Character Statistics

Now that we have a basic framework set up for our pause menu, we will now focus on the programming aspect of the pause menu.

In this chapter, you will learn how to link character statistics to the pause menu, as discussed in *Chapter 4*, *Pause Menu Framework*. By the end of this chapter, you will be able to link any other game statistics you would like to a UMG menu or submenu. We will cover the following topics in this chapter:

- Getting character data
- Getting player instances
- Displaying stats

Getting character data

At this point, the pause menu is fully designed and ready for data integration. In *Chapter 3*, *Exploration and Combat*, we had developed means to display some player parameters, such as the player's name, HP, and MP into CombatUI through binding Text Blocks with the **Game Character** variable in order to access character stat values held within **Character Info**. We will do this in a very similar fashion, as we did in the previous chapter, by first opening the **Pause_Main** widget and clicking on the Text Block that we will update with a value.

In this case, we have already designated locations for all our stat values, so we will start with the HP stat that we named **Editable_Soldier_HP**:

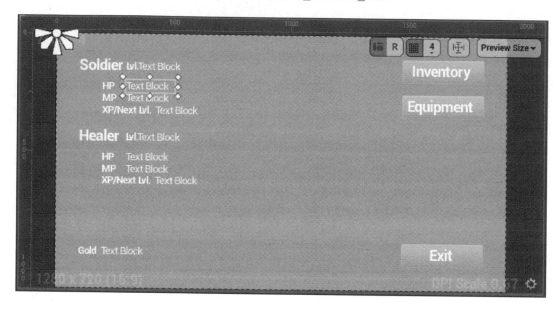

Navigate to **Content | Text**, and click on the drop-down menu of **Bind** next to the dropbox. Click on **Create Binding** under the drop-down menu:

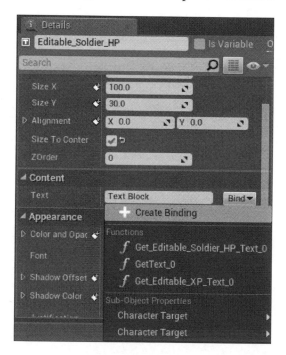

Once you have completed this process, a new function called `Get_Editable_Soldier_HP_Text_0` will be created, and you will automatically be pulled into the graph of the new function. Like in previous binds, the new function will also automatically have **FunctionEntry** with its labeled return:

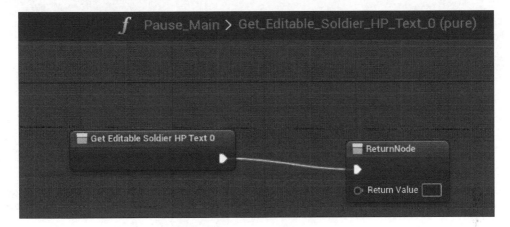

We can now create a new **Game Character** reference variable that we will again name **Character Target**:

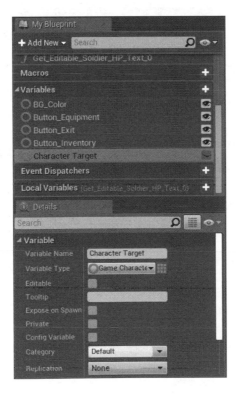

Then, we will drag our **Character Target** variable into the `Get_Editable_Soldier_HP_Text_0` graph and set it to **Get**:

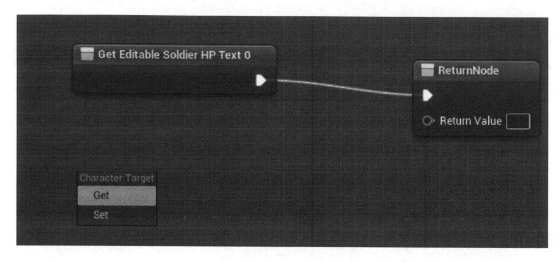

Next, we will create a new node named **Get HP**, which is located under **Variables | Character Info**, and link its **Target** pin to the **Character Target** variable pin:

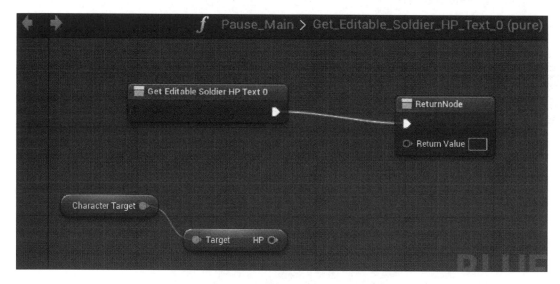

Lastly, link the HP stat in the **Get Editable Soldier HP Text 0** node to the **Return Value** pin of the **ReturnNode**. This will automatically create a **To Text (Int)** conversion node, which is responsible for converting any integer into a string. When you are finished, your `Get_Editable_Soldier_HP_Text_0` function should look like this:

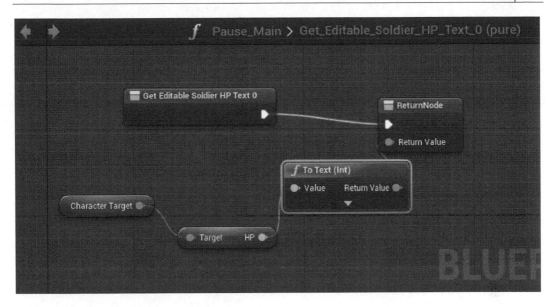

Getting player instances

If you were to test this now, you would see that a value gets created in our pause menu, but the value is **0**. This is not correct because our character is supposed to start with 100 HP according to the character's current stats:

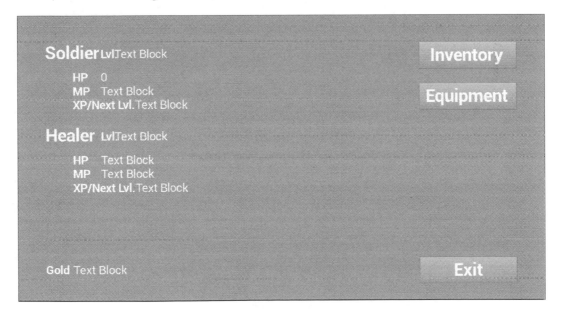

The problem occurs because the **Field Player** that accesses the pause menu never assigns any of our character data to **Character Target**. We can easily set the proper character target in Blueprint, but we won't be able to assign any of the character data without exposing our added party members to Blueprint. So, we must first head into RPGGameInstance.h and allow the exposure of our current game data to a **Game Data** category of Blueprint in the UProperty parameters:

```
UPROPERTY( EditDefaultsOnly, BlueprintReadOnly, Category = "Game Data" )
```

Your RPGGameInstance.h file should now look like this:

```
#pragma once

#include "Engine/GameInstance.h"
#include "GameCharacter.h"

#include "RPGGameInstance.generated.h"

/**
 *
 */
UCLASS()
class RPG_API URPGGameInstance : public UGameInstance
{
    GENERATED_BODY()

    URPGGameInstance( const class FObjectInitializer& ObjectInitializer );

public:
    UPROPERTY( EditDefaultsOnly, BlueprintReadOnly, Category = "Game Data" )
    TArray<UGameCharacter*> PartyMembers;

protected:
    bool isInitialized;

public:
    void Init();
    void PrepareReset();
};
```

Once you have saved and compiled your code, you should be able to properly call any created and added party members in Blueprint, and so we should have read access via the **Field Player** Blueprint.

Now, you can navigate back to the **Field Player** Blueprint and have it get **RPGGameInstance** by creating the **Get Game Instance** function node located under **Game**:

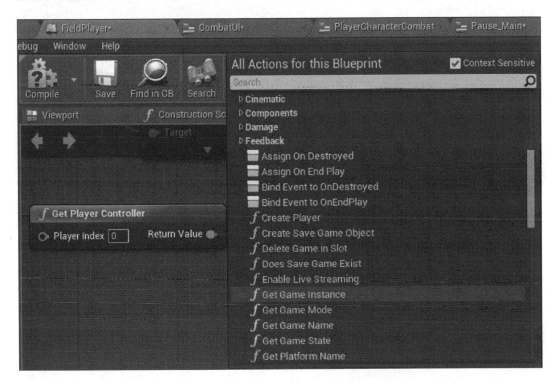

Have the **Return Value** of **Get Game Instance** cast to **RPGGameInstance**, which is located under **Utilities | Casting | RPGGameInstance**. Now that you've got an instance of the **RPGGameInstance** class, you can have the instance refer to the TArray of **Party Members**, which holds all your party members, by navigating to the category that you have created for it in **GameData** under **Variables**:

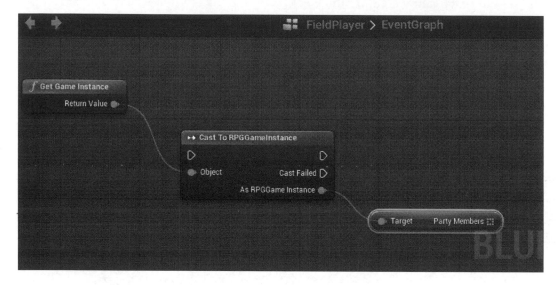

Here, we will need to point to the element of the array that holds our soldier character's stats, which is our first element or 0 index of the array, by linking the **Party Members** array to a **GET** function, which can be found by going to **Utilities | Array**:

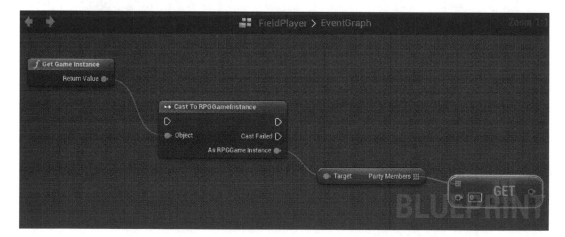

For additional characters, you will need to link another **GET** function to **Party Members** and have the **GET** function point to the element of the array that will point to any other characters (for instance, if you had a healer that is in index 1, your second **GET** function would simply list its index as 1 instead of 0 to pull from the healer's stats). For now, we are just going to focus on the soldier's stats, but you will want to get stats for every character in your party.

Lastly, once we have finished casting **RPGGameInstance**, we will need to set the **Character Target**, which we created in the pause menu, to our **Party Members**. To do this, right-click on your **Event Graph** to create a new action, but uncheck **Context Sensitive** because we are looking for variables that have been declared in a different class (`Pause_Main`). If you navigate to **Class | Pause Main**, you will find **Set Character Target**:

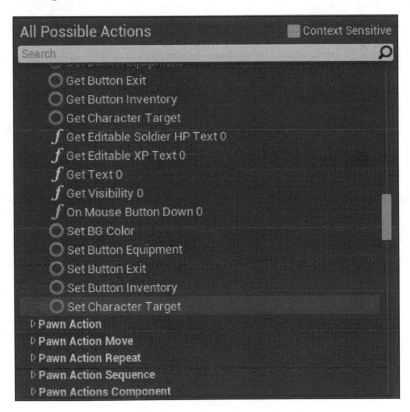

Here, simply link **Character Target** to the out pin of your **GET** function:

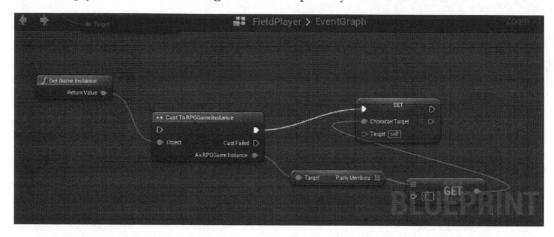

Then, set **Character Target** so that it is triggered after **RPGGameInstance** is cast:

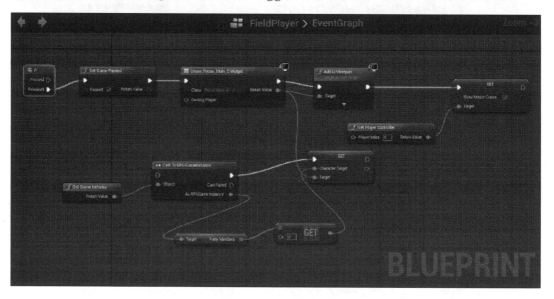

Displaying stats

Now, we will need to pick a good spot to cast **RPGGameInstance**. It would be best to cast **RPGGameInstance** after the pause menu has been created, so link the out pin of the **Set Show MouseCursor** node to the in pin of the **Cast To RPGGameInstance**. Then, link the **Return Value** of the **Create Pause_Main Widget** to the **Target** of **Set Character Target**. When you are finished, your **EventGraph** under **FieldPlayer** will look like this:

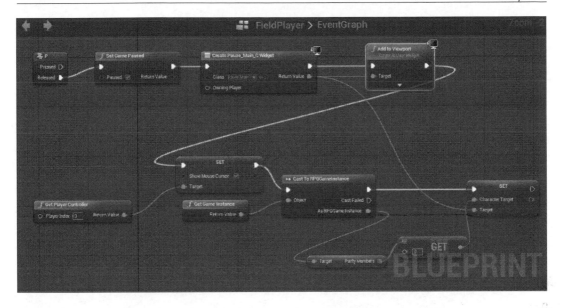

When you are finished, you will see that the HP of the soldier is displayed correctly as the current HP:

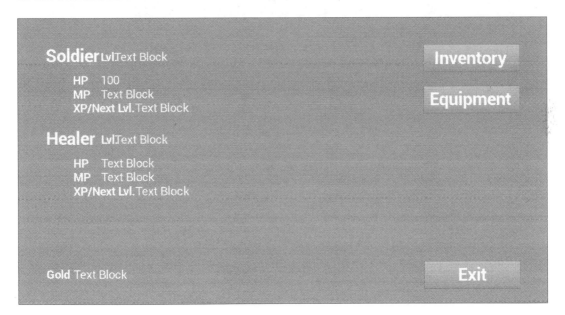

You can now add the remaining soldier stats to Text Blocks in **Pause_Main** from the pause menu by binding functions and then have these functions return values, such as the character target's MP and name. When you are finished with your soldier character, your **Pause_Main** should look something like this:

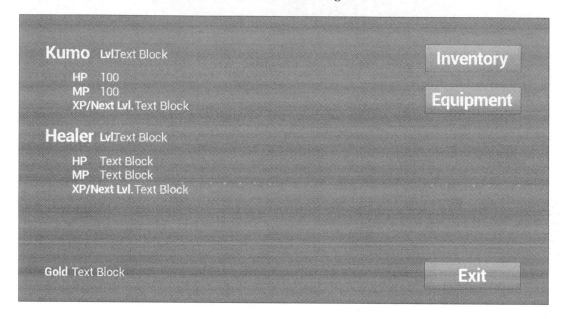

We do not yet have levels or experience, we will cover levels and experience in a later chapter.

If you have any other characters, make sure that you add them as well. As mentioned earlier, if you have additional characters in your party, you will need to go back to your **FieldPlayer** Event Graph and create another **GET** function that will get the indexes of your other party members and assign them to new **Character Targets**.

Let's now head back into the **Pause_Inventory** widget and bind character stats to their corresponding Text Blocks. Just like in **Pause_Main**, select a Text Block that you want to bind; in this case, we will grab the **Text Block** to the right of **HP**:

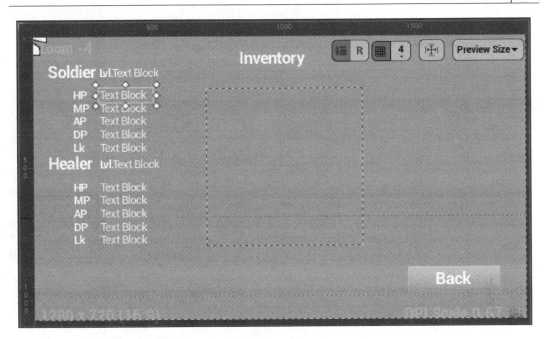

Then, simply create a binding for the Text Block, as you did for other Text Blocks. This will, of course, create a binding for a new function that we will return the HP status of the **Character Target**. The issue is that the **Character Target** that we created in **Pause_Main** is a **Game Character** variable local to **Pause_Main**, so we will have to recreate the **Character Target** variable in **Pause_Inventory**. Luckily, the steps are the same as they were; we just need to add a new variable and name it **Character Target**, and then make its type an object reference to **Game Character**:

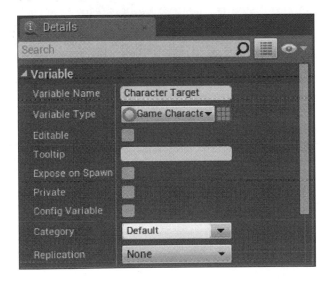

When you are finished, add the **Character Target** variable as a getter, link the **Character Target** variable to get the HP of your character, and link that value to **Return Value** of your **ReturnNode**, just like you did previously. You should have an Event Graph that looks pretty similar to the following screenshot:

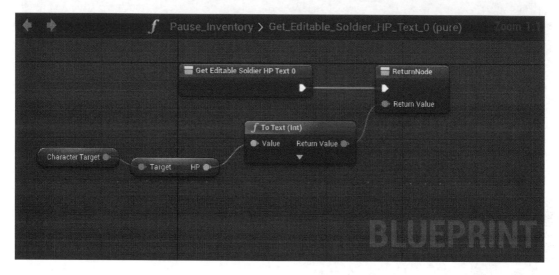

If you were to test the inventory screen at this point, you would see that the HP value would be 0, but do not panic, you don't need to do much critical thinking to correct the value now that **FieldPlayer** has a general framework for our characters. If you remember, when we cast **RPGGameInstance** after creating the **Pause_Main** widget in the **FieldPlayer** class, we pulled our added party members from our game instance and set it to **Character Target** in **Pause_Main**. We need to perform steps similar to these, but instead of beginning the retrieval of party members in **FieldPlayer**, we must do it in the class in which we created the **Pause_Inventory**, which was created in **Pause_Main**. So, navigate to the Event Graph of the **Pause_Main** widget:

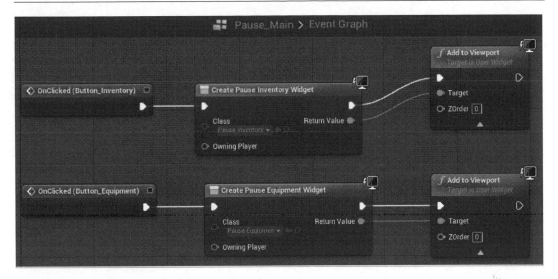

In the preceding screenshot, we see that we are creating both the **Pause_Inventory** and **Pause_Equipment** widgets by clicking on their respective buttons. When the screens are created, we remove the current viewport. This is a perfect spot to create our **RPGGameInstance**. So, as mentioned in the previous steps, create a **Get Game Instance**, which is located under **Game**. Then, set the return value to **Cast to RPGGameInstance** by going to **Utilities | Casting**, which will then reference the **Party Members** array located at **Game Data** under **Variables**. Here, you will use the **Get** function by going to **Utilities | Array**, and link it to the **Party Members** array, pulling index 0. This is what you should have done, and so far, the steps are identical to what you did in the **FieldPlayer**:

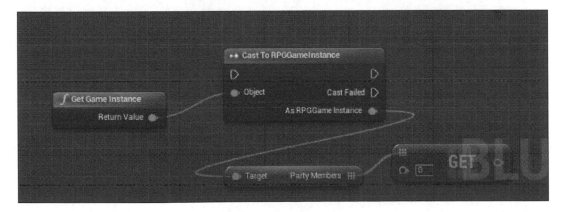

The differences set in when you set the **Character Target**. As mentioned earlier, we will set the **Character Target** variable of our newly created **Character Target** variable to **Pause_Inventory**:

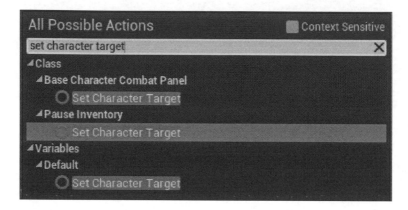

Once this is done, link the out pin of **Cast To RPGGameInstance** to the in pin of **Set Character Target**. Also, link **Get** to **Character Target**:

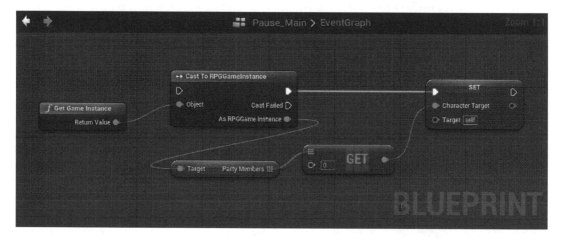

Lastly, link the out pin of **Add to Viewport** coming from **Pause_Inventory** to the in pin of **Cast To RPGGameInstance** to trigger the retrieval of the character stats, and link the **Return Value** of the **Create Pause_Inventory Widget** to **Target** of **Set Character Target**:

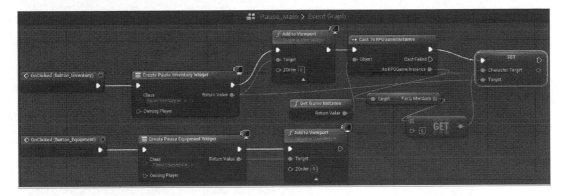

At this point, if you test the inventory screen, you will notice that the HP value is being displayed properly:

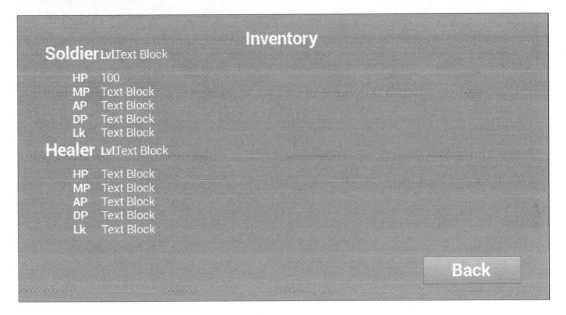

Now that you know how to create references to party members from **Pause_Main**, you can follow the same steps to set each party member as a character target in **Pause_Inventory**. But first, we need to complete all of the stat value displays in **Pause_Inventory** by creating bindings in each stat's respective Text Block and setting the **Return Value** of each Text Block to the value retrieved from **Character Target**.

Once you are finished with the soldier in your **Pause_Inventory**, you will see something that looks like this:

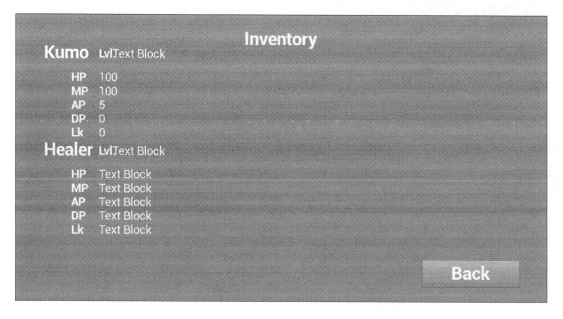

At this point, you can easily navigate back to **Pause_Equipment**, create a new **Character Target** variable, then set a **Party Members** to the **Character Target** variable on displaying **Pause_Equipment** in **Pause_Main**, just like you did in **Pause_Inventory**. The **Inventory** and **Equipment** buttons in the **Pause_Main** Event Graph should look something like this when you are done:

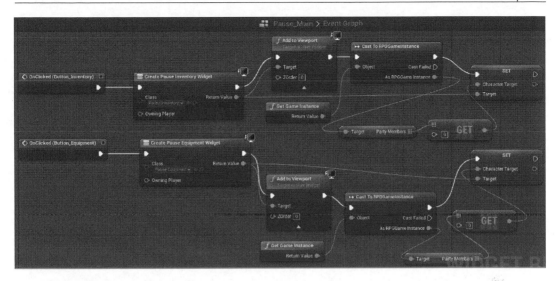

In the **Pause_Equipment** widget, we can only bind the **AP**, **DP**, **Lk**, and **Name** Text Blocks, as we will be leaving the weapons for later. If you bind these Text Blocks with the newly created **Character Target** in exactly the same way you bound the **Pause_Inventory** Text Blocks, your **Equipment** screen will look like this on testing:

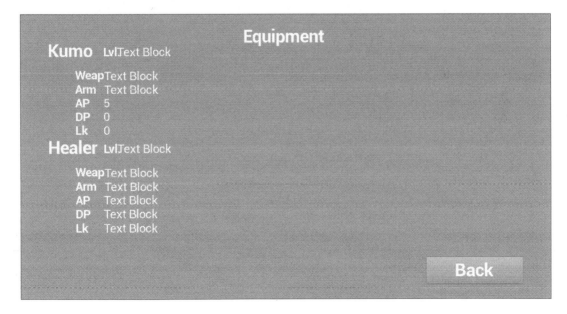

At this point, we have finished binding character stats to our pause menu screens for now.

Summary

In this chapter, we added the current character stats to the pause menu. Now that we are comfortable with UMG, we will be moving on to communicating with NPCs via dialog boxes, along with adding a shop to the game.

6
NPCs and Dialog

By now, you already have a player character by default that interacts with battles on the field, but the game is in dire need of **non-player characters** (**NPCs**).

In this chapter, you will create an NPC that will act as an information hub and shop owner. Since we have not yet given useable items and equipment to the character, or a reason for the character to have gold, the next logical step is to create a shop owner who will play the role of an NPC by talking to the player and offering the player business transactions when the player decides to interact with the NPC.

We will cover the following topics in this chapter:

- Creating the NPC Character Blueprint
- Interacting with the NPC
- Dialog box setup
- Creating an NPC welcome box
- Adding an NPC talk box

Creating the NPC Character Blueprint

To get started, we will need to create a new Character Blueprint class. Since we already have a location for characters, navigate to the `character` folder located in your **Content Browser** under **Content | Blueprints | Characters** (create a new `character` folder in `content/blueprints` if one is not there already, just to stay more organized; you can even drag your **FieldPlayer** Blueprint into the `character` folder if you'd like), and add a new character by clicking on **Add New | Blueprint Class**:

The **Pick Parent Class** window will pop up. This will allow you to pick a common parent class for your Blueprint class or create your own class:

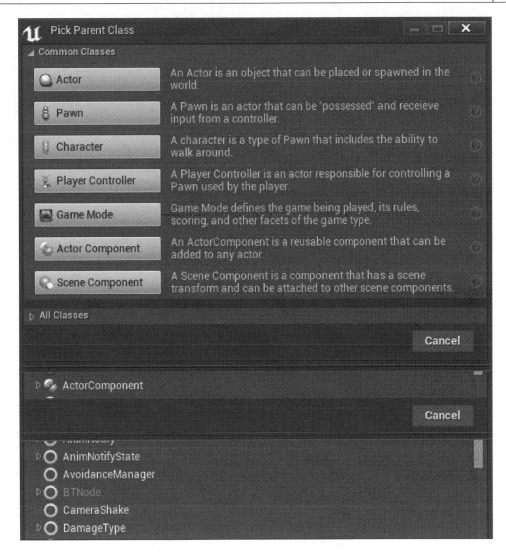

UE4 has a lot of common classes built in, which have a lot of the frameworks of several different types of classes already built for us. One of those classes is **Character** which allows us to work with a common character framework for use with any type of character pawn we want. So, from this window, select **Character**.

Once you have selected **Character**, a new Character Blueprint should now be in **Content | Blueprints | Characters**. Rename the character as **NPC_ShopOwner** since we will be using this character as the shop owner:

From here, open **NPC_ShopOwner** to enter the viewport of your new character:

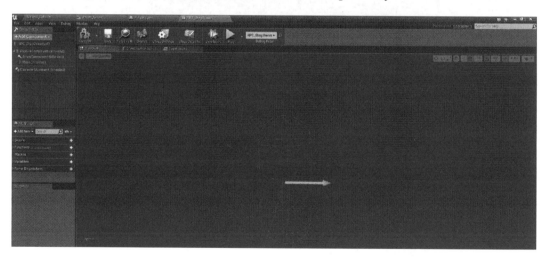

You should see that, as mentioned earlier, this class inherits `Character.h` which already has a framework for a lot of components. This will now make it easy for us to make a visible NPC. Within the **Components** panel, you will see **CapsuleComponent**, which holds inherited data such as **ArrowComponent** that determines which way the object is pointing, and **Mesh**, which holds an instance of a skeletal mesh.

Let us first apply a mesh and animations to our **Mesh** component. Since we are not creating character models and animations in this book, we can simply use built-in assets. First, click on **Mesh** within **Components | CapsuleComponent**:

From here, you will notice that your **Details** panel changes in order to display the **Mesh** variable and its components. For now, we will want to keep most of the defaults here since the character has everything we would want out of an NPC. However, the character does not have a mesh, so let's give it one by navigating to **Details | Mesh** and, in **Skeletal Mesh**, selecting the **None** drop-down menu that would house a skeletal mesh. Then, you should see all the skeletal meshes available in our project. In our game, there is a skeletal mesh called **SK_Mannequin**, we will select this as our skeletal mesh:

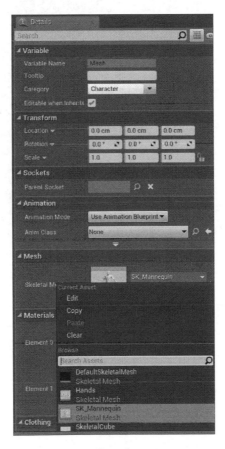

Now that we have selected a skeletal mesh, you should see it displayed in your viewport. At this point, you may notice that your skeletal mesh is much higher than the bottom of the capsule because the skeletal mesh's origin is at its feet and is attached to the origin of the capsule that is located in the middle of the capsule. There are a lot of ways to fix this problem, but the quickest way would be to reposition the character manually by bringing the character down on the Z axis. A value of **-90** for **Z Location** seems to work perfectly in this example:

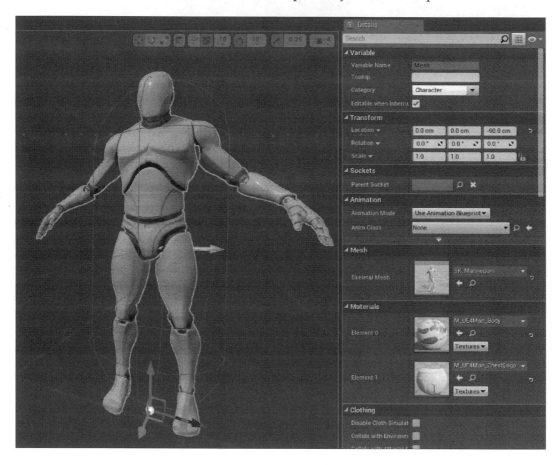

You will also want the character to be facing the right way. You can see that the character is faced the wrong way because the arrow component is pointing perpendicular to the way the character is facing. Simply adjust the character rotation on the Z axis. A value of **-90** for **Z Rotation** seems to do the trick:

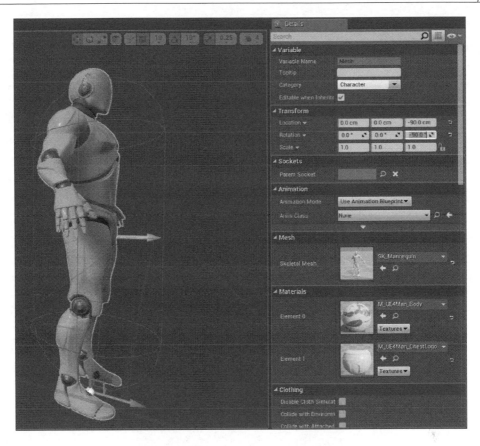

Lastly, we need to get the character out of the relaxed pose. So navigate to **Details | Animation** and select the **Anim Class** drop-down menu. In this drop-down menu, select **ThirdPerson_AnimBP**, which is the animation class for the character we selected. If you are using another character with a different animation class, be sure to select the animation class that is built for your character:

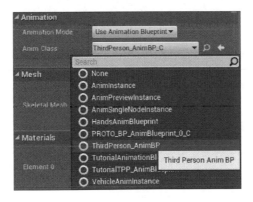

We also need a way to interact with this character. For this, we are going to create a volume that expands a certain distance in front of the character; this will be the area in which the player is able to interact with the NPC. To do this, we will need to add another component to **CapsuleComponent**. Navigate to the **Components** panel and select **Add Component | Collision | Box Collision**:

This creates a box collision at the character's origin:

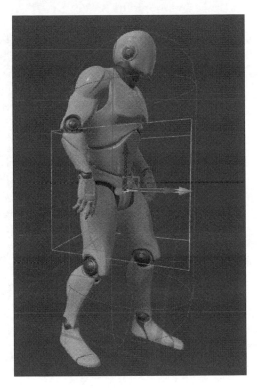

We are going to use this collision by calculating whether the player is inside the box or outside the box. If they are in the box, the player will be able to interact with the NPC; if the player is outside the box, the player will not be able to interact with the NPC. Since we want to make this as realistic as possible, the player should only interact with the NPC if the character is standing in front of the NPC. So adjust the location and scale of the box until it is in front of the character and sized such that the player can easily walk a forgivable distance in front of the NPC to interact with it.

For this character, I will edit the **Location X** value to be **60**, **Scale X** value to be **2**, **Scale Y** value to be **2**, and **Scale Z** value to be **3**:

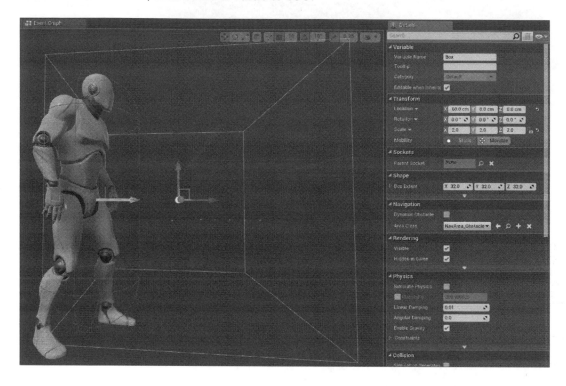

Finally, we want to give the collision box a type that does not block the player, but allows the player to enter the collision box. Navigate to **Details** | **Collision** and under **Collision Presets**, select **Trigger**:

This will essentially turn the collision box into a trigger volume that can be used to trigger events such as dialog and shop menus.

At this point, you can drag and drop your **NPC_ShopOwner** into your level:

If you playtest this, you should notice that you will collide with the skeletal mesh, but you will not collide with the trigger volume. You are now ready to create Blueprints to make this NPC interactive.

Interacting with the NPC

Now that you have made the NPC and volume that will trigger interaction with the NPC, it is time to program interaction with the NPC by using the trigger volume.

Let us first think about the logic. What we will want to do is only allow the player to interact with the NPC if the player is within the NPC's line of sight (in this case, the trigger volume). If the player is not within the trigger volume, we do not want to allow the player to interact with the NPC. In this case, we will need some sort of Boolean that will return *true* if the player is in the trigger volume and *false* if the character is not within the trigger volume. We also want to allow the player to press a key to interact with the NPC, but only when the Boolean we create is set to true, since the Boolean we create to keep track of the NPC trigger volume may span across multiple classes. Just like in the previous chapters, let's declare that global variable in `RPGGameInstance.h`. We will put the variable in the same `Game Data` category that our other global variables are in, but this time, instead of only allowing the Blueprint to read the variable, we need to allow Blueprint to write the variable since we will be switching the variable between true and false. We will add a Boolean called `TalkShop` as one of our public variables:

```
UPROPERTY( EditDefaultsOnly, BlueprintReadWrite, Category = "Game Data" )
bool TalkShop;
```

When you are finished editing `RPGGameInstance.h`, your header file should now look like the following:

```
#pragma once

#include "Engine/GameInstance.h"
#include "GameCharacter.h"

#include "RPGGameInstance.generated.h"

/**
 *
 */
UCLASS()
class RPG_API URPGGameInstance : public UGameInstance
{
    GENERATED_BODY()

    URPGGameInstance( const class FObjectInitializer& ObjectInitializer );

public:
    UPROPERTY( EditDefaultsOnly, BlueprintReadOnly, Category = "Game Data" )
    TArray<UGameCharacter*> PartyMembers;

    UPROPERTY( EditDefaultsOnly, BlueprintReadWrite, Category = "Game Data" )
```

```
   bool TalkShop;

protected:
   bool isInitialized;

public:
   void Init();
   void PrepareReset();
};
```

Compile the code and then head into the **NPC_ShopOwner** Character Blueprint. Select the **Box** component in the **Components** panel, and within the **Details** panel, scroll down to **Events**. You will notice that there are many different types of events that can be created here based around how the box is interacted with:

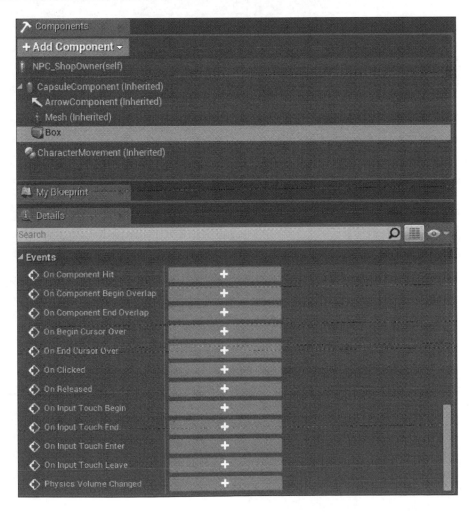

We are most interested in **On Component Begin Overlap** and **On Component End Overlap** because these are the events that will trigger if something either intersects the box or does not intersect the box. Let us first work on triggering an event if the player intersects the box. So, within **Details | Events | On Component Begin Overlap**, select **+**. This will automatically open **Event Graph** and create an **OnComponentBeginOverlap** event:

All we will need to do here is simply set the TalkShop Boolean that we created previously to true if the player intersects the box. To do so, first cast to the **FieldPlayer** using **Cast To FieldPlayer** located under **Utilities | Casting** and set the interaction component to the **FieldPlayer** object by linking the **OtherActor** pin within **OnComponentBeginOverlap** to the **Object** pin within the **Cast To FieldPlayer** node:

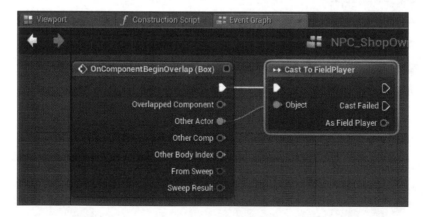

From here, we have **FieldPlayer** triggering a cast to **RPGGameInstance** using the **Cast To RPGGameInstance** node located under **Utilities | Casting**, whose **Object** pin is **Get Game Instance** since the TalkShop variable is located within **RPGGameInstance**:

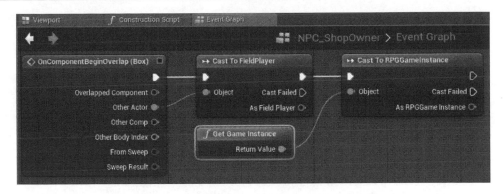

Lastly, create a **Set Talk Shop** action by unchecking **Context Sensitive**, navigating to **Class | RPGGameInstance**, and selecting **Set Talk Shop**:

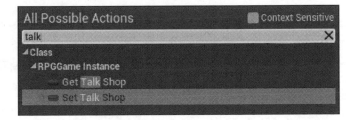

Have **Cast To RPGGameInstance** trigger the **Set Talk Shop** action and be sure that we are referencing the TalkShop variable within **RPGGameInstance** by linking the **As RPGGameInstance** pin from **Cast To RPGGameInstance** to the **Target** pin from **Set Talk Shop**. Also, be sure to set the TalkShop variable to true by checking the **Talk Shop** Boolean within the **Set Talk Shop** node. When you are finished, your Blueprint should look like the following screenshot:

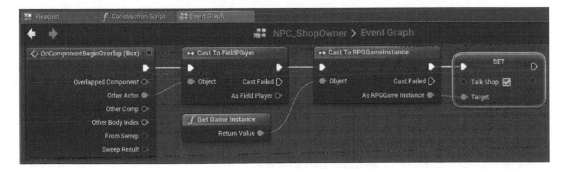

Now that we are finished creating the **Begin Overlap** event, let us create our player/key interaction and check whether or not the **Talk Shop** Boolean is true or false. Since the player controller won't have direct access to **NPC_ShopOwner**, we will need to create the key interaction either within the Field Player class or the Level Blueprint class. Because the NPC is specifically part of this particular level and different levels will most likely house different NPCs, it would make the most sense for the key and Boolean check to be located within the Level Blueprint. So at this point, navigate to **Blueprints | Open Level Blueprint** to enter the Level Blueprint.

Within the Level Blueprint, we will create a key event to the letter *E* by navigating to **Input | Key Events | E**. Then, upon release of the *E* key (because we want the player to commit to the key press), trigger **Cast To RPGGameInstance** whose object is **Get Game Instance** because upon the key press, we will want to check the status of the TalkShop variable that is located within **RPGGameInstance**:

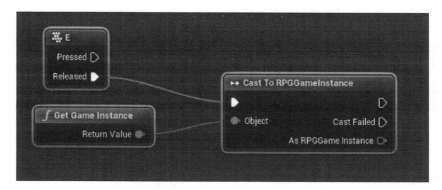

Reference the TalkShop variable by dragging out the **As RPGGameInstance** pin within **Cast To RPGGameInstance**, navigate to **Variables | Game Data** and then select **Get Talk Shop**, since we will be checking **Talk Shop**:

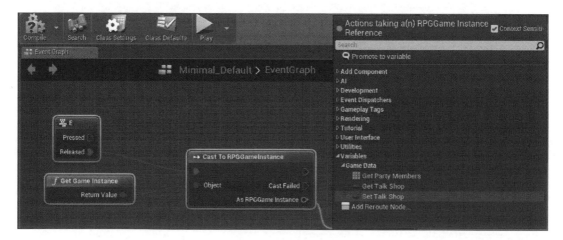

Now that we are referencing the `TalkShop` variable, we can check the condition of **Talk Shop** by creating a **Branch** statement located under **Utilities | Flow Control**:

Link the **Talk Shop** pin to the **Condition** pin within the **Branch** node to check the condition of `TalkShop`, and have the **Cast To RPGGameInstance** activate **Branch**:

Now that we have this framework set up, we can do something if the `TalkShop` condition is true or false. For now, we will just run a test by printing some text to the screen by navigating to **Utilities | Text | Print Text**, which will create a **Print Text** function. Link the **True** pin from the **Branch** node to the **In** pin of **Print Text**. When you are finished, your Level Blueprint should look like the following screenshot:

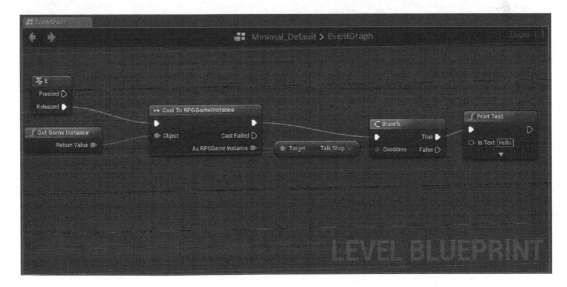

If you test this now, you should notice that if the player presses the *E* key outside the NPC trigger volume, nothing will happen; however, if the player presses *E* when they are within the trigger volume, text will appear on the screen. However, if we exit the volume and continue to press *E*, the text will continue to appear on the screen. This is because we are never setting the `TalkShop` Boolean back to `false`. Doing this is very simple. Navigate back to **NPC_ShopOwner** and select + under **Details | On Component End Overlap** to create an **OnComponentEndOverlap** event:

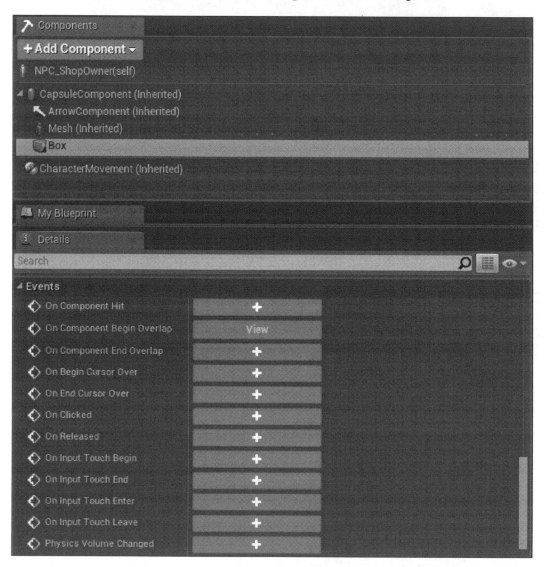

Since we have already created a reference to **Talk Shop** when creating the **OnComponentBeginOverlap** event, and set that reference to true, we can simply make the **OnComponentEndOverlap** event that does the exact same thing as the **OnComponentBeginOverlap**; however, instead of setting TalkShop to true, set TalkShop to false by making sure the **Talk Shop** pin within the **Set Talk Shop** node is unchecked. Your **OnComponentEndOverlap** event should now look like the following screenshot:

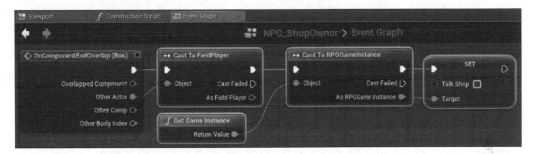

When you test this now, interaction with the NPC via the *E* key should only work if the player is intersecting the NPC's trigger volume as intended.

Dialog box setup

We are now ready to create dialog that our NPC will state to the character. To do this, we will first create a Widget Blueprint that will be responsible for housing all parent variables of the NPC, such as the dialog in the game, so that we can simply pull dialog anytime we need it by calling the dialog variable within the function. This process will be better than the hardcoding text in UMG because it will allow us to need only a single dialog UMG that we will dynamically place text into.

So let's first create a new Widget Blueprint by navigating to **Content Browser |
Content | Blueprints | UI** and then selecting **Add New | User Interface | Widget
Blueprint**. Then, name it **NPC_Parent**:

Once created, open the new Widget Blueprint and then navigate to the graph. From
here, head to the **My Blueprint** panel and select **+** to the right of **Variables**; this will
create a new variable. Name this variable **NPCDialog** and make it public by clicking
the eye to the right of the variable name:

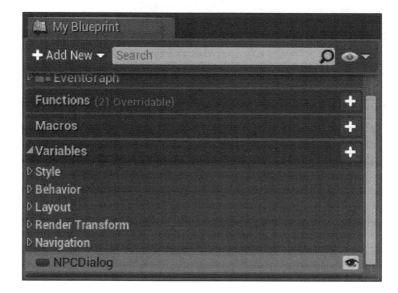

In the **Details** panel, change **Variable Type** to **Text** since we will be using text to display dialog. Also, click on the square icon to the right of **Variable Type** to make the variable a text array:

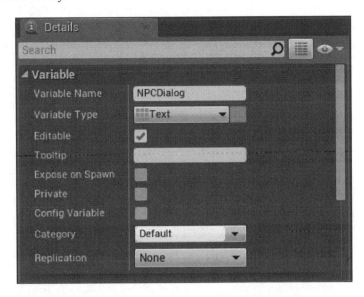

Next, scroll down to the **Default Value** tab within the **Details** panel to the area that contains elements of an array. By default, it does not have elements:

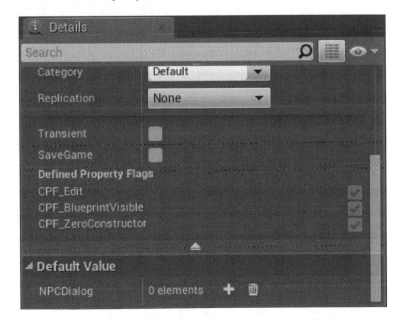

In **Details | Default Value**, click on + next to **elements** to add an element that will create a text box next to the element **0**. Put a value in this element by writing some text. You can write any form of text you want here; since at one point I plan to have the NPC give the player information, I will make the dialog say *You can check out your Character Status by pressing P when you are outside of battle*:

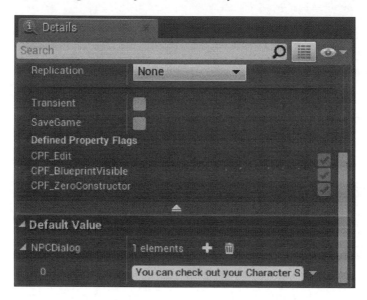

Since our NPC is a shop owner, they can greet us, for example, by saying *Greetings. I am Roy, the shop owner, what can I do for you?* You can add this text as a second element in the **NPCDialog** array:

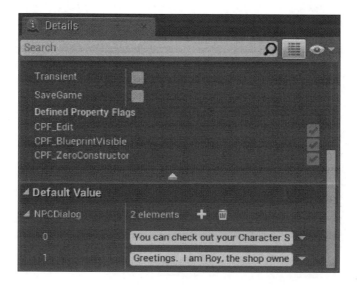

Whenever we need a new NPC variable that we may not want hardcoded, we can go back to this Widget Blueprint and add dialog like we did just now. Next, we can create the actual dialog for our NPC by navigating back to our **Content Browser**. Since we may end up having many different characters using the same dialog box just with different text in it, we may want to create another Widget Blueprint that just has a basic window and a button to exit the dialog box. In **Content Browser**, navigate to **Content | Blueprints | UI** and then select **Add New | User Interface | Widget Blueprint**. Then, name it **DialogBox**:

Open the new Widget Blueprint. From here, navigate to **File | Reparent Blueprint** and reparent it to **NPC_Parent**, which holds all our variables:

Since dialog boxes are rarely the size of the entire screen, we are going to create a Canvas Panel within our default Canvas Panel by navigating to **Panel | Canvas Panel** and dragging the new Canvas Panel within the parent Canvas Panel:

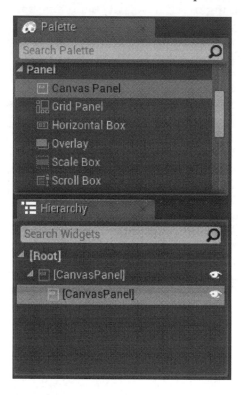

Rename this new Canvas Panel **CanvasPanel_DialogBox**. Also, anchor this Canvas Panel to the middle of the screen:

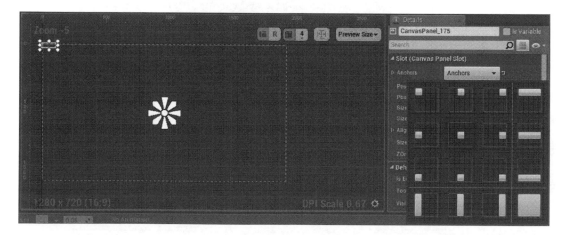

You may also want to resize the text box to hold a decent amount of text. I will resize this text box to have a **Size X** value of **1024** and **Size Y** value of **512**. You should also center the box by setting **Position X** to -1024/2 which is equal to **-512**, and **Position Y** to -512/2 which is equal to **-256**:

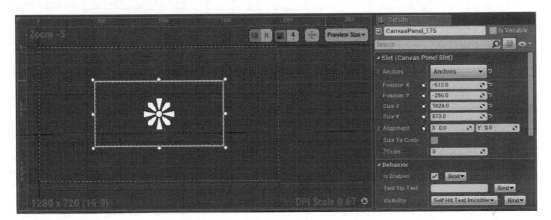

Within **CanvasPanel_DialogBox**, add an image from **Palette | Common | Image** that we can use to add a background color in a similar way to what we did for the pause menu:

In the **Details** panel, rename this image **BGColor** and position and resize it so that it is in the middle of the screen. This can easily be done by choosing a center anchor:

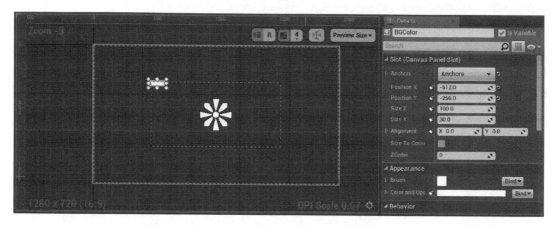

Resize and position this to be the same as the Canvas Panel, that is, the **Size X** value as **1024**, **Size Y** value as **512**, **Position X** value as **-512**, and **Position Y** value as **256**:

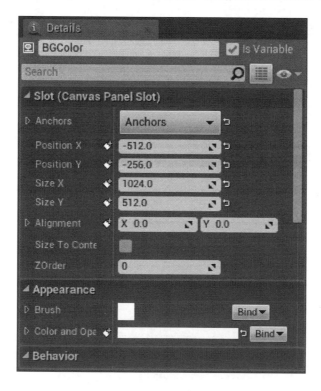

Lastly, under **Details | Appearance | Color and Opacity**, adjust the color to be the same as the other menus. In this case, we can select the color picker and pass in the linear hex value of **267FFFFF**:

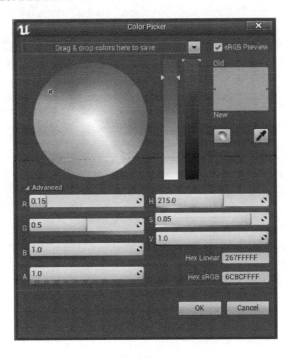

Next, let us insert an exit button to leave this menu by selecting and dragging a button from **Palette | Common | Button** into **CanvasPanel_DialogBox**:

Rename this button **Button_Exit** and position it towards the right-hand side of your Canvas Panel by first changing the size of your button to match the size of the pause menu buttons, which have the **Size X** value as **300** and the **Size Y** value as **100**. Then, position the button in the bottom-right of the Canvas Panel, by changing the anchor to bottom-right aligned. Then, use simple positions such as the one that gives 20 pixels of padding, that is, **Position X** as **-320** and **Position Y** as **-120**. You will also notice that the button is behind **BGColor**; simply change the **ZOrder** value to **1**:

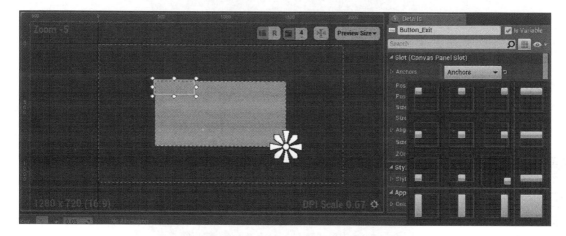

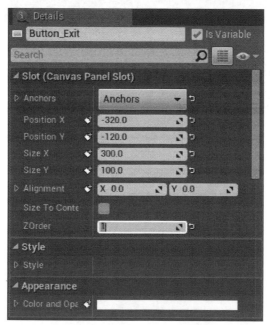

Now that you have a button created and positioned, add a Text Block to it. Rename the text **TextBlock_Exit** and under **Details | Appearance | Font**, change the font size to **48**. Also, change the content of the Text Block to **Exit**:

Program the button to exit as well, just like you did in the previous menu creations, by selecting the button, scrolling down to **OnClicked** in **Details | Events**, and then clicking on the **+** button. This will open up **Event Graph** and populate the **OnClicked** event for the exit button. Drag out the **Out** pin from the **OnClicked** event and select **Remove from Parent** located under **Widget**:

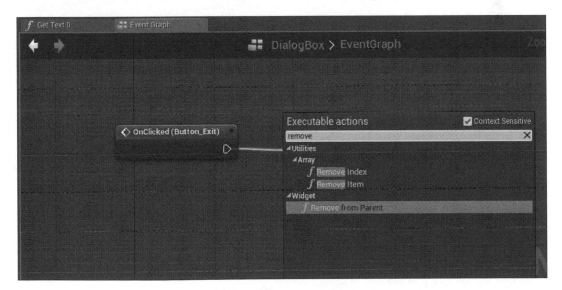

Navigate back to the **Designer** view and add a Text Block to **CanvasPanel_DialogBox**, name it **TextBlock_Dialog**, and have it take up most of the Canvas Panel. For this, we can position the Text Block to have a padding of 20 pixels by giving **Position X** a value of **20** and **Position Y** a value of **20**. We can also set the size of the Text Block giving **Size X** a value of **986** and **Size Y** a value of **300**. Lastly, set the **ZOrder** value to **1**:

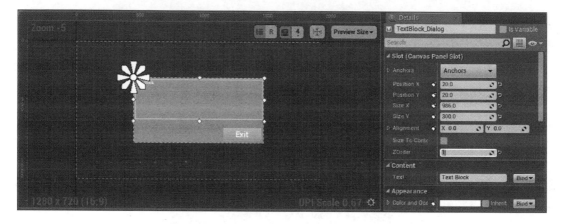

At this point, we are finished with creating the dialog box template. We can now move on to creating dialog boxes for our NPC.

Creating an NPC welcome box

Now that we have a template for our dialog boxes, let's use them by creating custom dialog boxes for our NPC that are based on what we just created. To stay organized, we should make a separate folder for NPCs since we will most likely have a lot more UMG and opportunities to use our dialog box outside of the NPC creation. So within **Content Browser**, navigate to **Content | Blueprints | UI** and create a new folder under **Add New**. Name this folder NPC and then navigate into the folder. Create a duplicate of the **DialogBox** Widget Blueprint that you made in the previous section and move it into the NPC folder. Name the duplicated widget **Shop_Welcome**:

Open the **Shop_Welcome** widget and select the **TextBlock_Dialog** Text Block. In **Details | Content**, create a new text binding that will then open up the graph:

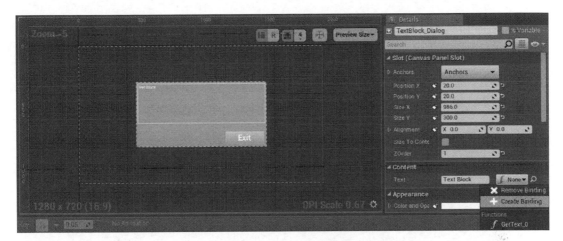

At this point, you can right click to find **All Actions for this Blueprint**, and under **Variables | Default**, you should find the **Get NPCDialog** variable which you can use:

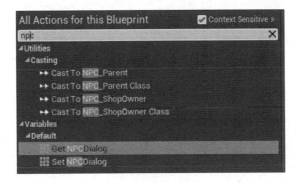

From here, drag out the **NPCDialog** array pin and select the **Get** function under **Utilities | Array**:

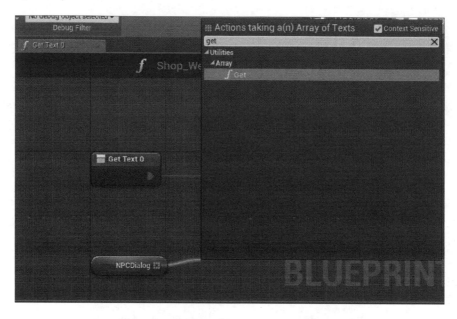

From here, you can select any of the text that is in **NPCDialog** by choosing the right element. Since the welcome text is in element 1, change the **0** in the **Get** function to **1**. To have this text return to the Text Block, link **GET** to **Return Value** of **ReturnNode**:

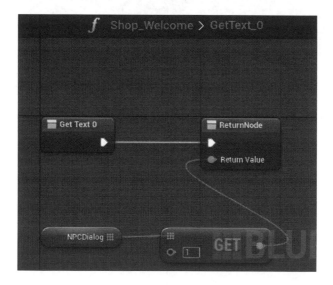

Since this is the welcome dialog box, we will still allow the player to exit, but we should also allow them to get general details from the NPC or visit their shop. So let's copy the **Exit** button and put place holders for both talking and shopping. Navigate back to the **Designer** view and make two more buttons on the left-hand side of the **Exit** button, one that says **Shop** and one that says **Talk**. You don't have to program these buttons yet since we do not have a shop or talk UMG yet:

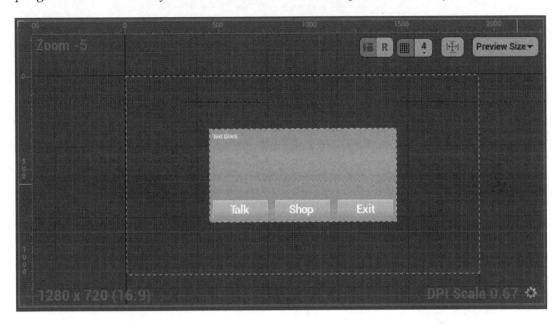

Next, make this screen appear at the proper time by opening the Level Blueprint that you started at the beginning of this chapter. Instead of printing text to the screen when the **Talk Shop** condition is true, link **Create Widget** under **User Interface** to **True**:

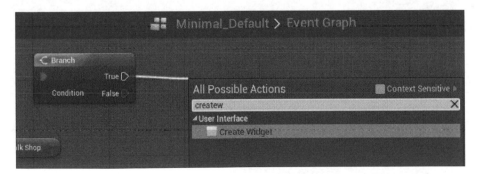

For the class, select **Shop_Welcome**:

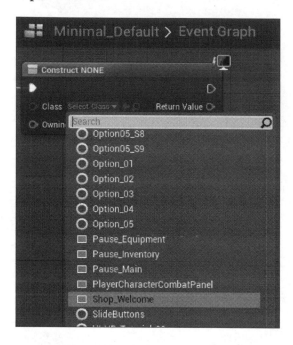

Lastly, display this to the screen by linking the Return Value pin of **Create Shop_Welcome Widget** to **Add to Viewport**, which is located under **User Interface | Viewport**:

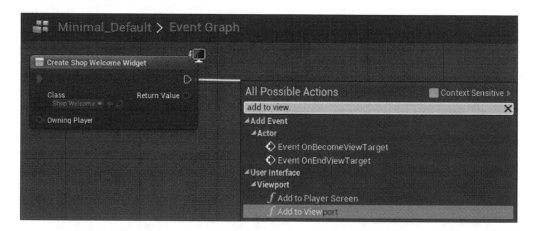

Also, give the player access to a mouse cursor by creating a **Get Player Controller** function under **Game** and linking its **Return Value** to **Set Show Mouse Cursor** located under **Class | Player Controller**. Finally, link the **Add to Viewport** node to the **Set Show Mouse Cursor** node and check **Show Mouse Cursor**. When you are finished, your Level Blueprint should look like the following screenshot:

If you playtest this now, you should be able to still go up to the NPC and press *E* to interact with him, but this time a dialog box will appear:

Congratulations, you have created your first dialog box. Now let us move on to making navigation buttons that open up other interactive widgets.

Adding an NPC talk box

Now that you have already created a dialog box that pops up when the player interacts with the NPC, you can easily add dialog for the player to see when they click on the **Talk** button. Simply duplicate the **DialogBox** Widget Blueprint that you made previously and place it in the NPC folder under **Content Browser** located in **Content | Blueprints | UI**. Rename the duplicated Widget Blueprint **Shop_Talk**.

We will now add some proper dialog to this menu by opening the **Shop_Talk** Widget Blueprint. Then, within the **Designer** viewport, select the Text Block that is already placed into your Canvas Panel.

Once selected, navigate to **Details | Content** and, within **Text**, select **Bind | + Create Binding**.

As always, this action will automatically bring you to the Graph Editor and set the **Get Text** function to return a null value from a **Return** node. The next steps are identical to the steps that you did when calling dialog from the **NPCDialog** variable in the previous sections. You must navigate to the **My Blueprint** tab and use the **GET** version of the **NPCDialog** variable.

Then, drag out the **NPCDialog** array pin and select the **Get** function under **Utilities | Array**. Lastly, have the **GET** function select the correct element of the **NPCDialog** array. In this case, we would keep element 0 selected since we set our dialog in element 0 earlier in this chapter. Once the proper dialog is chosen, link **GET** to **Return Value** of the **ReturnNode**. At this point, your Graph Editor should look like the following screenshot:

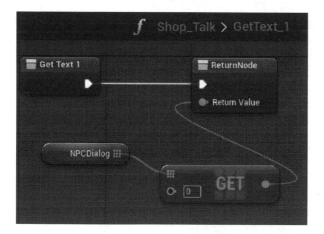

You are now finished with the **Shop_Talk** Widget Blueprint. You need to now bind it to the **Talk** button in the **Shop_Welcome** Widget Blueprint, so open the **Designer** view in **Shop_Welcome** and select the **Talk** button. In the **Details** panel, navigate to **Events** and press the **+** button next to **OnClicked**:

This should now create an **OnClicked** event bound to your **Talk** button and the Event Graph should now have automatically opened. From here, what we need to do is upon the button being clicked, we need to close the **Shop_Welcome** Widget Blueprint and open the **Shop_Talk** Widget Blueprint. These steps should be very similar to what you did many times previously when you opened and closed Widget Blueprints after button presses. Link the **OnClicked** event to **Remove from Parent** located under **Widget**, which will close your current Widget Blueprint. Then, link the **Create Widget** node to **Remove from Parent**, which is located under **User Interface**. Change the class of **Create Widget** to **Shop_Talk** so that your **Shop_Talk** Widget Blueprint is generated. From here, link **Add to Viewport** to **Return Value** of the **Create Shop_Talk Widget** node that is located under **User Interface | Viewport**. Also, be sure **Add to Viewport** is linked to the out pin of **Create Shop_Talk Widget** so that the Widget Blueprint is displayed in the player's view only after the **Shop_Talk** widget is created. When you are finished, your **EventGraph** for your **Talk** button should look like the following screenshot:

You may have noticed that the **Talk** button now works perfectly, but the text will get cut off:

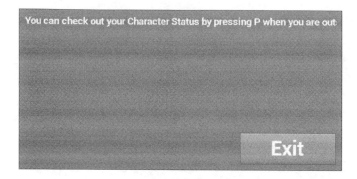

This is because we are not wrapping the text. To wrap the text, go back into the **Shop_Talk** Widget Blueprint and, in the **Designer** view, select the **Dialog** Text Block. Then, in the **Details** panel, navigate to **Appearance** and check **Auto Text Wrap**. This will ensure that the text is always wrapped around the content, which in this case will move the text to a new line when it hits the border of the Text Block. If you test the **Talk** button, the words should now wrap like this:

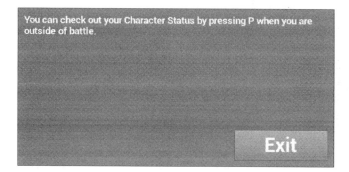

At this point, you should have the interaction working perfectly between the player and the NPC with all buttons working properly, with the exception of the **Shop** button.

Summary

In this chapter, we created an NPC that can communicate with the player through the use of a trigger volume and key binding. Now, we can display dialog from an array of strings at any point in our game. In the next chapter, we will transform our NPC into a shop owner and allow the player to purchase equipment from the shop.

7
Gold, Items, and a Shop

Now that you have created an NPC that talks to the player, it is time to allow the NPC to help the player. In this chapter, we will use the NPC as a shop owner, displaying items for the user to buy. Before we do this, the user is going to need some sort of currency to buy the items. We will cover the following topics in this chapter:

- Setting and getting gold instances
- Item data
- The shop screen framework
- The item button framework
- Linking the item data

Setting and getting gold instances

While we move on to making a shopping interface, via the **Shop** button, we must first be able to pull the currency in order to pay for items in the shop. In a previous chapter, we discussed and made placeholders for gold, but we did not actually create gold values. In this game, we would like gold to be dropped by enemies at the end of battle. In this case, enemies will need some sort of gold data that we can add to the player's gold data (eventually, items will need this gold data that is tied to them as well). In *Chapter 4*, *Pause Menu Framework*, we created a pause menu that has a gold placeholder, and we will now add gold to this pause menu.

First, let's add a Gold property to FEnemyInfo.h. Navigate to **Source | RPG | Data**, open FEnemyInfo.h, and add a Gold property of an integer data type to your EnemyInfo table, as follows:

```
UPROPERTY( BlueprintReadOnly, EditAnywhere, Category =
  "EnemyInfo" )
  int32 Gold;
```

We now need to tie the `Gold` property with our standard `GameCharacter` properties so that we can update any instance of an enemy with the proper gold value. Next, you will open `GameCharacter.h`, which is located in **RPG** under **Source**, and add a public `UProperty` to the `UCharacter` class for gold similar to that in `FEnemyInfo.h`:

```
UPROPERTY(BlueprintReadWrite,EditAnywhere, Category =
  CharacterInfo)
  int32 Gold;
```

Then, head into `GameCharacter.cpp` to set the return value of the gold that is equal to the value set in `EnemyInfo`, so that each instance of this particular enemy will return the amount of gold set in the enemy's data table:

```
character->Gold = enemyInfo->Gold;
```

When you are finished, the enemy's character information in `GameCharacter.cpp` will look like this:

```
UGameCharacter* UGameCharacter::CreateGameCharacter(FEnemyInfo*
enemyInfo, UObject* outer)
{
  UGameCharacter* character = NewObject<UGameCharacter>(outer);

  character->CharacterName = enemyInfo->EnemyName;
  character->ClassInfo = nullptr;

  character->MHP = enemyInfo->MHP;
  character->MMP = 0;
  character->HP = enemyInfo->MHP;
  character->MP = 0;

  character->ATK = enemyInfo->ATK;
  character->DEF = enemyInfo->DEF;
  character->LUCK = enemyInfo->Luck;
  character->Gold = enemyInfo->Gold;

  character->decisionMaker = new TestDecisionMaker();
  character->isPlayer = false;
  return character;
}
```

We now need to choose when to accumulate the gold, and in this case, we will accumulate the gold from combat. So, navigate to **Source | RPG | Combat**, open `CombatEngine.h`, and create a public gold variable that we will use to store all the gold won in the battle:

```
int32 GoldTotal;
```

When you have finished declaring the `GoldTotal` variable, the `CombatEngine.h` file will look like this:

```
#pragma once
#include "RPG.h"
#include "GameCharacter.h"


/**
 *
 */
enum class CombatPhase : uint8
{
 CPHASE_Decision,
 CPHASE_Action,
 CPHASE_Victory,
 CPHASE_GameOver,
};

class RPG_API CombatEngine
{
public:
 TArray<UGameCharacter*> combatantOrder;

 TArray<UGameCharacter*> playerParty;
 TArray<UGameCharacter*> enemyParty;

 CombatPhase phase;
 int32 GoldTotal;

protected:
 UGameCharacter* currentTickTarget;
 int tickTargetIndex;
 bool waitingForCharacter;

public:
 CombatEngine(TArray<UGameCharacter*> playerParty,
  TArray<UGameCharacter*> enemyParty);
 ~CombatEngine();
```

```
bool Tick(float DeltaSeconds);

protected:
 void SetPhase(CombatPhase phase);
 void SelectNextCharacter();
};
```

The next step that we need to perform is telling the engine when to give the gold to the player. As mentioned earlier, we want players to win gold from enemies that can easily be integrated into our combat engine. Navigate to **Source | RPG | Combat**, and open `CombatEngine.cpp`. Let's first scroll down to the `for` loop that we created in *Chapter 3, Exploration and Combat*, to check for a victory. Just above this `for` loop, declare a new `Gold` integer, and set it to `0`:

```
int32 Gold = 0;
```

This will assure that, if we don't have a victory and need to cycle through the `for` loop again, the gold gained in battle will reset to 0. Next, we need to accumulate the gold from every enemy killed; thus, within the `for` loop, we have `Gold` increment by each enemy's gold:

```
Gold += this->enemyParty[i]->Gold;
```

Your `for` loop will now look like this:

```
for( int i = 0; i < this->enemyParty.Num(); i++ )
{
  if( this->enemyParty[i]->HP <= 0 ) deadCount++;
  Gold += this->enemyParty[i]->Gold;
}
```

After the `for` loop, you will still have an `if` condition that checks whether the enemy party is dead; if the enemy party is dead, the combat phase will change to the victory phase. If the condition is `true`, it means that we won the battle; therefore, we should be rewarded with the gold from the `for` loop. Since the `Gold` variable that we want to add is in the `GoldTotal` variable, we simply set the local `Gold` variable to the new value of `GoldTotal`:

```
GoldTotal = Gold;
```

When you are finished, your `if` condition will now look like this:

```
if (deadCount == this->enemyParty.Num())
 {
  this->SetPhase(CombatPhase::CPHASE_Victory);
  GoldTotal = Gold;
  return false;
 }
```

Now that we have set enemies to drop gold after the player is victorious in battle, the next thing that we need to do is add gold to our game data; more specifically, it would be best to add it in `RPGGameInstance.h`, since an instance of the game will always be active. It would be unwise to add the gold data to a party member unless there is a specific party member who will always be in the game. So, let's open `RPGGameInstance.h` located in **RPG** under **Source**.

As a public property, add another integer to `Game Data` that we will call `GameGold`. Also, ensure that `GameGold` is read- and write-enabled because we want to be able to add and subtract gold; therefore editing of `GameGold` must be enabled:

```
UPROPERTY(EditAnywhere, BlueprintReadWrite, Category = "Game Data")
    int32 GameGold;
```

Now that we can create instances of `GameGold`, go to your `RPGGameMode.cpp` file where you originally set up the logic for the game over and victory conditions; in the victory condition, create a pointer to `URPGGameInstance` that we will call `gameInstance`, and set it equal to a cast to `GetGameInstance`:

```
URPGGameInstance* gameInstance = Cast<URPGGameInstance>(GetGameInstance());
```

We can now use `gameInstance` to add the total gold that we got from the battle to `GameGold`:

```
gameInstance->GameGold += this->currentCombatInstance->GoldTotal;
```

At this point, the value of `GameGold` that we are using as the player's gold will now be incremented by the gold won in the battle. The `tick` function in `RPGGameMode.cpp` will now look like this:

```
void ARPGGameMode::Tick( float DeltaTime )
{
  if( this->currentCombatInstance != nullptr )
  {
    bool combatOver = this->currentCombatInstance->
      Tick( DeltaTime );
    if( combatOver )
    {
      if( this->currentCombatInstance->phase == CombatPhase
        ::CPHASE_GameOver )
      {
        UE_LOG( LogTemp, Log, TEXT( "Player loses combat, game over" ) );
```

```
        Cast<URPGGameInstance>( GetGameInstance() )->PrepareReset();

        UUserWidget* GameOverUIInstance = CreateWidget
          <UUserWidget>( GetGameInstance(), this->
          GameOverUIClass );
        GameOverUIInstance->AddToViewport();
    }
    else if( this->currentCombatInstance->phase == CombatPhase
      ::CPHASE_Victory )
    {
        UE_LOG( LogTemp, Log, TEXT( "Player wins combat" ) );
        //add gold to total gold
        URPGGameInstance* gameInstance = Cast<URPGGameInstance>(GetGameInstance());
        gameInstance->GameGold += this->currentCombatInstance->GoldTotal;

        // enable player actor
        UGameplayStatics::GetPlayerController( GetWorld(), 0 )->SetActorTickEnabled( true );
    }

    for( int i = 0; i < this->currentCombatInstance->
      playerParty.Num(); i++ )
    {
        this->currentCombatInstance->playerParty[i]->decisionMaker = nullptr;
    }

    this->CombatUIInstance->RemoveFromViewport();
    this->CombatUIInstance = nullptr;

    delete( this->currentCombatInstance );
    this->currentCombatInstance = nullptr;
    this->enemyParty.Empty();
        }
    }
}
```

Now, you need to make sure that all your changes are saved and recompile your entire project (you may need to restart UE4).

We can now adjust the gold value of each enemy character that we have from the enemy's Data Table. In **Content Browser**, navigate to the **Enemies** Data Table located at **Data** under **Content**. In the Data Table, you will now see a **Gold** row. Add any value that you want to the **Gold** row, and save the Data Table:

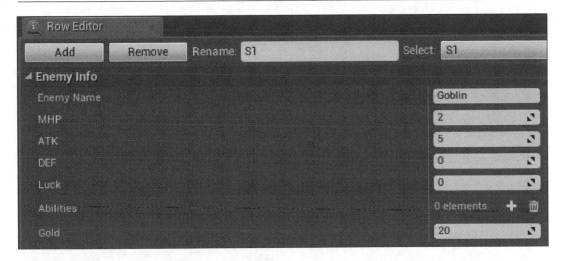

Now that an enemy has a gold value, there is a real value that is bound to the Gold variable in EnemyInfo that gets added to GameGold if the player is victorious in battle. However, we need to display that gold; luckily, we still have a placeholder for the gold in our pause menu. Open the **Pause_Main** Widget Blueprint, and click on the **Editable_Gold** Text Block that we created in *Chapter 4*, *Pause Menu Framework*. In the **Details** panel, go to **Content** and create a binding for the Text Block, which will open the graph for **Get Editable Gold Text**:

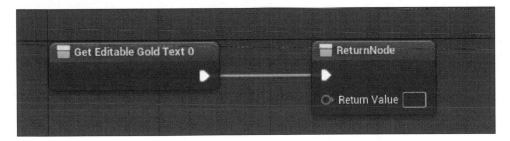

The first thing that we need to do is get the game instance of **RPGGameInstance** by creating a **Get Game Instance** function located under **Game** and setting it as an object of **Cast To RPGGameInstance**:

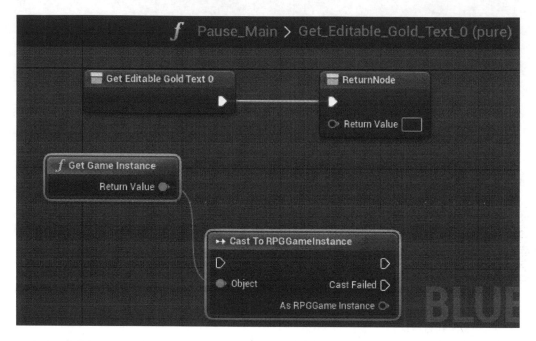

We can then get the GameGold variable from **RPGGameInstance**, which is the variable that stores the current gold total for the game. It is located in **Game Data** under **Variables**. Link it to the **As RPGGameInstance** pin in **Cast To RPGGameInstance**:

Lastly, link **Game Gold** to **Return Value** in **ReturnNode** and allow **Get Editable Gold Text** to trigger **Cast To RPGGameInstance**, which will trigger **ReturnNode**. Your **Get Editable Gold Text** binding will now look like this:

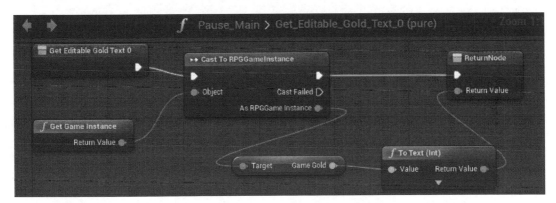

If you test this now, you will be able to get into battle, win gold from your enemies on victory, and now you will be able to see your gold accumulate in your pause menu. We can use these same variables to add to any menu system, including a shop.

Item data

Now that we are finished with the gold creation, we need to create one more thing before we make a shop, that is, items. There are many ways to make items, but it is best to keep an inventory and stats of items through the use of Data Tables. So, let's first create a new C++ `FTableRowBase` struct similar to the `CharacterInfo` structs that you previously created. Our files will be called `ItemsData.h` and `ItemsData.cpp`, and we will put these files where our other data is; that is, by navigating to **Source | RPG | Data**. The `ItemsData.cpp` source file will include the following two header files:

```
#include "RPG.h"
#include "ItemsData.h"
```

The `ItemsData.h` header file will contain definitions of all the item data that we will need. In this case, the item data will be stats that the player has, since items will most likely affect stats. The stats only need to be of the integer type and read-enabled since we won't be changing the value of any of the items directly. Your `ItemsData.h` file will look something like this:

```
#pragma once

#include "GameFramework/Actor.h"
#include "ItemsData.generated.h"

/**
 *
 */
USTRUCT( BlueprintType )
struct FItemsData : public FTableRowBase
{
  GENERATED_USTRUCT_BODY()

  UPROPERTY( BlueprintReadOnly, EditAnywhere, Category =
    "ItemData" )
    int32 HP;

  UPROPERTY( BlueprintReadOnly, EditAnywhere, Category =
    "ItemData" )
    int32 MP;

  UPROPERTY( BlueprintReadOnly, EditAnywhere, Category =
    "ItemData" )
```

```
    int32 ATK;

UPROPERTY( BlueprintReadOnly, EditAnywhere, Category =
    "ItemData" )
    int32 DEF;

UPROPERTY( BlueprintReadOnly, EditAnywhere, Category =
    "ItemData" )
    int32 Luck;

UPROPERTY( BlueprintReadOnly, EditAnywhere, Category =
    "ItemData" )
    int32 Gold;
};
```

At this point, you can recompile, and you are now ready to create your own Data
Table. Since we are creating a shop, let's create a Data Table for the shop in **Content
Browser** and in the `Data` folder by navigating to **Miscellaneous | Data Table**, and
then using **Items Data** as the structure.

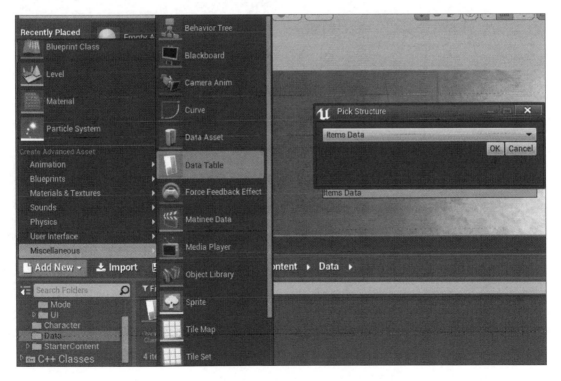

Name your new Data Table **Items_Shop**, and then open the Data Table. Here, you can add as many items as you want with whatever kinds of stat you would like using the **Row Editor** tab. To make an item, first click on the **Add** button in **Row Editor** to add a new row. Then, click on the textbox next to **Rename** and type in **Potion**. You will see that you have a potion item with all the other stats zeroed out:

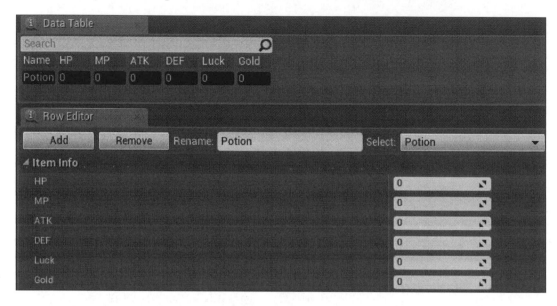

Next, give it some values. I will make this a healing potion; therefore, I will give it an **HP** value of **50** and a **Gold** value of **10**.

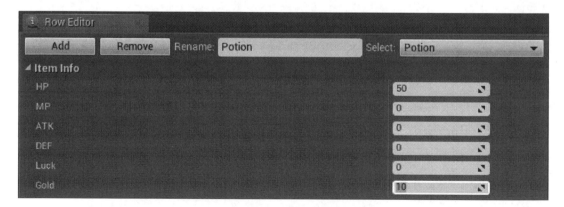

The purpose of this Data Table is also to store every item that our shop owner will carry. So, feel free to add more items to this Data Table:

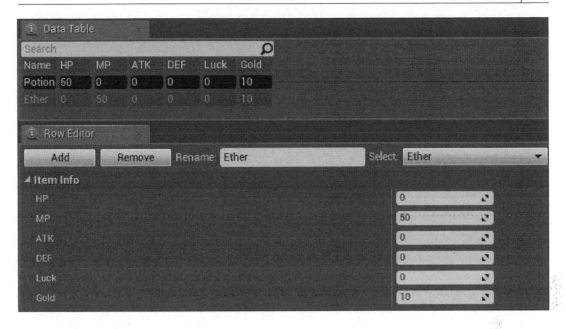

The shop screen framework

Now that we are done with creating items, we can move on to creating the shop. In the previous chapter, we created dialog boxes for our shop owner, and in one of the dialog boxes, we created a **Shop** button that, when clicked, will open up a shop menu. Let's create this shop menu by first creating a new Widget Blueprint by navigating to **Content** | **Blueprints** | **UI** | **NPC**. We will call this Widget Blueprint **Shop** and open it:

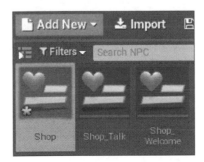

We will make the shop in a similar format to that of our pause menu, but we will keep it simple because all we need for now is a Scroll Box that will hold the shop's items, as well as an area for gold, and an **Exit** button.

To expedite this process, you can simply copy and paste the elements from your existing menu systems that you wish to reuse into the **Shop** Widget Blueprint. We can do this by navigating to **Content | Blueprints | UI** and opening the **Pause_Main** and **Pause_Inventory** Widget Blueprints, which we created in the previous chapters. From **Pause_Main**, we can copy the **Menu_Gold**, **Editable_Gold**, **Button_Exit**, **Menu_Exit**, and **BG_Color**, and paste them into the **Shop** Widget Blueprint.

We can also copy the **ScrollBox_Inventory** and **Title_Inventory** from the **Pause_Inventory** Widget Blueprint and paste them into the **Shop** Widget Blueprint. When you are done, your **Shop** Widget Blueprint will look like this:

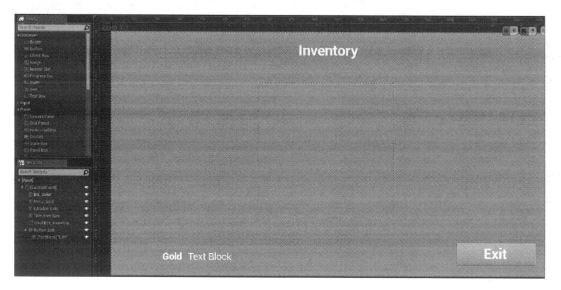

Here, edit the **Shop** Widget Blueprint so that the title reads as **Shop** instead of **Inventory**:

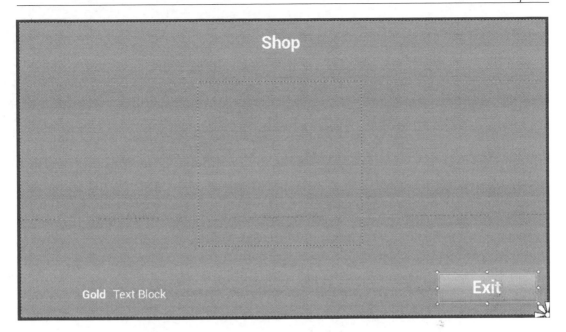

You will now need to link the **Shop** Widget Blueprint to the Shop button in the **Shop_Welcome** Widget Blueprint. To do this, open the **Shop_Welcome** Widget Blueprint by navigating to **Content** | **Blueprints** | **UI** | **NPC**, select **Button_Shop**, and then click on the + button to the right of the **OnClicked** event by navigating to **Details** | **Events**:

This will automatically open the graph with a newly created **OnClicked** event for **Button_Shop**:

Here, you can simply mimic the same actions you used to open the dialog boxes when the player clicks on the **Talk** button. The only difference is that, instead of creating a new **Shop_Talk** widget, the **Shop** widget will create the **Create Shop Widget** for you. The graph for **Button_Shop** will look like the following screenshot:

You will now be able to test the shop by talking to the NPC and clicking on the **Shop** button, which will now open the shop:

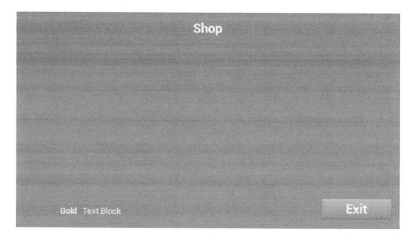

You will notice that nothing is yet visible in the shop, not even the gold. To display the gold on the screen, you need to repeat the steps you performed earlier in this chapter when you displayed the gold in the **Pause_Main** Widget Blueprint. But this time, open the graph in the **Shop** Widget Blueprint, and then create a binding for the **Editable_Gold** Text Block by navigating to **Details | Context**:

Your graph will automatically open, and you will notice a **Get Editable Gold Text** function with a **ReturnNode**. Since you will be getting the gold from the same game instance that you did when getting the gold from the **Pause_Main** Widget Blueprint, you can simply copy and paste all the nodes from the **Get Editable Gold Text** function into **Pause_Main**, and link them to the **Get Editable Text** function in the **Shop** Widget Blueprint. When you are done, the **Get Editable Gold Text** function in the **Shop** Widget Blueprint will look like this:

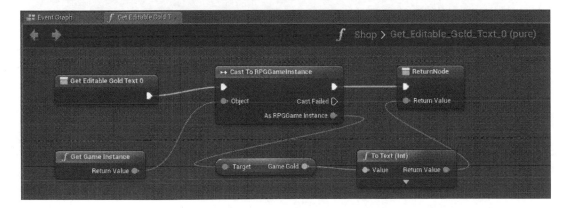

Next, we will create the **Button_Exit** functionality in the **Shop** Widget Blueprint by creating an **OnClicked** event (by navigating to **Details | Events**) for **Button_Exit**:

When the graph opens, link the **OnClicked** event to the **Remove from Parent** function:

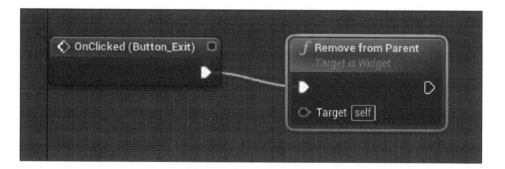

At this point, when you test the shop, you will see the gold and be able to exit the shop screen.

The item button framework

Before we link our items to the shop, we will first need to create a framework in which the items are placed in the shop. What we would like to do is create a button for each item that the shop owner sells but, in order to make the interface scalable in such a way that NPCs can hold different selectable items, it would be wise to create a Scroll Box framework that holds a single button with a default value for the item's text/description. We can then dynamically draw the button for as many items as the shop owner carries, as well as dynamically draw the text on each button.

To do this, we must first create a Widget Blueprint by navigating to **Content | Blueprints | UI** and call it **Item**:

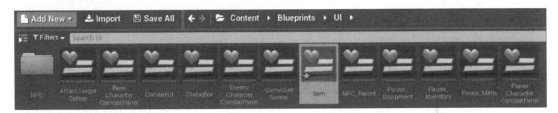

Open **Item**. Since we are going to make the items clickable, we will program a button. To make the button, all that we will need is the button itself and text for the button; we will not need a Canvas Panel because we will eventually be adding this button to the Scroll Box of our shop. So, from the **Hierarchy** tab, delete the Canvas Panel, and drag a button from **Palette**. We will name this button, **Button_Item**:

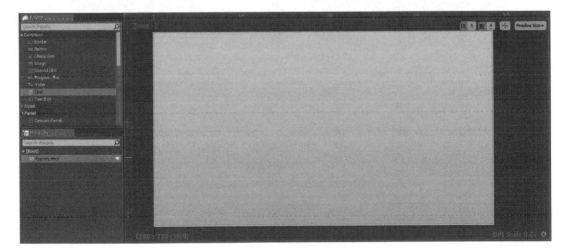

Finally, we will place a Text Block in the button that we just created and name it **TextBlock_Item**:

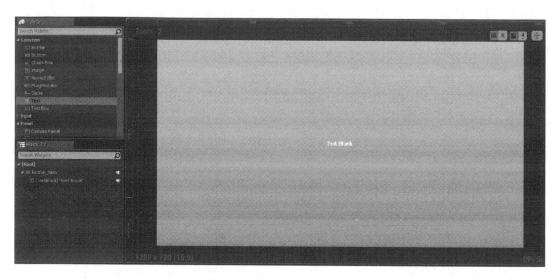

Once done, navigate to **Details** | **Content**, and create a binding for the text in the Text Block. This will automatically open the graph with a **Get Text** function:

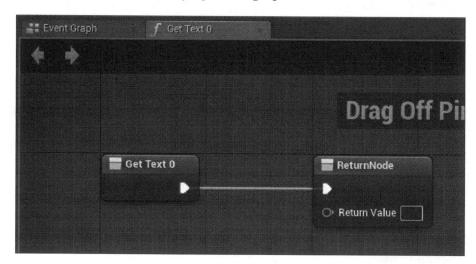

Create a new **Item** variable of the **Text** type:

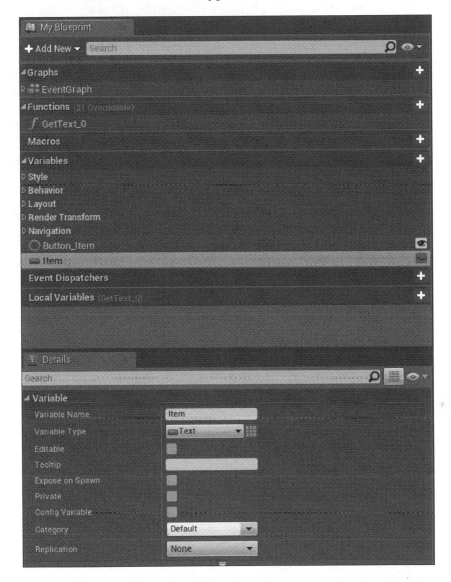

Drag the **Item** variable into the graph, select **Get** to drop in a getter for the **Item** variable, and then link it to the **Return Value** pin of **ReturnNode**:

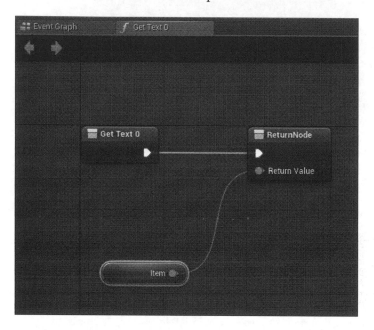

Linking the item data

It is now time to link the item data that we created at the beginning of this chapter to the shop using the **Item** button framework we just created. To do this, we will add a functionality to display every item in our **Items_Shop** Data Table using the **Item** button framework that we created in the previous section. First, open **Event Graph** in the **Shop** Widget Blueprint. Link the **Get Data Table Row Names** function located in Data Tables to **Event Construct**:

Then, from the **Select Asset** drop-down menu, select **Items_Shop**:

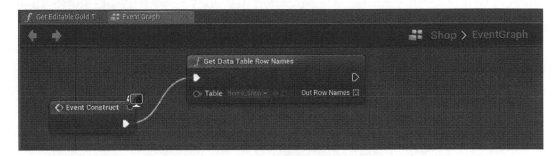

This will get the names of every item in the **Items_Shop** Data table that we created earlier in this chapter. Here, we need to create an instance of the **Item** Widget Blueprint for every item row. This will create a button for every item with the correct corresponding item name. To do this, create a **ForEachLoop** located at **Array** under **Utilities** and allow the **Get Data Table Row Names** function to execute it. Link the **Out Row Names** pin to the **Array** pin of the **ForEachLoop** so that every row in the Data Table becomes an element of the array in the **ForEachLoop**:

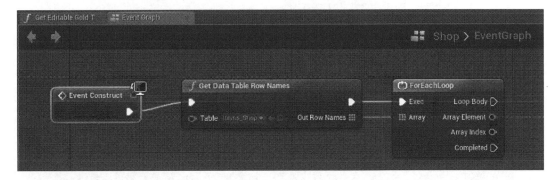

Next, we need to loop through each element of the array of row names and, for each row, we need to create a new instance of the **Item** Widget Blueprint. To do this, link the **Create Item Widget** action located under **User Interface** to the **Loop Body** pin in the **ForEachLoop**. Let the class instance be **Item** that can be selected from the **Class** drop-down menu in the **Create Item Widget** action:

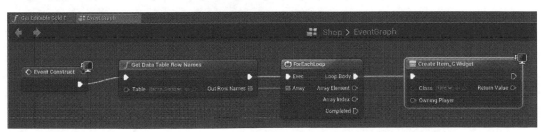

Then, for every item created, set the **Item** variable that is created for every **Item** widget instance to the value of each element in the array. You can create the **Set Item** action, by right-clicking anywhere in **Event Graph**, unchecking **Context Sensitive**, and locating **Set Item** by navigating to **Class | Item**:

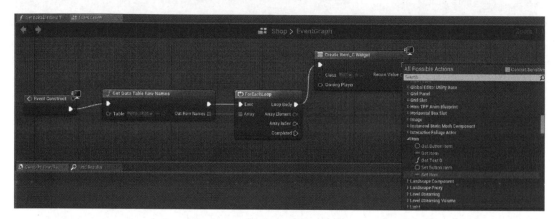

Create Item Widget can now launch **Set Item**, and set the **Return Value** pin value of **Create Item Widget** to the **Target** pin value of **Item**:

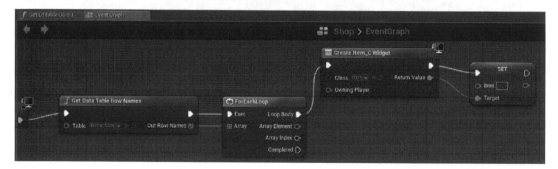

At this point, we have not yet set the element of the array to the item that we set in the **Item** widget; so, to do this, we can simply link the **Array Element** pin from the **ForEachLoop** to the **Item** pin in the **Set Item** action:

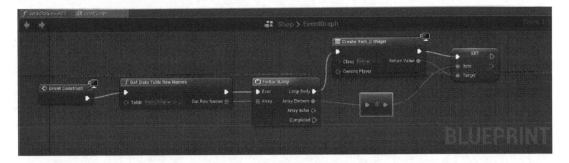

Lastly, we are going to have our Scroll Box that we created in the **Shop** Widget Blueprint hold all of our item instances. To do this, after we set each item to the correct name, we will add the item instance as a child to the **ScrollBox_Inventory** Scroll Box that we created earlier in this chapter. This is done by simply calling the **Add Child** function located in **Panel** under **Widget** after we set the item:

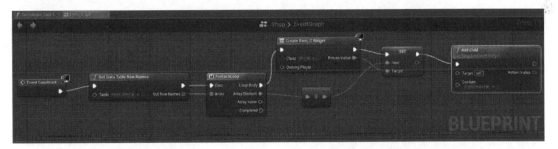

Then, we set the **Content** value of the child to the **Return Value** pin of the item:

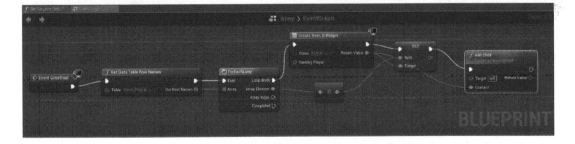

Lastly, the **Target** pin of the child needs to be linked to **ScrollBox_Inventory**, which can be dragged into your **Event Graph** from **Variables**. If you do not see the **ScrollBox_Inventory** variable in your variables, go back to the **Designer View**, select the **ScrollBox_Inventory**, and make sure **is variable** is checked:

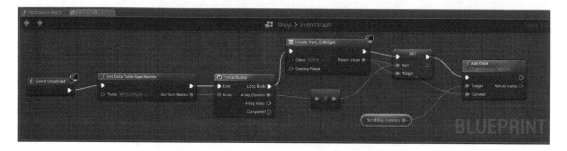

At this point, if you test your shop, you will see the shop populated with every item listed in your Data Table:

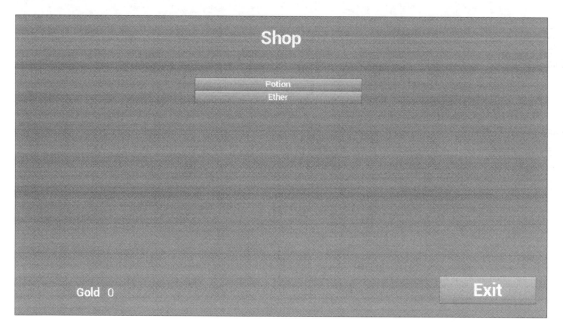

You will be able to add even more items to your Data Table and these items will automatically appear in your shop.

Summary

In this chapter, we created a currency system for our game along with the ability for our enemies to drop gold. We also created a new set of data that contains items and their stats, and we have now populated the shop owner's store to display the items currently for sale in the shop.

In the next chapter, we will add the buying functionality to the shop along with the usage of an item and consumption.

8
Inventory Population and Item Use

In the previous chapter, we learned how to add a shop, which holds items. In this chapter, we will go a step further by allowing a user to buy items from the shop and use those bought items in their dynamically populated inventory screen. Once done, we will use similar ideas to equip items to party members that will be used to increase the stats of the wearer.

By the end of this chapter, we will learn how to create logic in our **Shop** Widget Blueprint that populates the inventory Scroll Box in the **Shop** Widget Blueprint with the buttons created through the **Item** Data table from the **Item** Widget Blueprint. Now that we have the logic set up, we need to allow the user to interact with the buttons by being able to buy any item that they click on in the shop, so long as they have enough money. Since the issuer interacts with the dynamically populating buttons, it is important that we have our logic executed when the user presses a button, which is located in the **Item** Widget Blueprint.

If you have any other Blueprints in your **Event Graph** that you may have put together earlier, you can ignore them since an interaction will allow us to start over using some different methodologies.

First, we must note that the **Item** Blueprint will house logic that should happen anytime a button from that Blueprint is clicked. So, at the moment, we are planning to have the button populate the shop, but in the player's inventory, the logic would need to be different, depending on which screen we are on. This means that we will first need to find out which screen the player is on, and then fire off a series of actions based on the screen they are on. It would be easy to do this with Booleans from the **OnClicked** event, which will check to see which menu the player is in and branch off different logic, depending on which menu the player is currently in.

Since we are concerned with the difference between the behavior of the buttons in the **Pause_Inventory** screen versus the **Shop** screen, we must first create a Boolean that will stay active throughout the life of the character. In this case, we will use the Field Player to hold our important item variables.

In this chapter, we will cover the following topics:

- Creating the Field Player Booleans
- Determining whether the inventory screen is on or off
- Logical difference between inventory and shop items
- Finishing the inventory screen
- Using the items

Creating the FieldPlayer Booleans

Go to the Field Player by navigating to **Content | Blueprints | Characters**, and select **FieldPlayer**. Open **FieldPlayer** and navigate to **Event Graph**:

Here, we create a new variable under the **Blueprint** tab by navigating to **+Add New | Variable**. Next, we create a new inventoryScreen Boolean. Then, we need to make the variable public. This Boolean will be responsible for keeping true or false values, depending on whether the player is on the inventory screen. We may need more variables like these in the figure, but for now, we will just use this variable:

When you are finished creating the inventoryScreen variable, compile the Blueprint.

Determining whether the inventory screen is on or off

We will now set the inventoryScreen variable in its proper place. The best place to put this is when the inventory menu pops up. So, go to **Pause_Inventory** by navigating to **Content | Blueprints | UI**. In **Pause_Inventory**, locate the **Event Construct** in the Event Graph (if an **Event Construct** does not exist yet, create one), and from here, get every actor from the Field Player class by creating **Get All Actors of Class**, which is located under **Utilities** in the **Actions** menu:

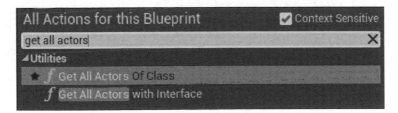

Under **Actor Class** in the **Get All Actors Of Class** function, change the actor to **Field Player**:

From the **Out Actors** pin, in the **Get All Actors Of Class** function, you will need to attach a **GET** function. This will take an array of all actors in your Field Player class and allow access to individual members of the class:

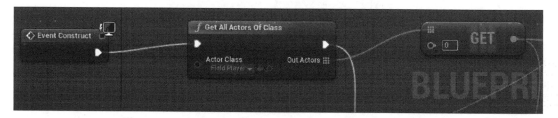

Lastly, open your all possible actions and uncheck **Context Sensitive**. Go to **Set Inventory Screen** by navigating to **Class | Field Player**:

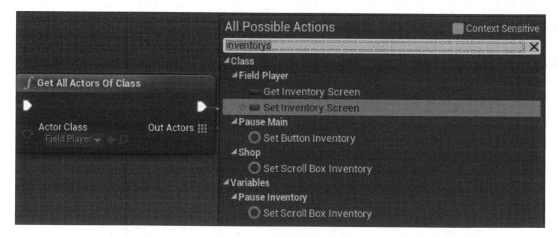

Once done, connect the **Target** pin of your **Set Inventory Screen** to the right-hand side pin of **GET**. Also, make sure that the **Inventory Screen** is checked, which means that we set the **Inventory Screen** to true here. At this point, you can also link **Event Construct** to fire off **Get All Actors Of Class**, which will activate the **Set Inventory Screen**:

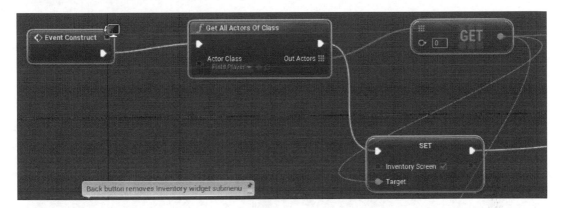

We will also need to make sure that the Boolean is set to false when the player leaves the inventory screen, so clone another **Set Inventory Screen** Boolean, and set it to false. Link the **Target** pin back to the **GET** from **Get All Actors Of Class**, and activate it when the inventory window closes:

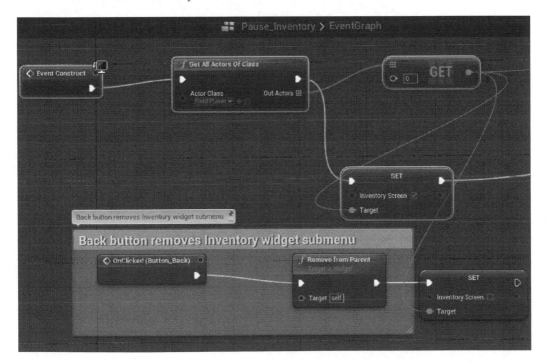

We will later come back to **Pause_Inventory** to add the button population logic, similar to the shop in the previous chapter. However, now that we have our Booleans set, we will be able to tell whether the player is viewing the inventory or is navigating the shop (if the Boolean is false).

Logical difference between the inventory and shop items

Let's now open the **Item** Widget Blueprint by navigating to **Content** | **Blueprints** | **UI**:

At this point, we should not have any logic for the button, which is necessary because it gives us the actions that the button will perform in conjunction with the game. To add a functionality to the button, click on the button, navigate to **Details** | **Events** | **OnClicked**, and then click on **+**:

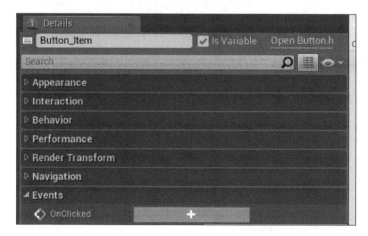

Here, we will need to do a few things. Firstly, we know that this Blueprint will be responsible for all of the button mechanics regarding both the shops and the character's inventory and the mechanics will be different since the character buys items from the shop and uses items from the inventory. Since these different game screens provide different actions, it would be wise to first check whether a user is in the shop or in their inventory. To do this, we should first bring in the **Get All Actors Of Class** function, and get all the actors from the Field Player class. Then, we need to link the **Out Actors** pin to **GET**. Finally, have the **OnClicked** event fire off **Get All Actors Of Class**:

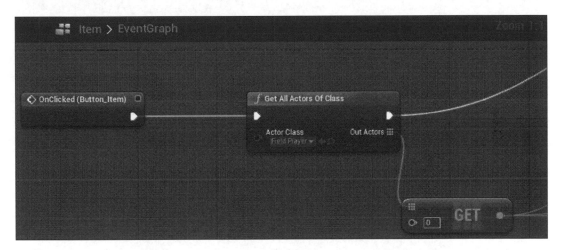

At this point, we can open our **Actions** window, and go to the **Get Inventory Screen** by navigating to **Class | Field Player**. You will need to uncheck **Context Sensitive** to see this option:

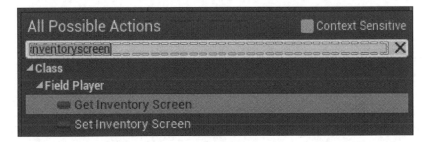

You will then link the **Target** pin of the **Inventory Screen** node to the blue **GET** pin. This will allow us to access the **Inventory Screen** Boolean from the Field Player class:

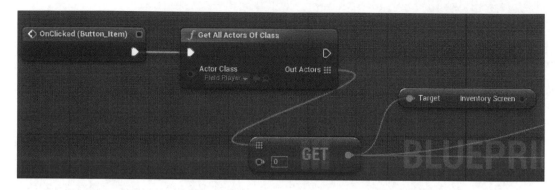

It is now time to create a branching system that will perform logic, depending on whether the player is shopping or whether they are in their inventory. We will use our **Inventory Screen** Boolean for this. Let's first bring in a branch by navigating to **Utilities | Flow Control** in the **Actions** menu:

Here, we link the condition of your branch to the **Inventory Screen** condition. Then, have the **Get All Actions Of Class** function activate the branch. At this point, when the player clicks on the button, we will check to see whether the **Inventory Screen** is true (or if the player is on the inventory screen). If they are not on the inventory screen, then it means that the player is on some other screen; in our case, the shop:

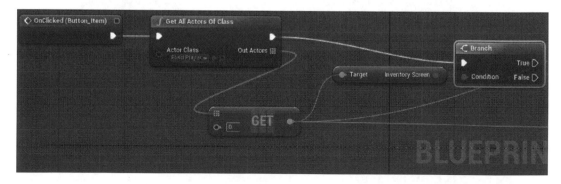

Before we continue with the rest of the **Item** button logic, we need to think about our logical flow. If the user is in the shop, and the user clicks on an item to be purchased, then if that person has enough money to purchase the item, the item should be placed into some sort of a collection or array that can populate the user's inventory screen. Because of this mechanic, we will need to seek some sort of global array that will be able to hold an array of items that the player has purchased. To do this, go to the **FieldPlayer** Event Graph and add a new text array named **arrayItem**. Also, make sure that this variable is set to public and is editable:

Finishing the inventory screen

Navigate to the **Pause_Inventory** Event Graph. While **Context Sensitive** is off, bring in the **Get Array Item** from the **Actions** window by navigating to **Class | Field Player**:

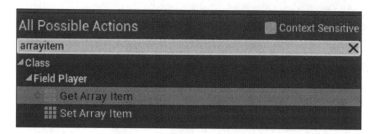

Once done, connect the **Target** pin of **Array Item** to **GET** so that you can get every item that is sent to that array once we populate the array in the **Items** Blueprint:

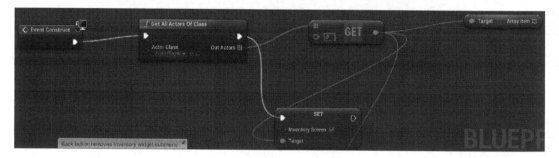

Now that we have the array of items in the player's inventory, we will now loop through each element, and create an item from every element in the array. To do this, create a **ForEachLoop** by navigating to **Utilities | Array**. Link **Array Item** from your **arrayItem** variable to the **Array** tab in the **ForEachLoop**. Then, have **SET Inventory Screen** activate the **ForEachLoop**:

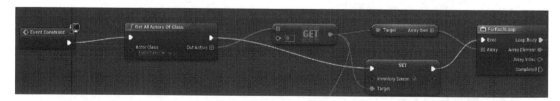

Just like what we did when populating the buttons for the shop, we would want this `for` loop to be responsible for adding buttons from the **Items** Widget Blueprint. So, in the body of the `for` loop, we need to create the **Item** widget by first navigating to **User Interface | Create Widget** in the **Actions** window:

Then, we need to change the **Class** dropdown to **Item**, and link it to **Loop Body** in the **ForEachLoop**:

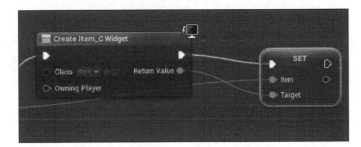

You will then need to set the text for each element in the array. So, open the **Actions** window and with **Context Sensitive** off, bring in **Set Item** by navigating to **Class | Item**.

Link the **Item** pin to the **Array Element** pin from the **ForEachLoop**. Then, set the **Target** pin of **Set Item** to the **Return Value** of **Create Item Widget** and have **Create Item Widget** activate the **Set Item**:

Lastly, we will need to add the **Item** widget to the Scroll Box that we created in **Pause_Inventory**. Simply create an **Add Child** node that is located at **Panels** under **Widget**. Then, link **ScrollBox_Inventory** from your variables to the **Target** pin of **Add Child** (if you do not see **ScrollBox_Inventory** as a default variable, make sure you go back into the Designer View of **Pause_Inventory**, select the **ScrollBox_Inventory**, and check **is variable**, then have the **Content** pin of **Add Child** be the **Return Value** of **Create Item Widget**). Finally, have the **Set Item** node start up the **Add Child** node:

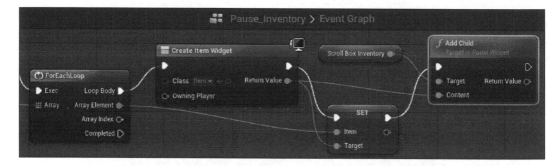

When you are done, your **Pause_Inventory** Blueprint will look like this:

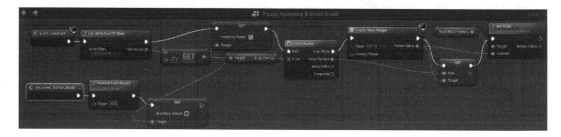

Buying items

Head back into the **Item** Blueprint. Where we left off before, we allowed that upon clicking a button, we would get all actors from the Field Player class. Here, we set up a branch that checks whether the **Inventory Screen** Boolean is true or false (which means that we check whether the player is on the inventory screen; if they are not on the inventory screen, we will perform the buying logic in our shop).

Let's first bring in a **Get Data Table Row** function located under **Utilities** in the **Actions** window:

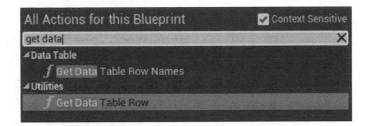

Then, set the Data Table to **Items_Shop**. This will allow us to get every row from the **Items_Shop** Data Table. Then, link the **False** pin from the branch that we created to the execution of **Get Data Table Row**:

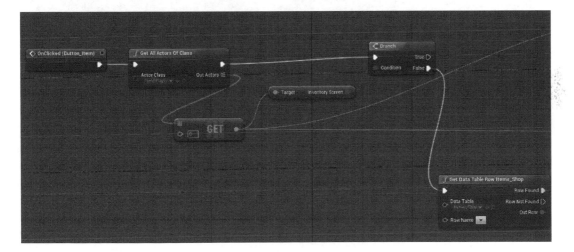

You may have noticed that we can select any row name from the Data Table. In this case, we just need to get the row name of the item that is currently selected. To do this, bring in **Get** of the **Item** text variable that you created in the previous chapter in this class. You need to link it to **Row Name** in the **Get Data Table Row** function, but these pins are not compatible. So, you need to first convert the text item to a string by left-clicking and dragging it from the **Item** node and then navigating to **Utilities | String | To String (Text)**. This will create the first conversion you need:

Lastly, you can just link this converted string to the **Row Name** pin in the **Get Data Table Row** function:

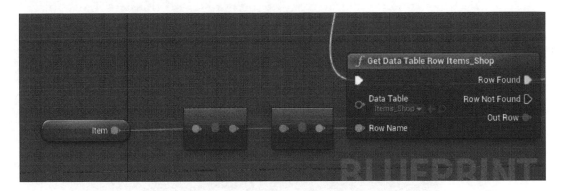

Once done, we have completed the logic for a specific item being selected in the shop. Now, we need to calculate the amount of gold that would be the *value* of each item and subtract it from our total gold. To do this, we must first get the RPG instance of the game so that we can call the game gold. However, since we will need this instance for a number of other variables in this Blueprint, we may want the game instance to be called part of our constructor. Create an **Event Construct** if you have not done so already. Next, link a **Cast To RPGGameInstance** object located at **Casting** under **Utilities**. Then, link the **Get Game Instance** object (located in the **Actions** window under **Game**) to the **Cast To RPGGameInstance** object:

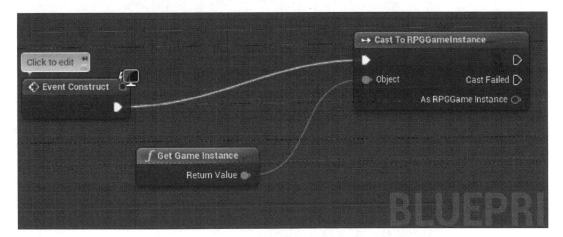

Since we will eventually need to access character parameters, such as HP and MP, when applying our items to the player, we will need to get all the party members, and set a Character Target similar to what we did in previous chapters. To do this, create a new variable:

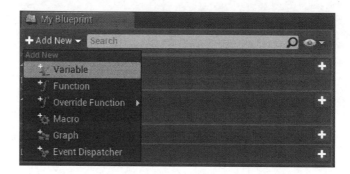

Then, go to **Details | Variable**, call the **Character Target** variable, and change its type to **Game Character**, which will reference our game character within the party:

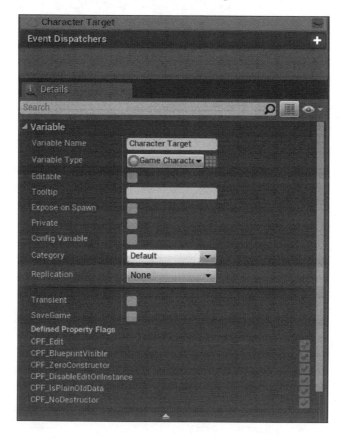

Then, from the **As RPGGame Instance** pin, drag out a line, and pick the **Get Party Members** variable by navigating to **Variables | Game Data**:

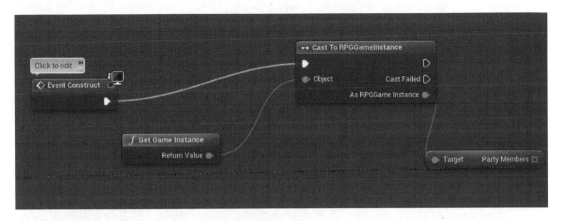

To the **Party Members** array, link a **GET** function. You need to link **GET** to the Character Target. So, bring in a **SET** version of the new Character Target variable that you created, and link the **GET** function to the **Character Target** pin in **SET Character Target**. Lastly, have the **Cast To RPGGameInstance** execute **SET Character Target**. When you are finished setting up the reference to the game instance and game characters, your constructor will look like this:

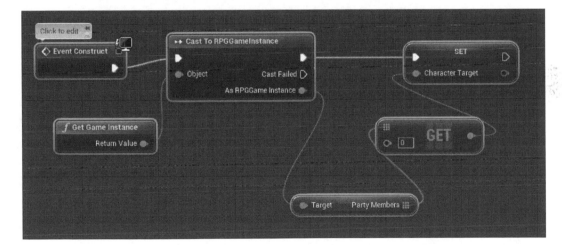

Now that we have set a reference to our current game instance, we can manipulate the gold. The next thing you need to do is navigate to your **Get Data Table Row** function. Here, left-click and drag the **Out Row** pin within the function, which will give you some limited options; one of these options is to create **Break ItemsData**. This will allow you to access all of the data for each item. Once done, you will have a box that shows all of the data that we created in our **Items_Shop** Data Table:

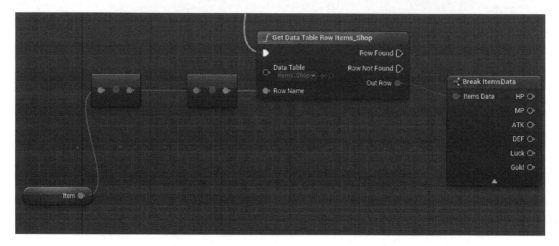

The logic is very simple. Basically, if the user has enough money, allow them to purchase an item and subtract the cost of the item by their game gold. If they do not have enough money, do not let them purchase the item.

To do this, we will create a **Get Game Gold** reference. This can be found by navigating to **Class | RPGGame Instance** if **Context Sensitive** is unchecked:

Once it is created, link the reference to **As RPGGame Instance** in the **Cast To RPGGame Instance**. You may also notice a **SET** pin that sets **HP** to **5** in the following screenshot; you may add one or leave it alone. This will just indicate that the player starts with 5 HP; this is being done for testing purposes when we test the player consuming a potion; if you decide to use **Set HP** for testing purposes, remember to remove it when you finish play testing:

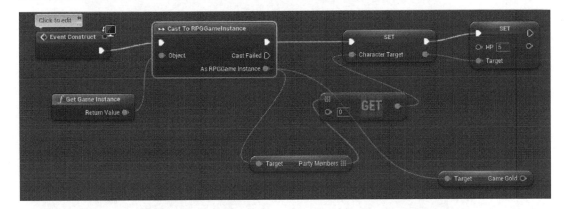

Now, we will subtract the game gold from the cost of the item being purchased. So, simply create a math function that subtracts an integer from an integer. This math function can be found by navigating to **Math | Integer**:

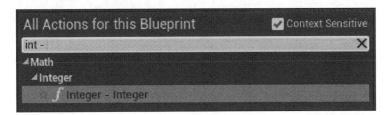

To do the math correctly, we will need to link the game gold to the top pin of the minus function and the gold from **ItemsData** to the lower pin. This will subtract our game gold from the cost of the item:

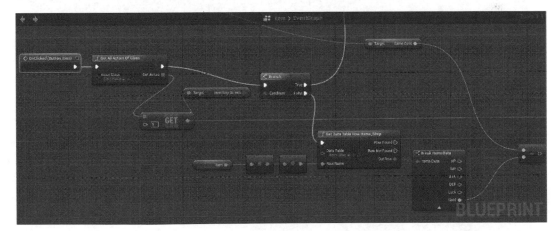

Here, we need to check whether the player has enough money to purchase the item. So, we will check whether the final product is less than 0. If it is, we will not allow the player to make the purchase. To make this check, simply use another math function, named **Integer < Integer**, located at **Integer** under **Math**. You will then compare the final product of the subtraction with 0, as shown here:

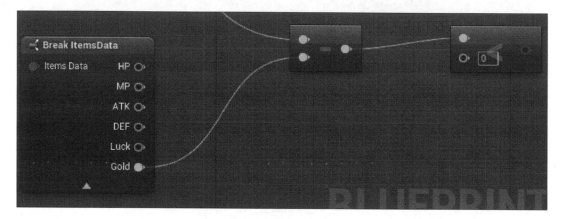

Next, create a branch by navigating to **Utilities | Flow Control**, and link the condition to the condition of the **Integer < Integer** function you just created. Then, link the **Row Found** pin from the **Get Data Table Row** to execute the branch so that if a row is found, the math can occur:

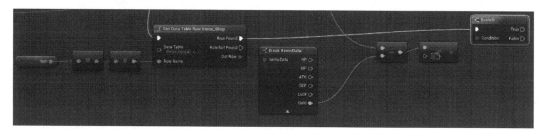

If the final result is not less than 0, then we need to set the game gold to the subtraction product. To do this, bring in the **SET Game Gold** function by navigating to **Class | RPGGame Instance** in the **Actions** window with **Context Sensitive** off:

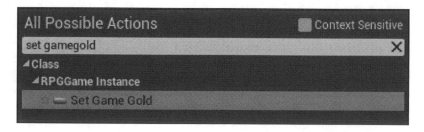

Link the **Target** pin of **Set Game Gold** to the **As RPGGame Instance** pin from the **Cast to RPGGame Instance** function. Then, link the **Game Gold** pin to the final product of the subtraction operation to get the remaining game gold:

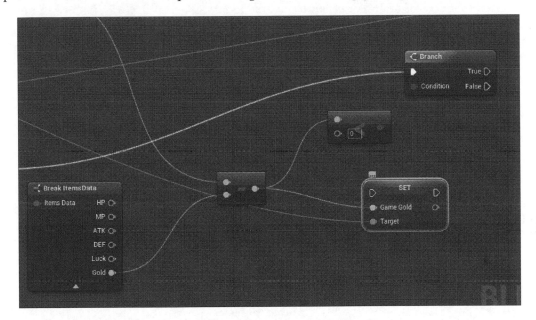

The last thing we need to do is link everything correctly. The remaining link is from the branch; if the less than condition returns false, then it means that we have enough money to buy the product, and we can change the game gold. So, next, link the **False** pin from the branch to execute **SET Game Gold**:

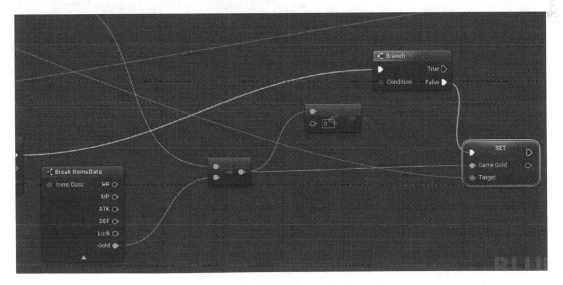

If you were to test this now, you would notice that items can be purchased flawlessly from the shop. However, the problem is that the items are never being populated from the shop to the player's inventory. This is a simple fix. Earlier in this chapter, we already set our inventory screen to be able to get an array that can be stored in the Field Player. We will simply use this array to add the items that we buy to the array, and then, retrieve these items when we open our inventory:

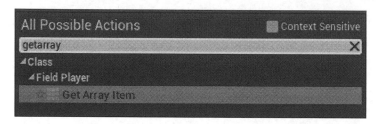

Since we already have a way to gather variables from the Field Player, we will bring in the **Get Array Item** variable by navigating to **Class | Field Player**.

We will link the **Target** pin of **Array Item** to the **GET** of the **Get All Actors Of Class** function so that we have full access over the `arrayItem` variable. We will then bring in an **Add** function by navigating to **Utilities | Array** in the **Actions** window:

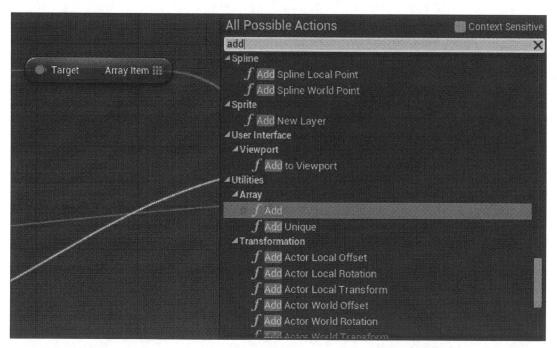

The **Add** function will allow you to add elements to an array while dynamically increasing its size (such as a list). To use this, you will link the array that you want to populate; in this case, **Array Item**. Then, you will need to link the item that you want to add to the array; in this case, **Item**. Lastly, you will need to execute **Add**. We will execute it after the **Gold** value is set. In essence, after the player buys the item, the item will then be added to their inventory:

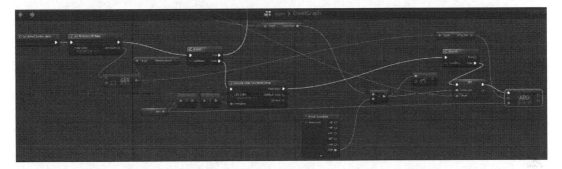

Your buying mechanics are now complete, and you can now test your shop. You will notice that items can be purchased and these purchased items populate your inventory.

Using items

Now that you have allowed items to populate the inventory, it is now time to make these items work. At this moment, you should still have a branch at the beginning of your item's **onClicked** button. So far, your branch just goes through a false routine because this routine indicates that the player is interacting with the buttons if they are in the shop. It is now time to create a routine for when the **Inventory Screen** Boolean is true, which means that the player is on the inventory screen.

The initial steps between where we created a **Get Data Table Row** function and set it to the **Item_Shop** Data Table (which takes an item row name and breaks the items into item data) are identical to our previous steps. So, we can simply copy and paste those portions from our previous steps into an empty area in this Blueprint:

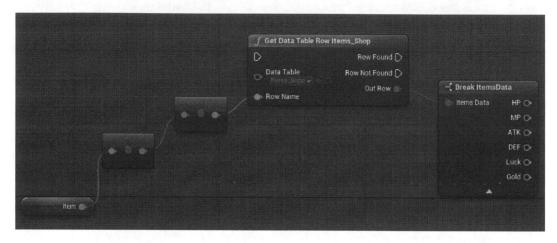

Next, we will link the **True** pin from our initial branch (that is activated by the **Get All Actors Of Class** function) to execute the **Get Data Table Row** function:

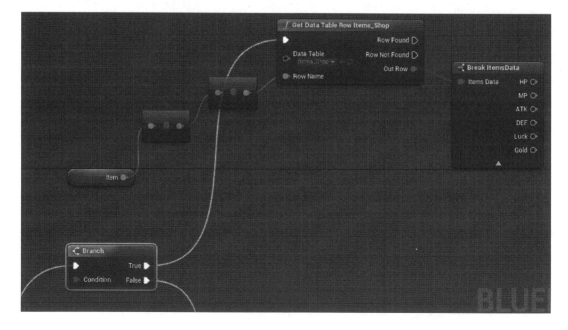

We will implement logic that is very similar to the logic that we implemented when purchasing items; but this time, we want to make sure that the user gets the correct amount set to them when using an item. Let's first start with the potion. The potion only uses the HP data. So, what we will need to do is add the HP data from the potion to the character's current HP. To do this, we will first need a Character Target variable. So, bring in a **Get Character Target** function from your **Variable** list:

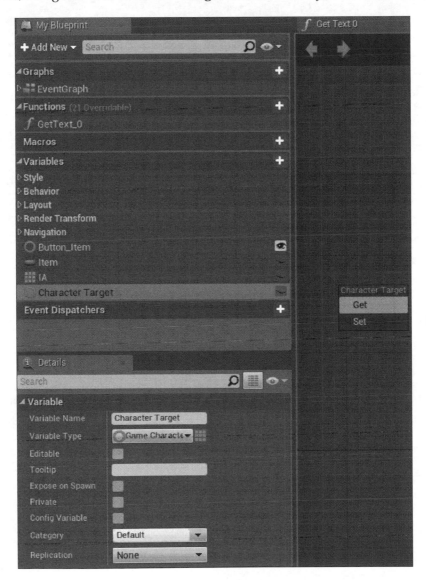

Once you do this, link the **Character Target** variable to **Get HP**:

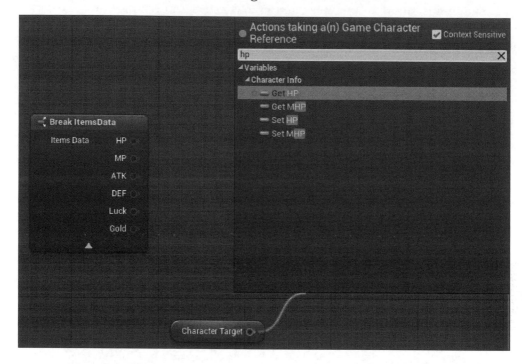

Now that you have access to the current player's HP, you can bring in the **Integer + Integer** function by navigating to **Math | Integer**. Simply link the **HP** pin from the **Break ItemsData** node to the top pin in the **Integer + Integer** function, and link the character HP to the bottom pin of the **Integer + Integer** node:

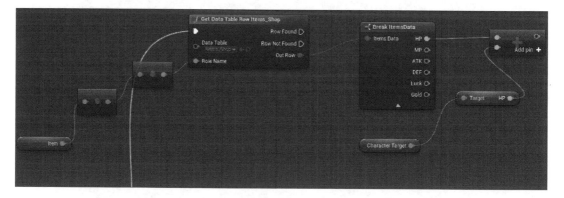

Here, we need to check whether the product of the addition is less than the character's maximum HP. If it is, we can use the potion. If it is not, we cannot use the potion. So, let's first bring in the **Get MHP** variable from **Character Target**, which shows what the character's maximum HP is like:

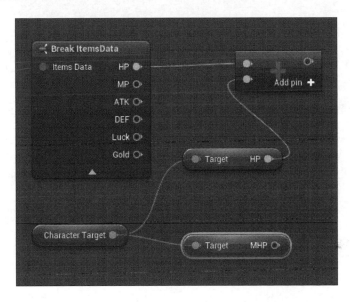

Now, we will need to bring in a condition that checks whether an integer is less than another integer. This can be found in the **Actions** window by navigating to **Math | Integer**:

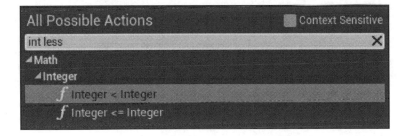

Next, link the final addition product to the upper pin of the **Integer < Integer** condition, and link **MHP** to the lower pin:

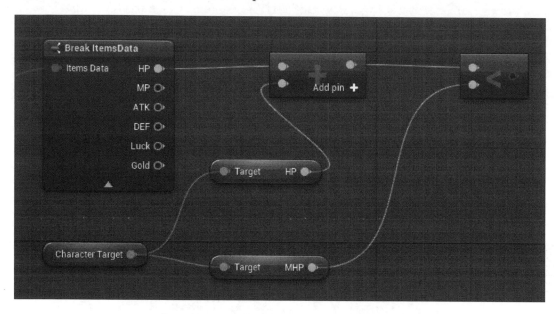

We will now make a branch that checks our condition. This branch should be activated only if a row is found (or if the user clicks on an actual item):

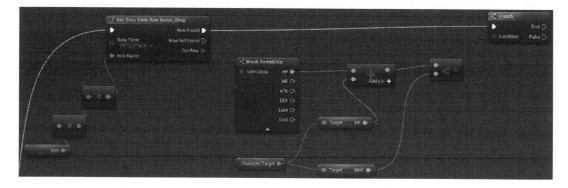

If the total HP is less than the maximum HP, then this would mean that the condition is true, and we need to remove the item from the inventory using the **Remove from Parent** function located under **Widget**. Then, we need to use the **SET HP** function by navigating to **Class | Game Character** and making it equal to the addition of the product item HP and character HP. We will also need to link the **Target** pin of the **SET HP** function to the reference to **Character Target**:

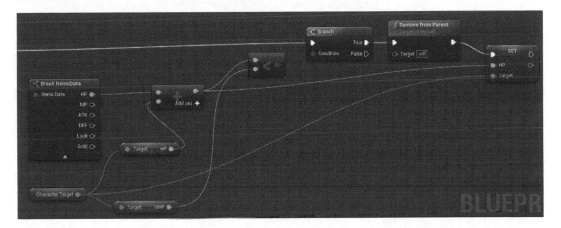

If you test this now, the character will be able to use potions, and the potions will be removed on use, but the user won't be able to fully heal because we are only testing to see whether the product of our addition is more than the maximum HP, which only accounts for situations where a potion's healing properties are not fully used. Therefore, the character may never be able to be 100% recovered. To fix this, we will simply create a routine for the **False** branch that will remove the item from the parent, and then, automatically set the HP to the maximum HP. This will solve our problem of not being able to heal our character all the way to their maximum health:

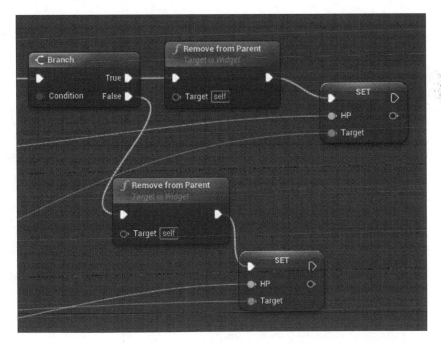

When you are done with this, your HP-based items' Blueprint will look like this:

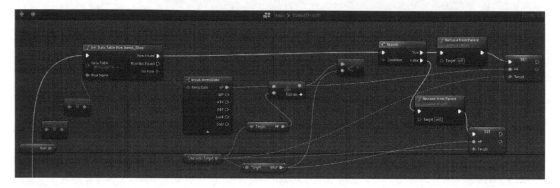

If you test this now, you will notice that all of your potions work perfectly in your inventory. The last potion that we did not finish is the ether, but the ether logic is exactly the same as the potion logic, though instead of checking the effects of HP, you are checking the effects of MP. Note that this logic is not specific to any one item, it is dynamic to the point where any item that affects these stats will run using this logic. So, if later on you have a mega potion, you will not have to redo any logic or add new logic, the mega potion is still considered an item and will apply the correct amount of HP that was given to it through the Data Table.

Summary

At this point, you now have your currency system that interacts with an NPC. You are able to buy items from the NPC and stock as many items as you want in your inventory, and then correctly use them. Using this knowledge, you should easily be able to create more items throughout the game using the same strategies that we covered in the last couple of chapters.

In the next chapter, we will dig deeper into useable items and work with equipping weapons and armor, which will temporarily change the stats of a player.

9
Equipment

In the previous chapter, we covered how to create useable items, populate them in a store controlled by an NPC, allow the player to buy items from the store, and use those items from their inventory. In this chapter, we will continue from where we left off by offering the player weapons and armor to equip themselves with.

We will cover the following topics in this chapter:

- The weapons Data Table
- Setting the weapon and equipment screen variables
- Creating the weapon button
- Revisiting the equipment screen
- Setting the equipment screen Text Blocks
- Correcting character stats when equipping

The weapons Data Table

Now that we have a decent framework for item creation, it will be very easy to create equipment. Since the **Items** Data Table reads all of the stats of the party members so that the stats can be modified if an item is used, we can expect equipment to modify all of the same stats; therefore, we can use the same structure for the **Equipment** Data Table, as we did for the **Items** Data Table.

So, at this point, we will create a Data Table for weapons by clicking on **Content Browser** and navigating to **+Add New | Miscellaneous | Data Table**:

Next, we can pick the **Items Data** structure since we will be calling the same data in the **Equipment** Data Table as we did in **Item** Data Table:

Then, name the Data Table **Weapons**:

We will use this **Weapons** Data Table to populate every weapon that we plan to equip on a character in the game. For now, we will only make a Data Table for one character's weapons, but you can use all of the following steps to create more weapon Data Tables for additional characters.

You can now open the **Weapons** Data Table, and just like our **Items** Data Table, we begin with creating data by clicking on the **Add** button and then naming the data. In this case, we will make our first weapon, a dagger, and then give the dagger some stats. Since the dagger is a weapon, we will just need to modify the **ATK** stat. Since we are keeping our examples simple, we are not utilizing other stats that many other RPGs have such as *accuracy* and *dexterity* because we do not have accuracy or dexterity in our RPG framework. However, if you decide to add these additional mechanics to your game later on, you will want to modify the appropriate stats in your Data Table that are associated with your equipment. You may also want to give the dagger a gold value if weapons hold a resale value in your game.

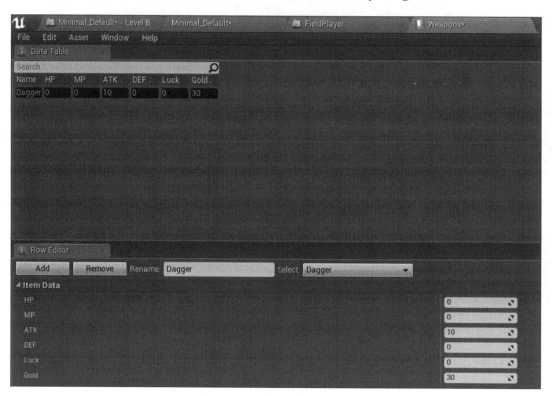

Setting the weapon and equipment screen variables

Now that you have a weapon in your **Weapons** Data Table, we can set up a framework to equip this weapon.

Just like the items that you created, you can choose to populate the weapons in a shop, you can choose to allow weapons to be picked up automatically from other NPCs in the field, or you can make them enemy drops just like you did with gold. Whichever method you choose, make sure that the weapons end up getting populated in your equipment screen in a similar way in which the items got populated in your inventory screen. At the bare minimum, we will need the character to hold an array of weapons. Navigate to the **FieldPlayer** Blueprint and open the Event Graph. Then, add a new text array variable that is similar to the **arrayItem** variable that you created in the previous chapter, and call it **arrayWeapons**:

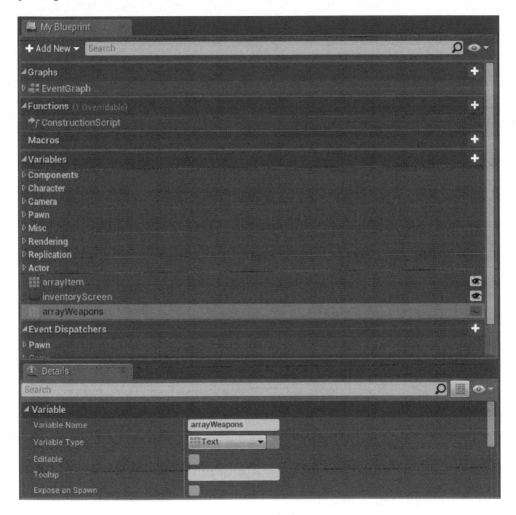

The major difference between the items and equipment is that we will be able to equip and unequip equipment rather than just *using* the equipment, so we will need to create a framework for this on our equipment screen. While we are in the **FieldPlayer** Blueprint, we can start creating this framework by also creating an equipmentScreen Boolean that we will eventually set to let the system know when the player is accessing the equipment screen. This will be needed when equipping weapons and armor just like the inventoryScreen Boolean was needed to allow the user to use items when accessing the inventory screen:

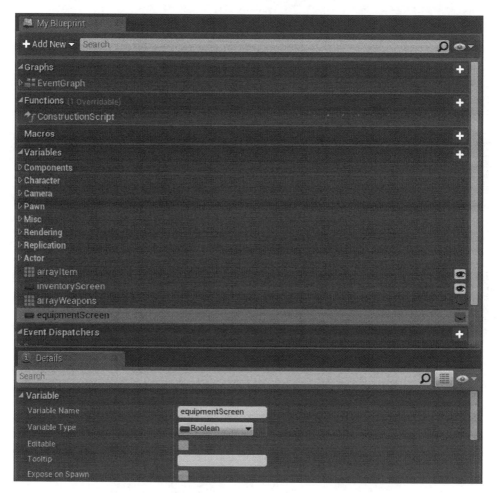

Now that the player can hold a weapons array and an equipment screen Boolean, we need to navigate to the **Pause_Equipment** Event Graph, and set the equipmentScreen Boolean to true when the event is constructed, and set it to false when the player leaves the screen. This is identical to the way in which we set the inventoryScreen Boolean in the **Pause_Inventory** Event Graph:

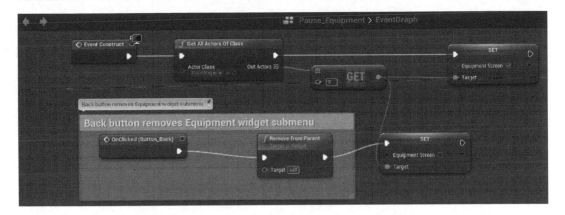

Creating the weapon button

Next, we can move on to populating the equipment screen. To do this, we first need to create a weapon button similar to the item button that we created previously. This weapon button will house all the logic that will be performed when the user presses the weapon button. Since the weapon button will be similar to the item button in a lot of ways, we can duplicate the item button and modify it to fit the weapon parameters. So, go to the **Item** Widget Blueprint by navigating to **Content Browser | Blueprints | UI**, and duplicate the **Item** Widget Blueprint:

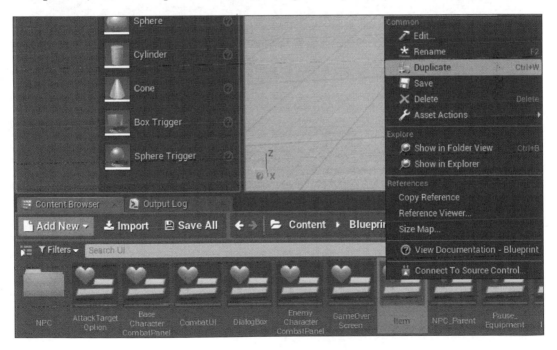

Then, rename it **Weapon**, as shown in the following screenshot:

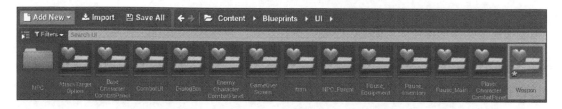

We can now open the **Weapon** Widget Blueprint and navigate to the Event Graph. Here, you will see an exact copy of the **Item** Widget Blueprint logic, and since the logic for equipping weapons will be similar to using items, we can just modify the Event Graph to fit it with what we want to happen when the user presses the weapon button.

First, we need to edit the section where the **OnClicked** event is located. We want the **OnClicked** event to find the `equipmentScreen` Boolean and check whether it is true, so we can remove the check for the `inventoryScreen` Boolean and replace it with the `equipmentScreen` Boolean:

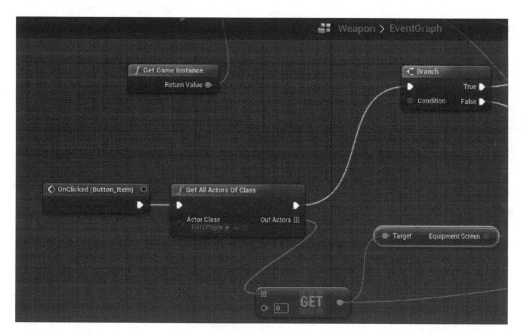

If the `equipmentScreen` Boolean returns false, the false branch will do nothing, and so we need to delete all of the false branch logic:

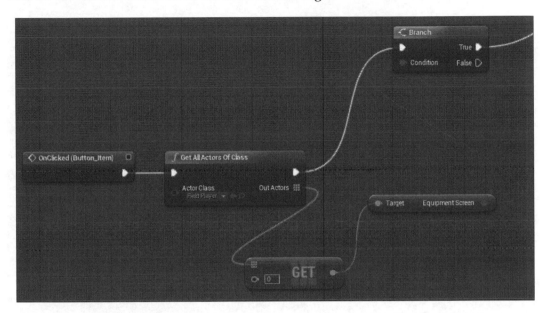

If the branch returns true, then we will set the **Get Data Table Row Weapons** function to get the **Weapons** Data Table:

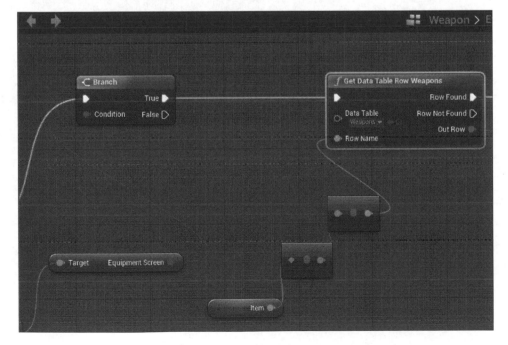

Then, from **Break ItemsData**, set it to break the data **ATK** stat, and set the **ATK** stat of the character accordingly:

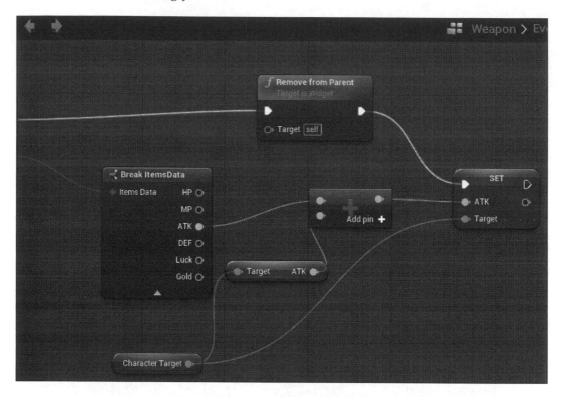

For now, the **OnClicked** event in your **Weapon** Event Graph will look like this:

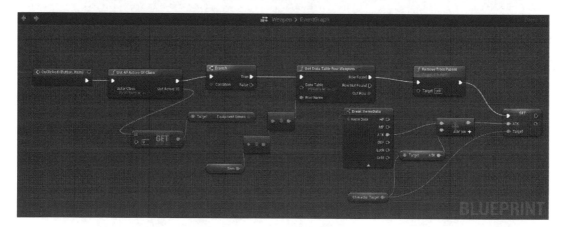

Also, make sure that you are still setting the **Party Members** stats to the
Character Target variable; otherwise, the base stats of the characters will
not carry over correctly:

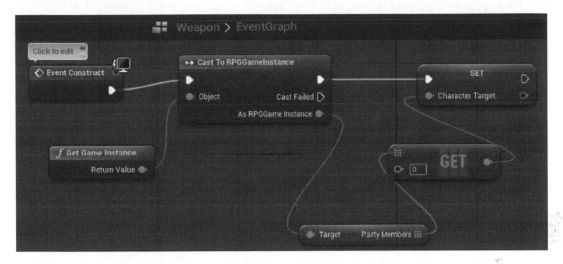

Revisiting the equipment screen

You may notice that if we stick to this Event Graph, we will merely be using each
weapon instead of equipping it because of the **Remove from Parent** function. We
will come back to edit this Event Graph later on in the chapter to properly set the
button to equip rather than use.

We will now populate the equipment screen. As mentioned earlier in this chapter,
you can choose how you want to populate the equipment screen. For simplicity of
this example, we will just populate the equipment screen as we did with the shop.
So, we will navigate back to the **Pause_Equipment** Widget Blueprint's Event Graph,
and use the same logic that we implemented to populate the shop screen; only this
time set the **Get Data Table Row Names** function to get the **Weapons** Data Table.
Then, set the **Create Widget** function to get the **Weapon** widget. Note that you
need to ensure that **is Variable** of the Scroll Box is checked in your **Designer** view;
otherwise, your Scroll Box will produce an error because it won't be found.

The Event Graph of **Pause_Equipment** will look like this when you are done:

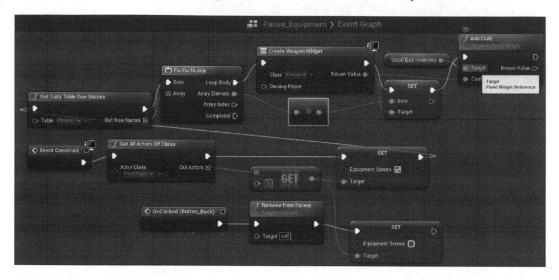

If you test the equipment screen now, you will notice that the weapons get populated in the Scroll Box, and if you use the equipment, the stats of the character go up and match the increased stats of the weapon. However, we still have some issues. The weapon is being used instead of equipped, and if we continue to use weapons, the stats end up climbing instead of getting replaced. Let's set the weapon to be equipped first rather than replaced.

Setting the equipment screen Text Blocks

Since we know that the equipment screen has Text Blocks on the right-hand side of the **Weapon** and **Armor** titles, which we created in *Chapter 5, Bridging Character Statistics*, we want to bind these Text Blocks to a text variable that will hold the names of the weapons and armor that we are equipping. Let's first navigate to our **FieldPlayer** Blueprint Event Graph, and create a text variable to hold the soldier's weapon name. We will call this text variable soldierWeapon:

Next, navigate to the **Pause_Equipment** Widget Blueprint's **Designer** view. Select the Text Block on the right-hand side of the **Weapon** title, navigate to **Details | Content | Text**, and click on the **Bind** drop-down menu to select **+Create Binding**:

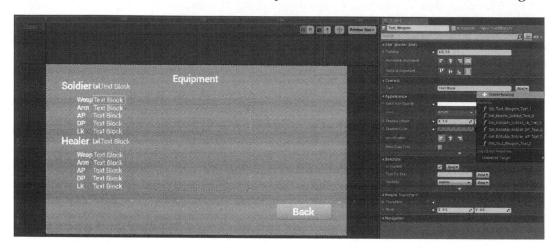

In the Event Graph for this binding, use the **Get All Actors Of Class** function to get all the actors of the **FieldPlayer**, and get the soldierWeapon variable and link it to the **Return Value** pin of **ReturnNode** so that the Text Block is able to draw the text that is saved in the soldierWeapon variable:

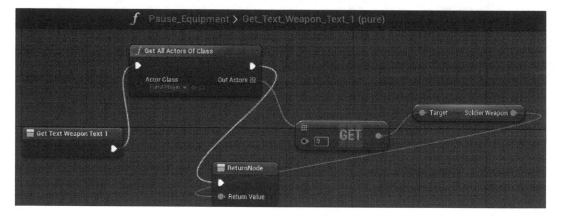

We can now set the text to the soldierWeapon variable by going back to the **Weapon** Widget Blueprint Event Graph and replacing the **Remove from Parent** function with **Set soldierWeapon**. The text value of soldierWeapon should be set to the **Item** variable that the user clicks on:

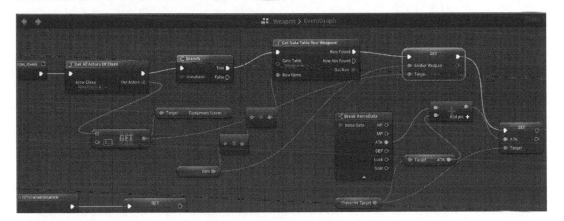

If you test the equipment screen now, you will notice that when the equipment button is pressed, the name of the weapon gets updated and the weapons will not be removed from the equipment screen.

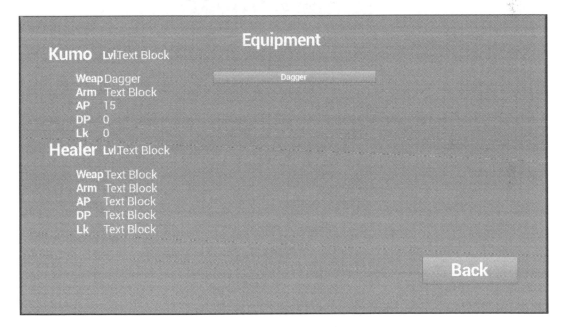

Correcting the character stats when equipping

The last thing that we need to do is adding some logic to make sure that the base stats do not continue to climb if the equipment is chosen more than once from the equipment screen. To do this, we need to create two variables in the **FieldPlayer** Blueprint. One variable will be a Boolean that keeps track of whether the soldier has a weapon equipped. The other will be an integer to keep track of the soldier's base attack stat. These elements together will allow us to create the logic in our weapon button that prevents the attack stat from climbing every time we click on a weapon.

So, first navigate to the **FieldPlayer** Blueprint and create a Boolean called **soldierWeaponEquipped**. Then, create an integer called **soldierbaseAtk**:

We specify these stats to be of a specific character and weapon equipment because if your game has more characters in your party, along with both weapons and armor for each character, you will need to differentiate between all the characters' statuses. Moreover, you may want to create a base status for every statistic because some equipment may change stats other than attack.

We can now create the logic using the new variables that we created. Navigate to the **Weapon** Widget Blueprint Event Graph. We need to modify some of our logic to tell when a weapon is equipped on the soldier. Create a **SET Soldier Weapon Equipped** function and set it to **true** after you have equipped the weapon (or pressed the button for the weapon):

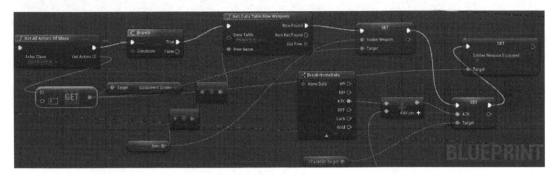

Remember that since this particular button equips the soldier's weapon only when it is pressed, if you have additional characters and/or different types of equipment, you need to create a different Widget Blueprint to accommodate these characters and equipment types.

Next, we need to create the logic to calculate the base attack. Since we have already used the Boolean to differentiate between when the soldier is equipping a weapon or not, we can use this logic to calculate the base attack stat. What we know in our game, by default, is that the character does not have a weapon equipped. So, what we can do is define the base attack stat as soon as we construct this Widget Blueprint, but specifically, when the soldier does not have a weapon equipped.

At this point, when the Widget Blueprint is constructed, get all the actors of the Field Player class using the **Get All Actors Of Class** function. After we have got all the actors of this class, get the `soldierWeaponEquipped` variable. Let's allow the **Get All Actors Of Class** function to fire off a branch that checks whether the `soldierWeaponEquipped` variable is true or false:

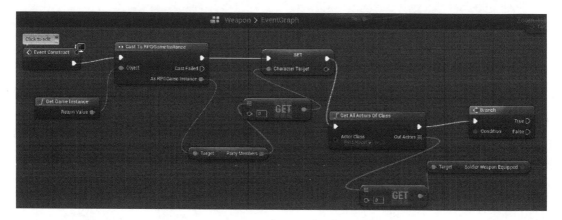

If the condition is false, set the **soldierbaseAtk** to the **ATK** variable of the character. When choosing a weapon, instead of adding the **ATK** of **ItemData** and the **ATK** of the current character's **ATK** stat, add the **ATK** of **ItemData** and **soldierbaseAtk** so that we can always use the base **ATK** variable when equipping a weapon rather than the current stat. This will prevent the **ATK** variable from climbing:

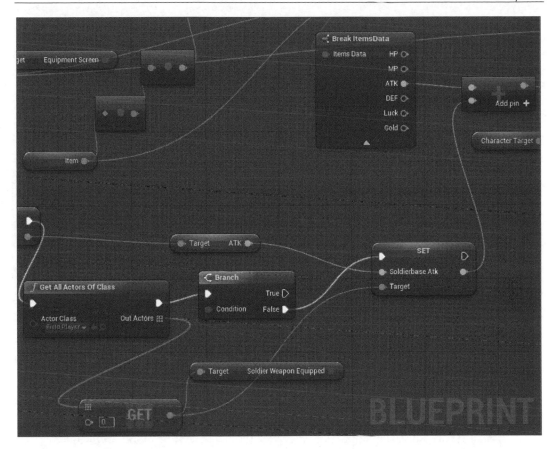

One major problem you will notice is that the attack stat will continue to grow if we exit the equipment screen and come back to equip an item. This is because we do not have logic in place for when a weapon is already equipped. So, when `soldierWeaponEquipped` is true, we need to find which weapon is currently equipped, and subtract its stats from the soldier's base stats in order to reset the base stats.

To do this, we will simply use the **Get Data Table Row Names** function to get the names of the items in the **Weapons** Data Table. For each name in the Data Table, we need to compare the name to the `soldierWeapon` variable from the Field Player class. If the names are equal, we get the row name from the **Weapons** Data Table using the **Get Data Table Row** function, subtract the **ATK** stat of the weapon from the `soldierbaseAtk` stat, find the absolute value of that operation using the **Absolute (Int)** function, and finally, set that number to the `soldierbaseAtk` stat:

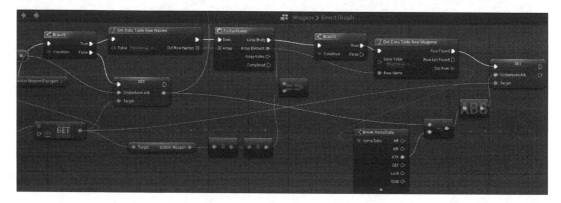

At this point, if you test the equipping of weapons, the attack stat will no longer climb.

This method will work since we do not have a leveling system in place yet. However, when we do have a leveling system in place, we will want to replace this **ATK** variable with the base **ATK** variable that we create for the leveling.

Summary

Now that you know how to equip and set stats for the soldier's weapon, you can use similar methodologies to create Data Tables, Blueprints, and logic for other characters and their equipment.

In the next chapter, we will create a leveling system for our game. We will learn how to allow enemies to give experience points to the player after they are defeated, which will then be used to level up characters in the game.

10
Leveling, Abilities, and Saving Progress

In the previous chapter, we covered how to create and apply equipment to the player, which when equipped, affects the stats of the player. In this chapter, we will allow the player to level up by setting up an experience system for each party member, allowing party members to gain experience from enemies when winning in combat. When each party member gains enough experience, they will level up and their stats will increase at each level that the party member has gained. We will also fix the combat damage settings so that attacks in combat will utilize character stats rather than hardcoded values. Once we have fixed the combat logic, we will then move on to creating an ability for our character that will be activated by gaining a level.

In this chapter, we will cover the following topics:

- XP and Leveling source code
- Data Table starting values
- Displaying levels and experience in the pause menu
- Applying the correct damage in combat
- Setting up the abilities array
- Abilities logic
- Saving
- Loading

XP and leveling source code

In order to allow party members to gain experience points from battle, we need to add experience points (which we will call XP) variables to our code. Moreover, the XP variables need to accumulate to a given XP cap (which we will call MXP for maximum XP), and if this cap is hit, the player will gain a level. The best way to do this is to add these variables to our source code, which we will then apply to every party member and enemy that we have in the game. The first thing we will do is add XP and leveling data to our Data classes. Navigate to **UnrealRPG | Source | Data** and open FCharacterClassInfo.h. In the FCharacterClassInfo : public FTableRowBase struct, add UPROPERTY to XP that will hold cumulative experience, MXP that will hold the experience cap to the next level, and Lvl that will hold the party member's current level:

```
UPROPERTY(BlueprintReadWrite, EditAnywhere, Category =
   "ClassInfo")
   int32 XP;

UPROPERTY(BlueprintReadWrite, EditAnywhere, Category =
   "ClassInfo")
   int32 MXP;

UPROPERTY(BlueprintReadWrite, EditAnywhere, Category =
   "ClassInfo")
   int32 Lvl;
```

Next, open FEnemyInfo.h, which is located in the same folder as FCharacterClassInfo.h. We need to add XP to the enemy's info because each enemy will give a certain amount of XP to party members. In the FEnemyInfo : public FTableRowBase struct, add a UPROPERTY to XP:

```
UPROPERTY(BlueprintReadOnly, EditAnywhere, Category = "EnemyInfo")
   int32 XP;
```

We will now need to use these variables in the GameCharacter instances of the game. Navigate to **UnrealRPG | Source** and open GameCharacter.h. In the class RPG_API UGameCharacter : public UObject struct, add UPROPERTY to XP, MXP, and Lvl:

```
UPROPERTY(EditAnywhere, BlueprintReadWrite, Category =
   CharacterInfo)
   int32 XP;

UPROPERTY(EditAnywhere, BlueprintReadWrite, Category =
   CharacterInfo)
```

```
    int32 MXP;

UPROPERTY(EditAnywhere, BlueprintReadWrite, Category =
    CharacterInfo)
    int32 Lvl;
```

Open `GameCharacter.cpp` so that we set game character instances equal to the party member and enemy data. First, in `UGameCharacter* UGameCharacter::CreateG` `ameCharacter( FCharacterInfo* characterInfo, UObject* outer )`, set the character's `XP`, `MXP`, and `Lvl` equal to the party member's data:

```
UGameCharacter* UGameCharacter::CreateGameCharacter(
  FCharacterInfo* characterInfo, UObject* outer )
{
  UGameCharacter* character = NewObject<UGameCharacter>( outer );

  // locate character classes asset
  UDataTable* characterClasses = Cast<UDataTable>(
    StaticLoadObject( UDataTable::StaticClass(), NULL, TEXT(
    "DataTable'/Game/Data/CharacterClasses.CharacterClasses'" ) )
    );

  if( characterClasses == NULL )
  {
    UE_LOG( LogTemp, Error, TEXT( "Character classes datatable not found!" ) );
  }
  else
  {
    character->CharacterName = characterInfo->Character_Name;

    FCharacterClassInfo* row = characterClasses->FindRow
      <FCharacterClassInfo>( *( characterInfo->Class_ID ), TEXT(
      "LookupCharacterClass" ) );
    character->ClassInfo = row;

    character->MHP = character->ClassInfo->StartMHP;
    character->MMP = character->ClassInfo->StartMMP;
    character->HP = character->MHP;
    character->MP = character->MMP;

    character->ATK = character->ClassInfo->StartATK;
    character->DEF = character->ClassInfo->StartDEF;
    character->LUCK = character->ClassInfo->StartLuck;
```

```
        character->XP = character->ClassInfo->XP;

        character->MXP = character->ClassInfo->MXP;
        character->Lvl = character->ClassInfo->Lvl;
        character->isPlayer = true;
    }

    return character;
}
```

Next, set each instance of the enemy character's XP equal to the XP enemy data:

```
UGameCharacter* UGameCharacter::CreateGameCharacter( FEnemyInfo*
    enemyInfo, UObject* outer )
{
    UGameCharacter* character = NewObject<UGameCharacter>( outer );

    character->CharacterName = enemyInfo->EnemyName;

    character->ClassInfo = nullptr;

    character->MHP = enemyInfo->MHP;
    character->MMP = 0;
    character->HP = enemyInfo->MHP;
    character->MP = 0;

    character->ATK = enemyInfo->ATK;
    character->DEF = enemyInfo->DEF;
    character->LUCK = enemyInfo->Luck;
    character->Gold = enemyInfo->Gold;
    character->XP = enemyInfo->XP;

    character->decisionMaker = new TestDecisionMaker();
    character->isPlayer = false;

    return character;
}
```

We can now add an XP framework to our combat engine. Open `CombatEngine.h`.
Add `XPTotal` as a public variable:

```
public:
    int32 XPTotal;
```

The `XPTotal` will be responsible for holding the total amount of XP gained from battle if all of the enemies have perished.

At this point, let's use the XP variables that we created to calculate the amount of XP gained from battle. Open `CombatEngine.cpp`. In `bool CombatEngine::Tick(float DeltaSeconds)`, add XP to our check for victory section. To do this, we will set the local `XP` variable to `0`, and for every enemy in the battle, we will accumulate the total amount of experience in the `XP` variable:

```
// check for victory
  deadCount = 0;
  int32 Gold = 0;
  int32 XP = 0;
  for( int i = 0; i < this->enemyParty.Num(); i++ )
  {
    if( this->enemyParty[i]->HP <= 0 ) deadCount++;
    Gold += this->enemyParty[i]->Gold;
    XP += this->enemyParty[i]->XP;
  }
```

If all of the party members have died, we will store the total XP of the enemies in our public `XPTotal` variable to be used outside this class:

```
// all enemies have died, switch to victory phase
  if( deadCount == this->enemyParty.Num() )
  {
    this->SetPhase( CombatPhase::CPHASE_Victory );
    GoldTotal = Gold;
    XPTotal = XP;
    return false;
  }
```

Lastly, we can add the XP gained to each party member in our game instance. To do this, open `RPGGameMode.cpp`. In `void ARPGGameMode::Tick( float DeltaTime )`, where we added a check to the victory phase, we will create a `for` loop. This `for` loop will cycle through every party member, and for each party member, we will set their current XP to be a cumulative of the XP gained from the battle:

```
for (int i = 0; i < gameInstance->PartyMembers.Num(); i++)
{
  gameInstance->PartyMembers[i]->XP += this->
    currentCombatInstance->XPTotal;
}
```

In this `for` loop, we can also check the current XP with the current XP cap for the level the player is currently at. If the current XP of the party member is more than or equal to `MXP`, the player will level up, gain increased base stats, and the XP cap to gain the next level (`MXP`) will increase:

```
if (gameInstance->PartyMembers[i]->XP >= gameInstance->
  PartyMembers[i]->MXP){
  gameInstance->PartyMembers[i]->Lvl++;
  gameInstance->PartyMembers[i]->MHP++;
  gameInstance->PartyMembers[i]->MMP++;
  gameInstance->PartyMembers[i]->ATK++;
  gameInstance->PartyMembers[i]->DEF++;
  gameInstance->PartyMembers[i]->LUCK++;
  gameInstance->PartyMembers[i]->MXP += gameInstance->
  PartyMembers[i]->MXP;
}
```

In this example, we kept our calculations simple by only allowing the stats to increase by one when the party member gains a level, and setting the cap to the next level to just be double of what the previous level was. If you like, you can come up with more complex calculations specific to your game here. Note that all the calculations used for differentiating stat numbers and for each party member can be done here.

When you are done, the victory condition will look like this:

```
else if( this->currentCombatInstance->phase == CombatPhase
  ::CPHASE_Victory )
{
  UE_LOG( LogTemp, Log, TEXT( "Player wins combat" ) );
  URPGGameInstance* gameInstance = Cast<
    URPGGameInstance>(GetGameInstance());
  gameInstance->GameGold += this->currentCombatInstance->
    GoldTotal;

  for (int i = 0; i < gameInstance->PartyMembers.Num(); i++)
  {
    gameInstance->PartyMembers[i]->XP += this->
      currentCombatInstance->XPTotal;

    if (gameInstance->PartyMembers[i]->XP
      >= gameInstance->PartyMembers[i]->MXP){
      gameInstance->PartyMembers[i]->Lvl++;
      gameInstance->PartyMembers[i]->MHP++;
      gameInstance->PartyMembers[i]->MMP++;
      gameInstance->PartyMembers[i]->ATK++;
      gameInstance->PartyMembers[i]->DEF++;
      gameInstance->PartyMembers[i]->LUCK++;
```

```
        gameInstance->PartyMembers[i]->MXP +=
            gameInstance->PartyMembers[i]->MXP;
    }

    }

    UGameplayStatics::GetPlayerController( GetWorld(), 0 )->
        SetActorTickEnabled( true );
    }
```

At this point, you can compile your source code and restart/open your project in UE4.

We are now done with creating the framework for our experience system in our source code, and we can now move on to providing specific starting values for each of these in our game.

Data Table starting values

In **Content Browser**, open the **CharacterClasses** Data Table by navigating to **Content | Data**. Here, we can change the starting values of our party members. For the soldier, we will have the starting XP as 0 because the party member should start with 0 experience. The **MXP** value will be **200**, which means that the Soldier will have to gain 200 experience points before making it to the next level. The **Lvl** value will be at **1** since we want each character to start at level 1:

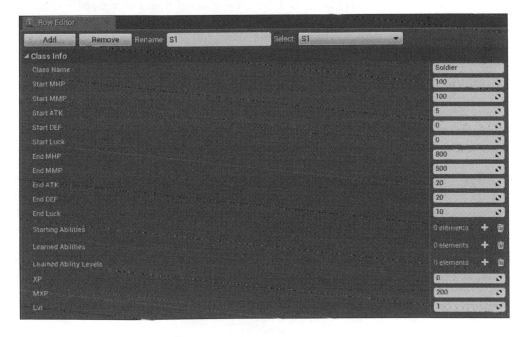

We should now set how much XP our enemies give. In the same folder, open the **Enemies** Data Table, where we have at least one enemy. For each enemy, we need to set a value for **XP** that will determine how much experience the enemy drops when they are killed. For this particular enemy, we set the **XP** value to **50**:

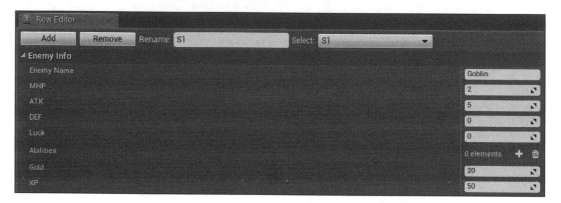

Displaying levels and experience in the pause menu

At this point, if you test the build, the party members will gain experience from battle and level up accordingly (you will be able to tell by watching the stats grow if a party member has gained enough experience to level up), but we will not yet display the proper level or experience points of the party members. We can easily do this by binding these values to our pause menu. Navigate to **Content | Blueprints | UI**. Open the **Pause_Main** Widget Blueprint. In the **Designer** view, select the **Editable_Soldier_Level** Text Block on the right-hand side of **Soldier Lvl** that we created in *Chapter 4, Pause Menu Framework*:

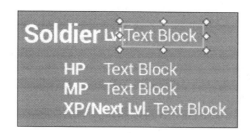

In the **Details** tab under **Content**, create a bind to that text by clicking on the **Bind** drop-down menu and selecting **+Create Binding**:

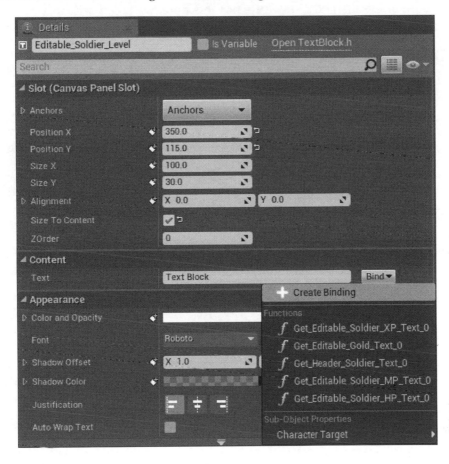

This will automatically open the graph of the **Get Editable_Soldier_Level_ Text** function. In the graph, we need to simply get the variables from the **RPGGameInstance**, like we did before, but this time, we are specifically getting the current **Lvl** variable and returning it as text:

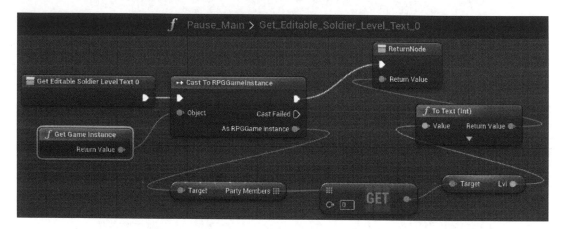

In this example, we are only getting the level for one party member (our soldier), which is in an index 0 in the array. If you have more than one party member, you will just need to change the index in your **GET** function to the proper index; for instance, an index of 1 will find the second party member in your array of party members and their stats, and would, therefore, return a different set of stats.

The only undefined Text Block that we have in our pause menu is the **Editable_ Soldier_XP** Text Block located on the right-hand side of the **XP/Next Lvl** text. Select this Text Block, navigate to the **Details** tab, and under **Content**, add a binding for the Text Block, like we did for our last Text Block, and the graph for the function labeled **Get Editable_Soldier_XP_Text** will pop up. Just like the last Text Block, we will get the correct party member's current data; in particular, we will get XP and MXP because we want this Text Block to show the cumulative XP and the XP needed to get to the next level:

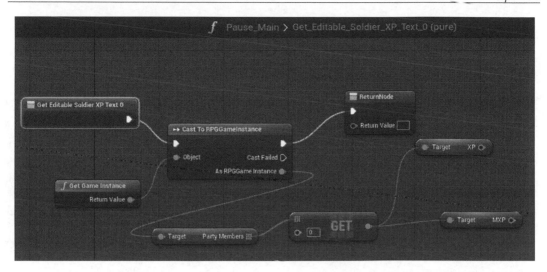

You will notice that **ReturnNode** can only take one **Return Value** pin, and we have two separate values. We can easily solve this problem using the **Append** function and appending the text. We will find the **Append** function by simply right-clicking on our Blueprint, navigating to **Utilities | String**, and selecting **Append**:

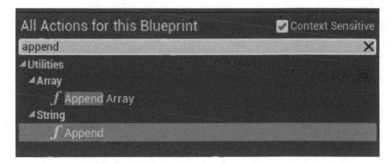

Append takes two strings at a time. Since the Text Block should have a / to separate the current XP with the XP needed to make it to the next level, we will need two **Append** functions. For the first **Append**, link **XP** to the **A** pin, and in the **B** pin, simply append a /:

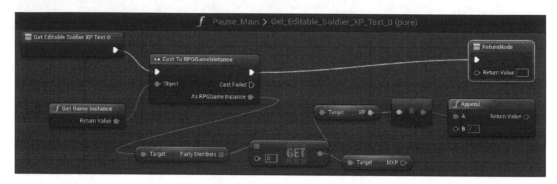

Next, create another **Append** function, and connect the **Return Value** of the first **Append** function to the **A** pin of the second **Append** function. Then, connect **MXP** to the **B** pin of the second **Append** function in order to have **MXP** append the last set of strings:

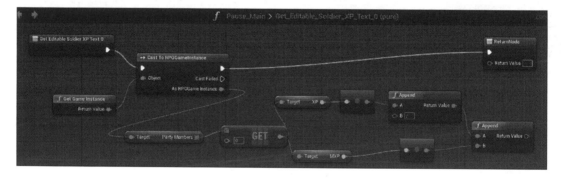

When you are done, simply connect the **Return Value** of the second **Append** function to the **Return Value** of the **ReturnNode**:

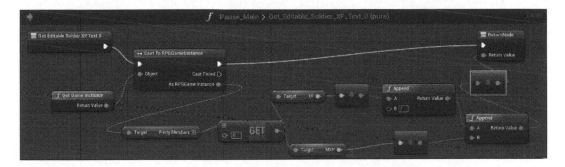

At this point, if you test your game by going into battle and leveling up, you will see that all of your stats will update correctly in the pause menu (the following screenshot is from after we have tested combat and gaining experience with foes):

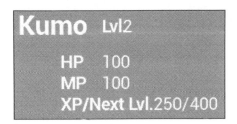

Applying the correct damage in combat

In battle, you will notice that the enemy and the player both do 10 points of damage no matter what. The current attack power and defense do not seem to be calculated. This is because, in *Chapter 3*, *Exploration and Combat*, when we created the combat actions, we hardcoded the damage to be `target->HP -= 10`, which means that no matter who is attacking, they will deal 10 points of damage to the player. We can easily fix this to use the actual stats of enemies and players by navigating to **Source | RPG | Combat | Actions** and opening `TestCombatAction.cpp`. Find `target->HP -= 10;` and replace it with `target->HP -= (character->ATK - target->DEF) >= 0 ? (character->ATK - target->DEF):0;`.

This is a ternary operator. When a target is attacked, whether it is a party member or an enemy, the target's HP will go down by the attacker's attack power minus the target's defense power only if this result ends up being the same or greater than 0. If the result is less than 0, then HP will default to 0. When you are done, void TestCombatAction::BeginExecuteAction(UGameCharacter* character) will look like this:

```
void TestCombatAction::BeginExecuteAction( UGameCharacter*
  character )
{
  this->character = character;

  // target is dead, select another target
  if( this->target->HP <= 0 )
  {
    this->target = this->character->SelectTarget();
  }

  // no target, just return
  if( this->target == nullptr )
  {
    return;
  }

  UE_LOG( LogTemp, Log, TEXT( "%s attacks %s" ), *character->
    CharacterName, *target->CharacterName );

  target->HP -= (character->ATK - target->DEF) >= 0 ? (character->
    ATK - target->DEF):0;

  this->delayTimer = 1.0f;
}
```

Setting up the abilities array

In *Chapter 3, Exploration and Combat*, we created a character class info for learned abilities, which was done in FCharacterClassInfo.h, which is an array used to hold an array of abilities for each character that inherits a class. We need to extend this array so that it is adopted by any game character to hold abilities that they learn throughout the game. To do this, open GameCharacter.h by navigating to **Source | RPG**. In class RPG_API UGameCharacter : public UObject, add a public UPROPERTY to learned abilities and allow it to be editable anywhere:

```
UPROPERTY(EditAnywhere, BlueprintReadWrite, Category =
  CharacterInfo)
  TArray<FString> LearnedAbilities;
```

Next, open `GameCharacter.cpp` located in the same folder, and set `LearnedAbilities` to be equal to `LearnedAbilities` from the class info that we created the variable in:

```
character->LearnedAbilities = character->ClassInfo->
   LearnedAbilities;
```

This will allow each instance of a party member to hold its own `LearnedAbilities` array that we can now edit either in code or in Blueprint. Your game character will now look like this:

```
UGameCharacter* UGameCharacter::CreateGameCharacter(
  FCharacterInfo* characterInfo, UObject* outer )
{
  UGameCharacter* character = NewObject<UGameCharacter>( outer );

  // locate character classes asset
  UDataTable* characterClasses = Cast<UDataTable>(
    StaticLoadObject( UDataTable::StaticClass(), NULL, TEXT(
    "DataTable'/Game/Data/CharacterClasses.CharacterClasses'" ) )
    );

  if( characterClasses == NULL )
  {
    UE_LOG( LogTemp, Error, TEXT( "Character classes datatable not found!" ) );
  }
  else
  {
    character->CharacterName = characterInfo->Character_Name;

    FCharacterClassInfo* row = characterClasses->FindRow
      <FCharacterClassInfo>( *( characterInfo->Class_ID ), TEXT(
      "LookupCharacterClass" ) );

    character->ClassInfo = row;

    character->MHP = character->ClassInfo->StartMHP;
    character->MMP = character->ClassInfo->StartMMP;
    character->HP = character->MHP;
    character->MP = character->MMP;

    character->ATK = character->ClassInfo->StartATK;
    character->DEF = character->ClassInfo->StartDEF;
    character->LUCK = character->ClassInfo->StartLuck;
```

```
character->XP = character->ClassInfo->XP;

character->MXP = character->ClassInfo->MXP;
character->Lvl = character->ClassInfo->Lvl;
character->LearnedAbilities = character->ClassInfo->
  LearnedAbilities;
character->isPlayer = true;
}

return character;
}
```

Once done, compile and restart the editor. We can now create a spot in our game where we can hold and use abilities. In this game, we will choose to use abilities in battle only, but if you want to use abilities elsewhere, for example, outside battle, you can easily accomplish this by following similar steps. Since we will be applying abilities in battle, let's add a new abilities button to our combat interface. In the editor, navigate to **Content | Blueprints | UI**, and open the **CombatUI** Widget Blueprint.

In the **Designer** view, create a Combo Box that will allow us to have a drop-down menu with multiple entries, which we will use to hold and select our abilities, and place them in the **characterActions** Canvas Panel:

Resize the Combo Box to the same size as that of the **Attack** button, and place it in alignment with the **Attack** button:

Lastly, rename the Combo Box to fit to the elements that will be contained in the Combo Box. We can name this **ComboBoxString_Abilities**, and check **Is Variable**:

Now that we have a Combo Box that can hold abilities, it is now time to populate the Combo Box with appropriate abilities. Open the **CombatUI** Event Graph. Since we are concerned with having the correct abilities that are accessible during battle, it would be best to populate the Combo Box with abilities as soon as the **CombatUI** is created. To do this, create an **Event Construct** by navigating to **Add Event | User Interface**:

Connect the **Event Construct** to **Cast To RPGGameInstance**, which will get all the party members, so that we can get and set the proper abilities:

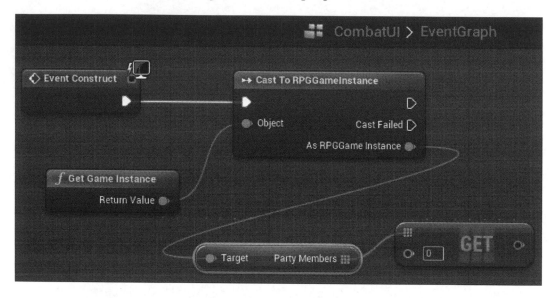

What we can do here is set an ability for one of the party members (in this case, the soldier) by getting an index 0 of the **Party Members** Array. We will give the Soldier an ability called **Attack x2** if the Soldier has reached level 2. To do this, we will get the current level of the target using the **Lvl** variable and compare it with the integer 2 using the **CompareInt** macro:

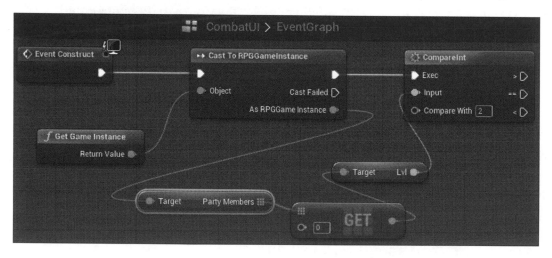

If the **Lvl** variable is more than or equal to 2, we can set the first element of the **LearnedAbilities** array to **Attack x2**:

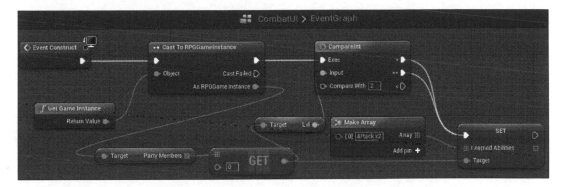

After we have populated the array with the new **Attack x2** ability, we can now populate the Combo Box with every ability that we have by simply executing a **ForEachLoop** and cycling through every element of the array, and adding it to the Combo Box using the **Add Option** function by navigating to **Combo Box | Add Option**:

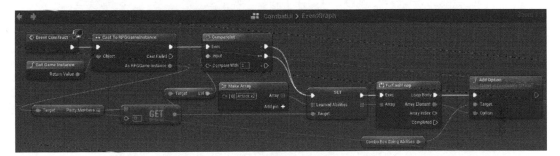

This is a very simple way to add combat abilities to an abilities drop-down menu in accordance with party member levels. If you want to create more abilities, all you need to do is simply compare your level with another level using the **CompareInt**, and you can add more abilities to the **LearnedAbilities** array. If you end up having additional characters in the game, it is best to create a new Combo Box for each party member, get that party member from whichever index they are in the **Party Members** array, and then add abilities to their own **LearnedAbilities** array like we did with the Soldier.

You should now be able to test this and see that when the player presses the Combo Box, **Attack x2** will appear if the Soldier party member hits level 2:

Abilities logic

We can now create a logic for our **Attack x2** ability. As the name suggests, **Attack x2** should perform an attack that does double damage. Before we apply this sort of logic, we must first create an event that occurs after selecting the ability from the Combo Box and pressing it. Head back into the **Designer** view. In the **Details** tab, navigate to **Events**, and press **+** next to the **OnOpening** event:

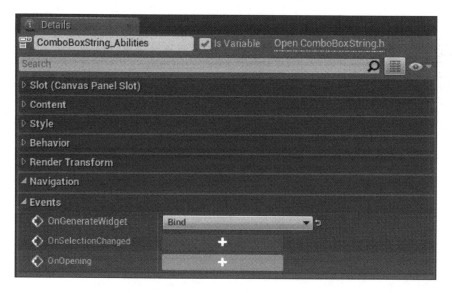

This will create an **OnOpening** event in your Event Graph. By selecting and clicking on the ability from the Combo Box, we need to first clear all the children from the **Panel** Widget using the **Clear Children** function, similar to what we did by clicking on the **Attack** button. This will prevent multiple buttons of the same target from popping up:

Next, we will check whether the **Attack x2** ability has been opened by first calling the **Get Selected Option** function located under Combo Box (you will need to turn off **Context Sensitive** for this):

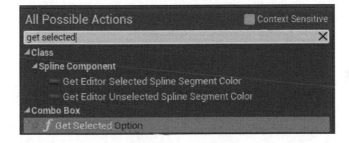

We set the **Target** of **Get Selected Option** to the **Get Combo Box String Abilities**:

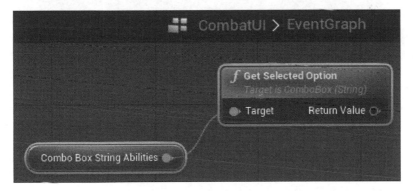

Then, check whether the selected option is equal to **Attack x2**:

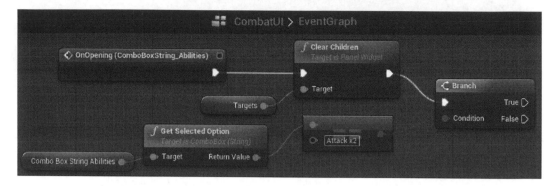

If it is equal, this means that we have selected **Attack x2,** and we will then get the **RPGGameInstance**. However, we need to first check whether the party member has enough MP to use the ability. In this case, we will set the ability to use 10 MP, so let's make sure that the party member has at least 10 MP before using the ability:

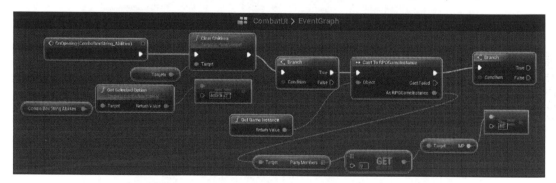

If the player has enough MP to use the ability, we will use a logic that allows the player to perform an attack that does double damage. Since the player will be doing double damage, this means that it will be easy to multiply the **ATK** variable of the player by two; however, we do not want the **ATK** variable to be doubled forever, only for this turn. To do this, it would be best to create a local variable that will temporarily hold the base **ATK** value so that on the next turn, we can reset the **ATK** value back to its normal value. We can easily do this by creating a local integer called **Temp Atk**, and set **Temp Atk** to the party member's **ATK** value:

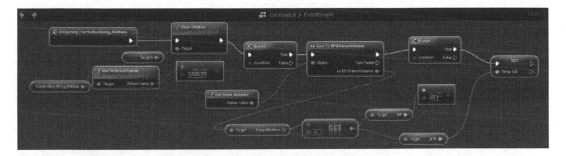

Next, we will set the **ATK** value of the party member to double its value by multiplying it by two, and set the **ATK** variable to the product of that operation:

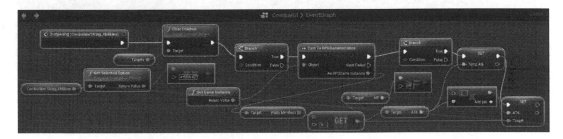

We also need to set a Boolean to tell when we have used **Attack x2**. Because if we have used it, we need to subtract MP from the party member, and set our **ATK** variable back to normal. To do this, we need to create a local Boolean, which we will call attackx2. After we set the attack to be double, set attackx2 to true, and allow the **CombatUI** to show all the available enemy targets by connecting **SET attackx2** to the **Get Character Targets** function:

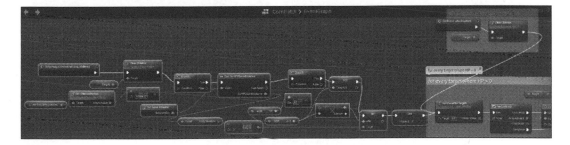

Once this is done, we can reset the `attackx2` Boolean to false, set the **ATK** variable back to its normal value, and remove 10 MP from the party member for using the ability. The best place to do this is after the **Event Show Actions Panel** occurs again, when the character actions become visible and the targets become invisible. After the targets become invisible, we will check whether the `attackx2` Boolean is true. If it is true, we will set it to false, and then set the **ATK** value equal to the **Temp Atk** value. Then, we subtract 10 from the party member's MP variable:

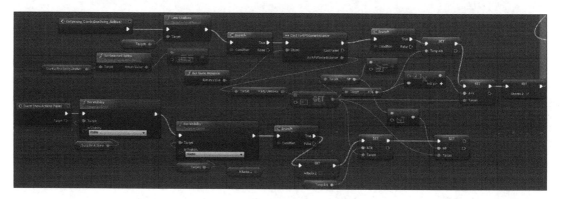

Saving and loading game progress

The last thing that we will focus on is saving and loading game progress. Saving and loading can be done in many ways, but at its heart, saving the progress revolves around specific variables that you would like to save.

Saving

Most games save a lot of different variables, such as the level or area the player is in, the player's stats, the player's inventory, and gold. In our example, we will choose to save the player's gold, but using the method that we are about to perform, you can easily figure out how to save all the other progress in the game.

To start with, create a new Blueprint class in **Content Browser** by navigating to **Content | Blueprints**. The **Pick Parent Class** window will pop up, and from **All Classes**, select **SaveGame**:

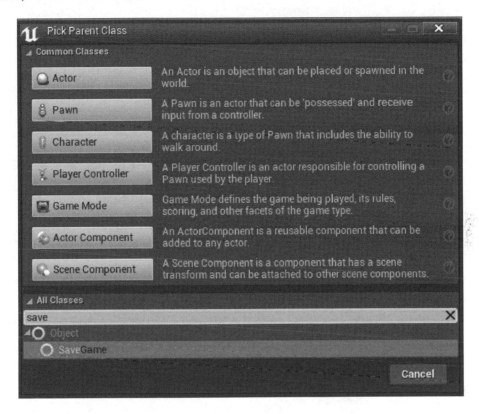

Name this class **NewSaveGame**, and open the class. The purpose of this class is to hold the values of every variable that you would like to save. As mentioned earlier, for this example, we will be saving the gold variable, but if you would like to save more variables, the **NewSaveGame** class that you just created will store those variables as well. At this point, add a new variable to this class from the **Add New** variable in the **My Blueprint** tab. Name it **Gold**, and make its variable an **Integer** type:

Now that you are done, it is time to find a good spot for the game to be saved and the gold variable to be saved. Since we already have a pause menu and learned how to add buttons to the pause menu in the previous chapters, it would be easy to create a new button that we can call **Save** in the **Pause_Main** Widget Blueprint and add an **OnClicked** event to it:

Once you click on **+** next to the **OnClicked** event, the Event Graph will open up, and you will see the **OnClicked** event for your **Save** button. Here, allow the button, when pressed, to create a save game object. To do this, create **Create Save Game Object** whose **Save Game Class** is set to **New Save Game**, and allow it to start when you click on the button:

Here, we will need to create a new variable of the **Save Game** type, and we will call this variable **save**:

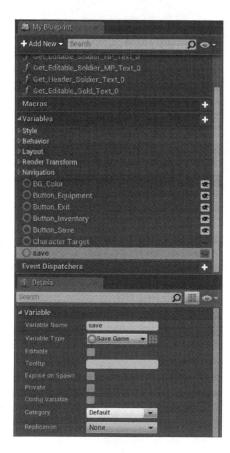

Here, we will create a **SET Save** variable in our Blueprint, and pass the **Return Value** of the **Create Save Game Object** function to **SET Save**:

We will now need to cast the **NewSaveGame** class so that we can set the **Gold** variable that we created to the game's gold. To do this, cast **SET Save** to **NewSaveGame** by connecting the **Save** value to the **Object** of **Cast To NewSaveGame**:

Next, allow **Cast To NewSaveGame** to fire off a **Cast To RPGInstance** whose **Object** is a reference to **Get Game Instance**. We are doing this so that we can get an instance of the **GameGold**, so link the **As RPGGame Instance** pin from **Cast To RPGGameInstance** to the **Get GameGold** variable from the RPG instance:

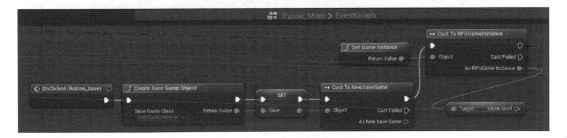

Now that we are getting the game gold, we can set the game gold's value to the **Gold** variable from the **NewSaveGame** class by linking the **SET Gold** to fire off when the **RPGGameInstance** is cast, and then linking the **GameGold** value pin to the **Gold** value pin and the **Target** pin of **SET Gold** to the **As New Save Game** pin from **Cast To NewSaveGame**:

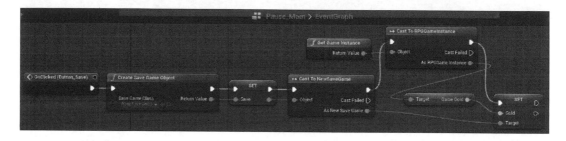

This particular method will allow us to save whatever the current game gold is to our **Gold** variable in the **NewSaveGame** class. Note that if you want to save more variables, set the values of those variables just like you set the value of the **Gold** variable by adding a **SET** node for each individual variable that you have.

The last thing we will need to do is create a save game slot, which will hold our save game object. To do this, create a **Save Game to Slot** action, which you will find under **Game** in your **Actions** window:

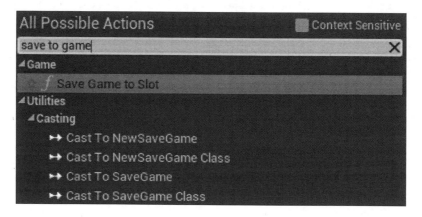

Create a slot name for this; in this example, we will use **A** as **Slot Name**. Link the **Save Game Object** pin of **Save Game to Slot** to the **Save** value pin, and allow the **Save Game to Slot** to fire when the **Gold** variable is set:

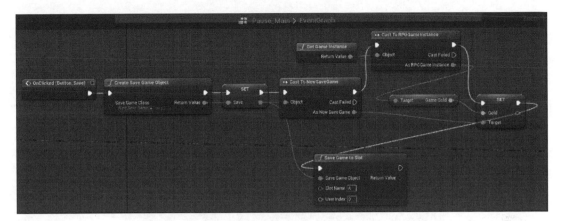

We are now done with the saving part of the game. We will now move on to loading a game slot.

Loading

Just like saving, loading can be done in a number of ways. In our game, we will simply load the player's save data on launching the game. To do this, open the **FieldPlayer** Blueprint since we know that the FieldPlayer will always exist in our game.

Next, we will create a **Load** variable of the **Save Game** type similar to what we did when we saved the game, so that we can properly cast the variables and their values from **NewSaveGame**:

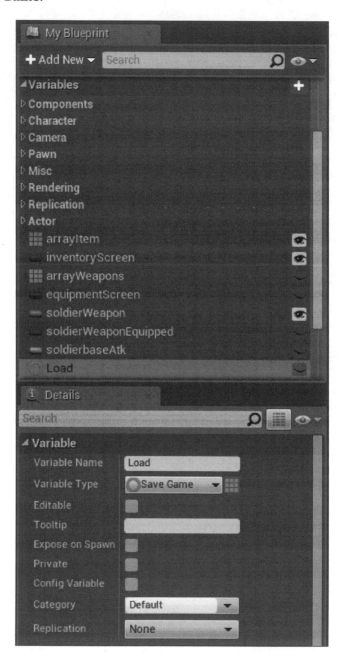

Here, we will create an **Event Begin Play**, and from **Event Begin Play**, we will call the **Does Save Game Exist** function from the **Game** category in the **Actions** window, and under **Slot Name**, we will look for **A** since we named our save slot **A** in the previous section:

From **Does Save Game Exist**, we will call a branch; if **Does Save Game Exist** is true, we will call **Load Game from Slot** and its **Slot Name** will also be **A**:

At this point, we have created a logic where, when the game starts, we check whether the saved game in slot A exists. If it does exist, we load the game from slot A; if it does not exist, we do nothing.

We can now set the **Load** variable that we created in the beginning of this section whose data type is **Save Game** to the **Return Value** of **Load Game from Slot** and cast it to **NewSaveGame** similar to what we did with our save game data:

Note that since we now have access to all the variables in **NewSaveGame**, it means that we have access to the gold value that we saved. So from here, we get the gold value from **Cast To NewSaveGame** so that you have whatever value was stored in **Gold** since the player last saved, and you will need to set the **GameGold** value from **RPGGameInstance** to **Gold** from **NewSaveGame**:

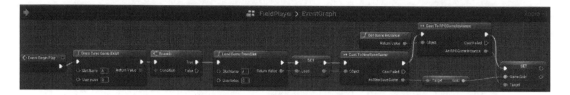

Just like when we created the saving logic, in this loading logic, if there are any other variables you need to load, you can easily do so by getting more variables from the **NewSaveGame** class and setting it to other variables from the **RPG Game Instance**.

You can now test this by simply playing the game, doing battle to get the game gold, saving the game with the **Save** button that we created in the pause menu, and then closing the game. When you reopen the game, you will notice that the gold you had when you saved the game is automatically loaded when you start the game. Using this framework, feel free to save other game variables such as your status and inventory

Summary

We now have a solution to allow party members to earn experience, gain levels with enough experience gained, and earn abilities through hitting specific levels. We have also fixed the combat system to allow party members and enemies to do damage based on their stats, as well as allow party members to use abilities in battle. Additionally, you now have the ability to save and load player progress throughout the game. Using the framework covered in this chapter, every party member can level up, and you can easily add more abilities to various party members, use them in battle, and players can save their game at any time and then come back to continue from where they left off.

At this juncture, you have successfully completed a working framework for a turn-based RPG. You have core gameplay working with the ability to allow a party of characters to explore a world in isometric 3D. You can battle enemies with new-found abilities and equipment and interact with NPCs by conversing with them and buying items and equipment with gold you earned from defeating enemies. And just like most other RPGs, you can level up through gaining experience, as well as save game status so players can come back to continue their games at a later date.

Your quest is not over yet though! Now that you know the basics, venture off to add more content to your game, like additional enemies, party members, NPCs and equipment. Through this process, create levels of your own using the framework and content you have created for yourself through following this book.

Index

Thank you for buying
Building an RPG with Unreal 4.x

About Packt Publishing

Packt, pronounced 'packed', published its first book, *Mastering phpMyAdmin for Effective MySQL Management*, in April 2004, and subsequently continued to specialize in publishing highly focused books on specific technologies and solutions.

Our books and publications share the experiences of your fellow IT professionals in adapting and customizing today's systems, applications, and frameworks. Our solution-based books give you the knowledge and power to customize the software and technologies you're using to get the job done. Packt books are more specific and less general than the IT books you have seen in the past. Our unique business model allows us to bring you more focused information, giving you more of what you need to know, and less of what you don't.

Packt is a modern yet unique publishing company that focuses on producing quality, cutting-edge books for communities of developers, administrators, and newbies alike. For more information, please visit our website at www.packtpub.com.

Writing for Packt

We welcome all inquiries from people who are interested in authoring. Book proposals should be sent to author@packtpub.com. If your book idea is still at an early stage and you would like to discuss it first before writing a formal book proposal, then please contact us; one of our commissioning editors will get in touch with you.

We're not just looking for published authors; if you have strong technical skills but no writing experience, our experienced editors can help you develop a writing career, or simply get some additional reward for your expertise.

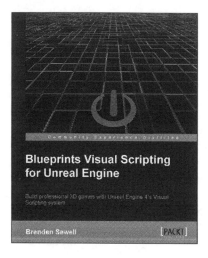

Blueprints Visual Scripting for Unreal Engine

ISBN: 978-1-78528-601-8   Paperback: 188 pages

Build professional 3D games with Unreal Engine 4's Visual Scripting system

1. Take your game designs from inspiration to a fully playable game that you can share with the world, without writing a single line of code.

2. Learn to use visual scripting to develop gameplay mechanics, UI, visual effects, artificial intelligence, and more.

3. Build a first person shooter from scratch with step-by-step tutorials.

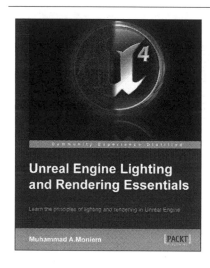

Unreal Engine Lighting and Rendering Essentials

ISBN: 978-1-78528-906-4   Paperback: 242 pages

Learn the principles of lighting and rendering in the Unreal Engine

1. Get acquainted with the concepts of lighting and rendering specific to Unreal.

2. Use new features such as Realistic Rendering and Foliage Shading to breathe new life into your projects.

3. A fast-paced guide to help you learn lighting and rendering concepts in Unreal.

Please check **www.PacktPub.com** for information on our titles

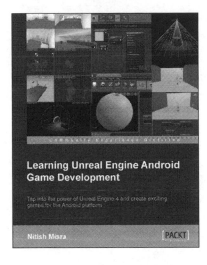

Learning Unreal Engine Android Game Development

ISBN: 978-1-78439-436-3   Paperback: 300 pages

Tap into the power of Unreal Engine 4 and create exciting games for the Android platform

1. Dive straight into making fully functional Android games with this hands-on guide.

2. Learn about the entire Android pipeline, from game creation to game submission.

3. Use Unreal Engine 4 to create a first-person puzzle game.

UnrealScript Game Programming Cookbook

ISBN: 978-1-84969-556-5   Paperback: 272 pages

Discover how you can augment your game development with the power of UnrealScript

1. Create a truly unique experience within UDK using a series of powerful recipes to augment your content.

2. Discover how you can utilize the advanced functionality offered by the Unreal Engine with UnrealScript.

3. Learn how to harness the built-in AI in UDK to its full potential.

Please check **www.PacktPub.com** for information on our titles